CAMILLE CLAUDEL

CAMILLE CLAUDEL

UNE FEMME

by

ANNE DELBÉE

Translated by
Carol Cosman

MERCURY HOUSE
San Francisco

Published in the United States by
Mercury House
San Francisco, California

United States Constitution, First Amendment: Congress shall make no law respecting an establishment of religion, or prohibiting the free exercise thereof; or abridging the freedom of speech, or of the press; or the right of the people peaceably to assemble, and to petition the Government for a redress of grievances.

Mercury House and colophon are registered trademarks
of Mercury House, Incorporated

Printed on acid-free paper
Manufactured in the United States of America

Library of Congress Cataloging-in-Publication Data

Delbée, Anne.
  [Femme. English]
  Camille Claudel: une femme / by Anne Delbée; translated by
Carol Cosman.
    p. cm.
  ISBN 1-56279-026-9
  1. Claudel, Camille, 1864-1943.   2. Sculptors – France – Biography.   I.
Title.
NB553.C44D4413   1992
730'.92 – dc20   92-11176
[B]   CIP

5 4 3 2 1

for Pierre B.

The Flesh
and the Spirit

ONE DAY I opened *L'Oeil écoute*.
It was a beautifully illustrated edition. Inside were some magnificent essays: "April in Holland," "Jan Steen," "Nicolas Maes." Commentaries I'd never read before on Rembrandt, on three of his paintings.

In addition, Paul Claudel had found a way of describing a certain aspect of Spanish painting. This was in a piece called "Spiritual Flesh." I was fascinated. Great sensuality mingled with the most ardent mysticism.

And then, discreetly placed at the very end, another essay: "Camille Claudel." Some day, sooner or later, someone – you or I – would open the book and turn to this page.

Who was she, this beloved sister? That question leaped out from every line. Once again I hear the first words of that essay. I hear them, and her.

"My little Paul!"

Her voice hasn't stopped echoing.

Who was she? This "proud girl in her triumphant burst of beauty and genius, dominating, often cruel" in her power over Paul's early years.

Who was she?

"A strong forehead, magnificent eyes, deep blue, a large mouth marked even more by arrogance than sensuality, a thick mane of auburn hair cascading down her back."

Who was this girl who suddenly called to me through her brother?

She had loved Auguste Rodin to the point of madness. July 1913: "Outside the ambulance was waiting. So much for thirty years!"

I read and reread. Impossible. She had died in 1943. Thirty years in an asylum. The long night of hell, the dark night of the soul – no.

Claudel was drawing to a close. Nine pages! Only nine pages there in my hands. In my heart.

"The rest is silence."

Brangues, June 1951.

No, not that! I would not close the book. I stayed there, repeating the beautiful words that mark Hamlet's death.

But it had been four centuries since that part had been played. All the rest would not be silence. Because the most remarkable thing was not that she was Paul's sister, Auguste Rodin's lover, that she was beautiful and "mad."

No, what struck me most deeply, what kept me from closing the book, was the fact that she was a sculptor. A nineteenth-century sculptor of genius. Paul Claudel described the strange figures down to the last one, Perseus, the man who kills without looking. The man who kills without . . .

The beautiful, tall girl with magnificent dark blue eyes.

"An impressive manner full of courage, frankness, genius, gaiety. A woman who had great gifts."

Thus began my search; this book represents one stage of it. There are years to go. For who could ever imagine that we have said everything there is to say on the subject of Camille Claudel?

This book takes us a step closer to her, calling to us from her confinement, another lock opened. There she is, signaling, smiling with her two beautiful, earth-covered hands. There she is, the female sculptor, the woman who gave life to unique forms.

I will follow the labyrinth that leads toward her, even if I lose my way from time to time.

She is there, she is waiting, there is no time to lose, I see her face crying in the night, half-buried,

Une Femme: A Woman

ANGERS, 1982
Night

The Final Hour

The bell tolls three melancholy notes.

PAUL CLAUDEL, *Journal*

ALONE.
Tiny, minuscule, she has just stepped onto the huge white marble floor, and the whole page trembles.

The pillow. She feels the edge of the linen. She can barely see the fabric. Beyond it? No. Just that little space near her eye. The pillowcase is scratchy on her face. She feels the roughness of the material. Anything else? No. Her body seems wrapped in a shroud. Already! They have left her this infinitesimal interval. Still a few more seconds. Perhaps.

She has moved her head. Delicately. Too much effort. She thought she was moving her head. Only a slight intake of breath. On the hospital pillow, a woman hides her cheek.

Slowly, she turns inward, far away from them. Far from the world. Far from its stings. She escapes. No one notices this.

She withdraws her little hand from their great paws. Her two beautiful hands beat their final cadence on the dirty sheet.

No one is present at this moment when the woman dies.
The hospital.

Alone.
She embarks. She has waited so long to leave. The bridge is beginning to vibrate. Paul should have taken her to China!

Twice she had hoped, so hoped he would. She makes the decision. All alone. Why keep waiting on their good will? Men of good will!

A weak smile traces itself one last time on the beautiful, proud lips, pale and slightly cracked.
There on the light pillow.

The sea is rippling. She throws down the gangplanks. Camille is hurrying. The boat is swaying lightly. She grabs the oars. On the great ship's tall masts the huge sails unfurl, the great wings now strike the water warmed by the rising sun.

This sheet. She feels the rough sheet under her hands. She scratches, for hours . . .

Hours of work to polish the marble. Silence! She is working. The four little old women chatter and chatter. Under the sea. All green. Camille hears their twittering. Silence, the mad gargoyles!
Along the mouth. A corner of saliva. A little foam.
The green water beneath her streams swiftly. Light pierces the cloudy sea. She stands at the prow of the boat. Coiled. Reverberating. A throbbing music calls to her, draws her down. No one is steering the boat.
Mysteriously, she recognizes the music. It's the little siren on the rock of green onyx. She is blowing on a shiny metal flute. Lost in the middle of the ocean. There, below, she is drawing her on.

On the pillow. The face turns ivory and the lips are whistling.

Camille follows the melody, coming closer. Closer still. The musician is no longer there. The light grows dazzling. Camille can see the tiny metal flute abandoned on the rock. She tries to grab it. Blinded, she drops the shiny instrument.

A nun is leaning over the pale face. She takes a small mirror in her hand. She looks at the faint fog gently clouding the mirror. She will return in a little while.

She moves across the proud marble. She has set down her other foot. She slides, she slides on the clear expanse. Her feet slip about on the mirrored slab, warming it. The room is too bright – crystal chandeliers – she waltzes, splashed with light, she turns round and round. She holds out her two magnificent arms. She is dressed in a nimbus of tulle, a collar of exquisite lace around her neck.

She invites the musician to dance with her. She whispers in his ear: "No comment, Monsieur Debussy." He smiles, leans toward her, his flimsy hat askew. She presses him against her, but she no longer feels his body. He is more and more diaphanous; all she holds in her hands is a simple jacket the color of the moon. Monsieur Rodin is there, dressed in gray. She clutches at him. He seems deaf. She pulls his beard – hard. Very hard. He too has disappeared. But she can feel his hand weighing on her, closing around her heart. She tries to lift it off, to pry apart the gripping fingers. She is suffocating. The dancers surround her. She cries out, words they do not hear. She is gasping for air.

In the bed. The light body takes up very little space. The alabaster face has stiffened slightly. The hands fly forward.

All those black clothes. Those dark top hats – snapping like bullets. They are approaching. She pushes back. She scratches. She wants to catch them. The bodies crumble. She's left with dried husks between her bruised fingers. Then she starts to run. The stones slip away. She escapes. She hoists herself up with all the strength of her thirteen years, mastering the turning earth, the stone against her body. She goes forward, violent, vindictive, willful.

Untiring, she climbs up the dizzying incline. Before sunrise she has reached the top of the cliff of her childhood years. The beach of white sand flies under her young feet. The dawn awaits the result of the struggle. The riders have formed a circle. They hide their faces under high, pearl-encrusted helmets. Their armor is opalescent. Their shields lustrous. They are silent. A terrible stillness. Their spotless standards wave in the empty air. Noiselessly.

They stand gigantic – powerful – armed. The great beast rages, protected by the compact tunic of hard chainmail.

The stone Geyn undergoes a monstrous awakening.

At his feet, a monster of a little girl observes him. Her two eyes wide open. She has waited patiently. The time has come to end his deep sleep.

Now she can attack him.

With her bare hands, all alone.

No one is there in the mirrored hospital room. On 19 October 1943. The Montdevergues hospital is filled with other patients that day.

She is seventy-nine years old.

Children of the Moon

Listen! Nearby there is a beautiful woman
A woman is sleeping nearby,
And at this very moment, her head resting on her arms,
She offers her body and her beautiful face, full of
savage pain
To the white light of the moon.
Her name is Galaxaure.

PAUL CLAUDEL, *L'Endormie*

S HE RAISED her head abruptly.
"Cami-i-i-lle."

The child's voice in the distance. She burst out laughing. A harsh laugh for this girl of thirteen. She was not mean, but she wanted to be alone. The first to penetrate the forest of Tardenois, alone to devour the wind galloping over the great plain of Champagne, alone to meet the princes, the stones.

"Cami-i-i-lle."

Her brother's voice down there. She hesitated for a moment – "My little Paul" – and smiled tenderly, overcome with remorse. Calling to her, he sounded half-girl, half-boy, his thin voice at once piercing and poignant. The boy was always around, ready to hurt himself. He was probably running across old Dambrune's fields, trying to join her. She was already at the edge of the woods. With great boyish strides, as her mother would say – her mother! In a rage she gave a big kick at the soaked earth, which burst into a thousand black drops. She started walking again, violently. Her boots sunk heavily into the damp, clayey soil. The crude earth that she kneaded with her adolescent tread – a young, unbridled, and insolent girl – her reddish brown mane slipping gradually onto her still frail shoulders. A sudden desire to grasp handfuls of the mud. The earth gave off an acrid, burning odor. She squeezed it with her hands, grasping it. The young girl breathed it in, wiped it on her face. The wind rose, a storm was coming, raging beyond Reims, the bitter earth, smoking like the turds old Jacquin's big draft horses dropped behind them. She began to shout, wanting to shout forever, to give vent to an overwhelming desire, to be abandoned, indecent. Then she attacked the Chinchy butte at a run.

She wanted to be the first up there, on top of the Geyn. First to dominate the giant. To look out at the horizon extending all the way to Paris – that's what they said in the village: "Just think, Paris is only three hours from Villeneuve." Even opening her huge eyes as wide as possible, she could never catch a glimpse of the city.

Alone, to dominate this country wasted by squalls, alone, in the middle of the nineteenth century.

"Cami-i-i-lle."

The child was behind her, half hidden by the dusk. His voice weaker now. She hesitated – a little, yet a little – but the hour was so beautiful, so elusive and dangerous. As they said in the village, it was the hour "between dog and wolf." It was the wolf she wanted to meet this evening, without anyone to distract her or force her to run away.

This was the kind of rendezvous she had secretly sworn to keep as she lay last evening in her cold, narrow bed. They were all asleep. She was alone with the silence. She was keeping sleep at bay – sleep, she laughed at it – she loved to put it in harness, to slow or quicken its pace at will. It was her best bedmate, but she would decide when to let herself slip into its arms. And last night she did not want it.

Now she heard only the wind and her steps crackling over the first pine needles. Her brother Paul was too far away now. The others must be preparing the simmering soup. "The Claudels," as they said in the village, with a certain sharpness in their voices – admiration? hatred? – Camille had often surprised them talking.

"They keep too much to themselves. It's unhealthy for the children."

"And those constant arguments . . ."

"Their uncle is the village priest. He isn't so proud."

9

The village of three hundred families fanned local hatreds.

Happily, there was the forest, the rough, luminous earth she found again during every vacation. And then there were the stones. It was the stones she had spoken to the night before, as she lay in the hollow of her bed, while sleep, like a banished lover, hung its head.

The stones – noble, untouchable. They knew the future. Hundreds of years old, they answered her each evening when she came to question them. Camille hurried, she was running now, heedless of the clawing trees, she knew the way, and her toughened feet tore up the sandy soil that slipped out from under them.

Paul would join her. He knew where to find her. He had been seven years old and she just eleven the first time they had escaped from the family house. Half bold, half blustering, they had gone the three kilometers separating the presbytery from the butte; holding hands, they could not have said which of them was leading the other toward the dark forest.

Two years had passed, she was no longer such a timid child. This evening, too, the house was far away, but she was relieved. At times she would have liked to run away for good. She would look down on them small, small, smaller still: the little village square next to the little house stuck onto the little church, which stood in its imposing little way over the churchyard . . . little tombs. Death.

There she was. Crouching in the shadows. First among them all. Ancient crones, proud young goddesses, wounded perhaps, dying, in forgotten confinements, upright youth, males.

There she was, the plump old woman, she seemed to be blowing a horn, her cheeks rounded, body tensed with the supreme effort. Camille looked at her and remembered the hunt she'd gone on with her father. The buck on his haunches, raising his pretty head; one last time those brown eyes had seen the woods tremble. Standing before him, the fat man with his horn had blown the final *hallili.* Her father had explained it to her – the death call. She'd looked from the thick red belly of the musician holding the horn to the animal's elegant chest. Then she'd run and put her two arms around the steaming neck dripping with sweat. Her father had cried, "Camille!" The dogs were growling, ready to jump on her. The hunters were silent. The buck had rested his head on her shoulder for a moment. She could still feel his heart beating wildly. Someone had carried her away. She knew nothing more. The death knell, the final *hallili* . . . She would often repeat the word to herself like a distant summons.

The old woman was looking at her, Camille had stopped for a second to catch her breath. Despite her fat cheeks, the old woman seemed so small, so lost. Camille loved to caress her wrinkled forehead. How long had she been standing there at the entrance to the woods?

Eternal guardian, Melusina bent with the dreams of childhood. Camille sometimes stopped for a long chat with her.

But this evening she scarcely had time to blow her a kiss. Paul was surely on her heels. The path turned right, then left. Then she was face to face with them, one was squat, shriveled, the other rising up as if caught in a whirlwind.

The first seemed to hide a terrible secret. Sometimes she seemed to remember the child who went away, abandoned her – and now she had aged, forever petrified. Sometimes she was struck by a ray of sunlight, illuminated, then she seemed to smile, as if once again the rosy arms stretched toward her. Perhaps she'd killed her child in a fit of madness. Camille remembered the ghastly story Victoire, their old housekeeper, told on winter evenings in front of the fire. No, not that!

On the other side were the happy lovers, embracing. The stone, cleft in two, seemed wrapped together. The girl often wondered: will they separate, will they find themselves again? For who could say whether the kiss, suspended at this moment, was beginning or ending? They seemed to dance, perhaps to spin together, almost separate already.

The stones. The reality of this rediscovered forest. The stones were watching her. She ran faster. Toward the Geyn. Always faster.

There they were, in the middle of the path. Camille had named them "the gossips." She loved to sit with them. There were three of them. They seemed to be informed about the latest village news, but sometimes Camille came upon them telling stories more than a thousand years old.

Stooping, hunched over, they talked and talked incessantly, silently. This evening, however, they were dozing and Camille did not have much time.

She climbed ever higher. The rain began to fall. The child felt nothing. She moved among her companions. The path became more slippery. Indifferent, Camille plunged on. Someone was calling her –

the call from the Geyn. The wind blew harder. The purple sky seemed torn in places. The path was treacherous, but Camille knew the weight of the earth that slipped away beneath her. The trees helped her, gnarled, thin, dark-skinned.

Here, she turned. There, she went under the old tree that was losing its hairlike needles, one by one, and broke with a muffled sound. There again, she stepped over a hillock of twisted roots, gray dwarves – she called them "the gnomes" – they seemed to want to hold her back with their deformed little arms. Their rough knees often gave her tiny scratches or made her lose her balance. This evening she stepped over them confidently, because he was there.

Colossal, white, bending forward slightly as if he were crushing the valley, dominating all else, these shadow people and the familiar shapes, he stood looking at her, draped in his white cloak. "The giant" faced Camille. Both of them luminous in the moonlight. Who had petrified the other in this extraordinary encounter, the girl or the giant stone? The adolescent's eyes shone dark blue, almost black, like onyx. She would have liked to be its master, its maker, she would have liked to have made this stone with her own hands. The child's eyes glowed with a savage, almost cruel determination. Suddenly she came closer: the standing stone, like the old male who feels death approaching, did not look away. She was against him, her nose against the nostrils of the beast, she leaned against him and caressed him slowly, patiently, for a long time.

Like a traveler weighed down by his heavy coat, lowering his head a little and stopping for a moment on his way, lost in his memories – he had been standing there for ages, between centuries past and future. The girl looked at the eternal stone, the girl looked at the Geyn. She was straight, lithe, her thirteen years resonant in the dusk; he, silent, secret, inscrutable. She was prepared to defy the god. She wanted to understand. Where did this beauty come from, this power and her sudden joy, she, who was so small, who defied heaven itself?

The smooth body, the brutal death in a thunderous burst, she wanted him even in his death throes. Sometimes she'd had the temerity to strike him. Then he reduced himself to dozens of white suns and cruelly mocked her, she, a mere mortal. She understood. She had chosen. She knew now what she wanted. The answer was there. She would not be someone who waits.

The rain began to fall harder, more angrily. The child felt nothing.

She went across the field of sand that covered the butte like powdered sugar sprinkled on a cake. The wind lifted the sand around her. It blew maliciously. She seemed so fine, a siren stranded on that alien shore. They said that a long time ago, a very long time ago, the sea had come all the way there – a beach of white sand stranded there, too, a moonscape.

Camille went to the extreme edge of the cliff. Camille surveyed the plain, the whole countryside. She glimpsed the future down there. Her future.

Suddenly the wind undid her hair ribbon. Her hair swirled around her face like so many gold serpents.

The black face smeared with mud was hardly visible under the darkening sky. The storm raged. The sky flashed white. She was warm, warm with her frantic efforts, warm like an expectant lover.

If the sea were still there, she would have thrown off her clothes and plunged into the water. She pulled off her jacket – the sweater she had stolen from her cousin – and left her shirt open. She threw off her shoes as if she were preparing to plunge in, digging her two feet into the sand still damp with rain; her oversized pants, also taken from her cousin, stuck to her legs like huge gaiters. If her mother had seen her going out like this! Happily, the cape had hidden everything. My God, the cape! It must have fallen off somewhere along the way. Camille was distraught for thirty seconds and then burst out laughing. The idea of having left her undergarments, her skirt, her little boots, and her bodice in her cousin's granary made her laugh. That was where she'd left the cape. Camille was happy – she began to sing a strange, raucous tune, an old counting rhyme:

> Do you want to eat some cress
> When we're going to Lièsse.

Closer and closer to a chant, to a kind of prayer. Suddenly she rolled around in the sand like a cat, cooling herself in its dampness. With her hair full of sand, an ancient warrior, her face smeared with mud, she stood up.

"Camille!"

Paul cried out at the sight of this apparition. Camille burst into her great loud, guttural laugh and took his hands.

"My little Paul!"

"If Mama could see you, she would say you're a basilisk."

"A what?"

"*Basilisk.* It's an imaginary serpent whose look can kill."

"Thanks a lot, Paul! The things you know about!"

Camille pummeled him with her fists. Now they were rolling around together, repeating their childhood games. The sand was flying, Camille squeezed him with her two strong arms. She was a head taller than he, but the little boy was tough and violent. He gave her a few kicks. In a rage, Camille set her hands on the ground and flattened herself on him, victoriously straddling her victim. Nothing more to do. But what was this odd, hot feeling? The girl's shirt was unfastened. Camille crushed him with her entire length, her nose in the sand. The child felt her hot breast near his cheek. He wanted nothing more. Why did he feel so defeated? How had she done it, this big sister? He no longer wanted to fight, he was shivering.

"You're cold." Camille pummeled him with great thumps and rubbed him vigorously to warm him up. She snuggled him against her, gathering up her sweater. She covered their two bodies.

The moon was a little higher in the sky. Two children's faces lit by the moon. Two pairs of blue eyes, one darker, the other clear, terribly clear.

"Tell me a story."

Camille would have preferred to keep quiet, to listen to the wind dancing with the trees.

The Story of the Donkey and the Stone

"On a path bordered by thick grass and sharp branches, a path full of obstacles, a donkey was walking at daybreak; he was stumbling here and there, distracted, browsing on leaves and dreaming of the nice carrot he would nibble when he arrived. When he arrived . . . but where was he going? And what carrot was waiting for him? No one could tell, and he least of all.

"At a turn in the path, a luminous stone, hot from lying in the sun, watched him coming. Smooth and white, free of any attachments. The donkey was nuzzling a nice fat dragonfly hovering under his nose when his little hoof planted itself a few steps from the stone. In a moment it caught him on the end of his toe, just as the dragonfly stung him boldly on his right nostril. Surprised, the donkey stopped and asked himself how even such a charming dragonfly could have hypnotized him like that. His long eyelashes flapped three times in astonishment and the dragonfly flew away. However, the charm still held him. His hoof was caught. He capered about, leaping here and there, bucking on this side and gamboling on that. Nothing would do, and suddenly the snorting donkey lost his balance and sat down on his haunches. Then the donkey thought. What had happened to his front paw? He flapped his eyelashes three times and looked at his long paw. Nothing. Another flap of his eyelashes did no good. He pulled his paw casually. It resisted. He hung his pretty head, flopped his long ears, and tried to think again.

"'Come on, paw, be a good fellow, move a little.'

"Nothing happened, and it even seemed to him that it was trembling, as if someone were caressing his hoof.

"What do you know, it was even pleasant, very pleasant, very, very pleasant. Then the donkey stretched out his other paw and gently lowered his stomach to the ground and put his muzzle between his two hooves.

"Now, what was that? A white carrot? Under his nostril, the donkey discovered the stone, the pretty stone embedded in his foot, perfectly adapted to its shape.

"'How splendid you are, beautiful stone!' said the donkey, half closing his sea-blue eyes. 'Are you the one who's holding back my paw? No, don't let me go. Here, I'll give you the other hoof, too, if you like.'

"'Hello, oh fine donkey, I stopped you because you were going hither and thither, and I wanted to ask you for a kiss.'

"'Here is a kiss for you, little sun. May I please stay near you? For it is day and your skin is so smooth.'

"'Your lips are sweet, don't go away, but take care. I am fixed, intractable, fatal. They say I'm as hard as stone, and if my body is sharp, my heart beats like a sun. But I can make you fall whenever I like.'

"'Oh stone, you too must take care. There, where I left my hoofprint, no one will ever set foot again, for I will never move. They say that I am stubborn as a mule.'

"And the two embraced and did not leave each other. And the sun went down like a body surrendering.

"Night fell. The stone was cold, but the donkey kept her warm. The donkey was afraid, but the stone held him tight.

"Then came the dawn. When people took the path to town early in the morning, at the bend in the road, between the thick grasses, they cried out in amazement. And shocked, they closed their eyes and pulled their aprons over their heads.

"In place of the stone lay a beautiful young girl made of white gold and black jade. In place of the donkey was a young boy with great sapphire eyes.

"They were naked, and their fingers clasped forever. As solid as the stone, as stubborn as the mule – this was their love."

"But you, you are only a donkey. No, a cock without a comb!"

Camille pushed him. And together they went rolling down the slope. The boy got up, furious, when the branches stopped them. Furious and ready to scratch her face. Camille looked at Paul. The sister looked at this little brother. She smiled. Camille smiled at a boy who had the same eyes as hers, only a little lighter.

Her mouth curved gently: "My little Paul, don't be angry." She took him by the hand. It was dark all around. Except where they stood. The moon was shining. Two children.

"Listen, I'll tell you my secret. I would like to be . . . I would like to make sculptures! I saw a book of statues, you know, like I make with the earth. I know now. I want to be a great sculptor!"

The boy looked at her, amazed. In the moonlight her eyes were shining – a wild girl. He had never seen her eyes look so beautiful. Everyone in the village said so – neighbors, cousins, the peasants. Dark blue, at times violet or green, they changed like water beneath the sky, and always that deep, wrenching color. His sister was beautiful, really. Other people had dead eyes. She really looked at things. Her eyes shimmered as if she were making every human being, every object more resplendent.

"What is it, Paul? Paul?"

Suddenly that look of hers frightened him, and he fled, running away.

"Paul, Paul, wait for me, come on!" Now she was calling after him. Not for long. Camille shrugged her shoulders. After all, this evening was hers. In any case, whenever she came home her mother would not say a word to her. Well, sometimes she scolded her. And anyway, what did she have to be afraid of? She walked all alone.

She was stronger than all the village boys her age. She was often the one who led the games with her cousins. And she had her little knife. She always kept it with her. She loved to quarter a piece of fruit, scrape out the center, peel the rind. She loved to get down to the pit, then try to reconstruct it starting from the center.

She began the descent calmly. She felt cramped, confined in the family house. Her father was the only one who could understand what she was feeling this evening. But she dared not confide her secret to him. If he should ever fail to understand, she would have no more hope.

Her father. Her father's smile. She was troubled when he looked at her, but she felt they understood each other. She was only thirteen years old. He was about to turn fifty-one. Slim, with lovely wrinkles at the corners of his eyes, making them even more extraordinary. Nearly eighteen years older than her mother. She loved that slightly emaciated face, the small beard that seemed to be emerging from shadow, painted by Rembrandt, his golden eyes . . . She was sure that he had golden eyes. Camille stopped in her tracks. How could her father and mother live together? Marriage! She was overwhelmed with disgust. She thought of their big bed, she didn't understand. And here she was, the child of that union – of that mother, heavy, thick, closed. Her father – his mouth held out to kiss her earlier that evening, he'd gently placed his slightly scratchy lips on her forehead . . .

Camille had forgotten what time it was. Her eyes were open on the night. Camille looked at the great black space that swept around her. She surveyed its contours. The gift? She knew the language of lines, of curves, of angles. They alone gave life to the flesh, the soul received things, just as beings did. She was never mistaken.

"You are my little sorceress," her father had whispered in her ear. This was after she had described the characters of Crapitoche the cat, of Uhry the mountain guide, of Paillette the laborer. "All you have to do is look!" She had modeled their hearts in advance. Light and shadow. It was all there.

A little sorceress and her will-o'-the-wisp father, she wanted to go to him. He must be worried – for Paul would say nothing. When Paul came in, he would sit silently in a corner or get furiously angry if someone meddled with his things, but he would not answer questions. Quite the contrary. The more they asked him, "Have you seen Camille?" the more he would button his lip.

She picked up her cloak. "My ribbon!" Too late. It was probably up there in the sand. She wasn't afraid of the path parting the night. The Chinchy butte, or the Devil's Gift.

The villagers said you shouldn't go there at nightfall, but was she afraid of the devil? Certainly not of the devil! The villagers said that he filled his sack with creatures who stayed out too late on his mountain. Well, she would go back to see him. She would love to see him. She knew that he took a human shape, she saw him as terribly human, even banal, which made him all the more dangerous, since people were always looking out for someone deformed and ugly. No, he must be ordinary, universal. Then she called to him, and at his silence shot him a disdainful look.

"Play hide-and-seek as much as you like. I can play that game, too. Let's see who wins!"

Her mother was terribly afraid of this monster, she said prayers so he wouldn't single her out. Yet she never went to Mass, they never went to Mass. Her father laughed at the old women hurrying to Sunday morning mass, but out of politeness no one joked when their uncle the priest came to dinner. Camille walked quickly, her hands in the pockets of her pants. She was not so warm now. They would surely have eaten. So what, she would grab a hunk of bread and cheese. Perhaps her father would give her a little apple brandy to warm her up. She was quite cold now. Her damp clothes stuck to her. She was suddenly afraid. She did not want to stay in this family, she was not like her sister, Louise, who already wanted to get married, though she was two years younger. She wanted to leave, she wanted to be an artist, but how could she tell them, how could she do it? Suddenly the future was like an abyss – vertigo, emptiness. The girl started running, fleeing toward the house, she was galloping, her heart beating – she was only thirteen years old – it was too hard to dream of Paris so soon!

The village street echoed under her boots. There was still the awful cemetery where she liked to scare herself, and the terrifying church with its dark nave. There was a little light . . . In a moment it would be warm. In the kitchen. Then she calmed herself, pulled herself together. She loved the contest, the adversary, only the void suddenly made her afraid. If she could see the devil right there, she would not be afraid. But naturally he was a coward, like the other village boys. When they were in a group, they strutted and swaggered and preened. Like a bunch of roosters! The show-offs! Camille shouted at them:

"Here come the hunters!" They might attack . . . but she saw young Fambrune. All alone on the narrow path. She had brushed against him . . . A little chicken! His comb limp. Come on, there would only be a dozen of them! And anyway, all she had to do was to look them in the eye, their ugly foreheads, their hooded eyelids. Wasn't she a basilisk after all!

Camille pushed open the door. Her mother raised her head and began to shout. Everyone looked up: Victoire, Paul, Louise, Uncle . . . Then Camille cried, "I've seen the devil!"

She burst out laughing. She leaned against the door, covered with black mud, she had braided her hair. Half-deer, half-unicorn, she was defiant. Them and their boiled food. Seated in a circle. So satisfied. She swaggered, she had decided: she would go far away. The noise of the spoons. "Close the door, would you?" "But I . . ."

She had forgotten that she was hobbling. She hobbled in, tip tip tap, tip tip tap. Her father was not there.

Letter *from the Asylum*

My dream would be to go back to Villeneuve and never leave again, I would rather live in a barn at Villeneuve than in first-class accommodations here. . . .

I feel regret watching you spend your money on a lunatic asylum. Money that I could use to make beautiful sculptures and live a pleasant life! What a terrible misfortune! I could weep. . . . What happiness if only I could be at Villeneuve again. Lovely Villeneuve, there's no place like it on earth!

Journey to Villeneuve . . . left 26. Villeneuve 27,
28, 29 June. The two old people in the old, broken-
down house with the old housekeeper and the cricket in
the kitchen hearth. At V. I am always "overwhelmed
by the pathetic."

PAUL CLAUDEL, *Journal*

LOCKED UP. Locked up. How long? She is around seventy-seven years old. She doesn't know anymore. An endless eternity of mornings, evenings, nights . . .

She tried to keep exact count of every year, every day, every second. Not to make them a gift of it. Sometimes, when the moon follows its path across the sky over the asylum, she breathes in the odor of the earth. A single whiff makes her drunk. The earth of Villeneuve. Then the worst tortures begin. Quickly she gets up – jumps out of the iron bed, slips on the underskirt, the skirt, the calico, the woolen stockings, takes her boots in her hand. She descends the stairs and breathes. Breathes in the good earth that stretches out under her legs – the earth of Villeneuve galloping free in the early mornings. She hesitates, oh – the cloak. Take the cloak of love and slip out of the family house. Standing up, she walks and broods in the narrow cell. The bad odors suffocate her, invade her entire body. Filth. They are still sleeping. Quickly slip on the underskirt, the skirt – and it begins all over again, endlessly. Forever. Escape quickly.

She goes back to bed. Agitated. Sometimes they say she is agitated. How old is she now?

How old is she? Seventy-four? "My little Paul." And he never goes back to Villeneuve. The house completely changed.

"I have no more attachment to it. Discouragement and the temptation to despair."

How difficult it is to be content.

He listens to the rusty weathervane and she is no longer there. The little poet who pursued Galaxaure through the woods, the white-skinned Galaxaure, "certainly the most beautiful of the forest maidens," he is left sitting there – she has left him. That was how many years ago . . . he isn't sure anymore, perhaps sixty.

Step by step I go over all of the poet's work – pages that are inexplicable, inexplicable to me. Simply because she is always calling to me under the harsh beam of the night:

"Look at her, on her knees, that woman's pain swallowed up in the light," because it is the little poet of *L'Endormie,* "walking gravely with measured steps, lifting his legs. As if he had wanted to wipe his feet on the moon."

The cricket in the hearth!

The two old people beneath the moon.

And she, scratching at the door with her two beautiful, torn, earth-covered hands.

The earth of Villeneuve.

The Devil
in the House

S HE LOVED the white dawns at Villeneuve. Her family was still
sleeping. Sometimes she would tiptoe down the stairs, careful not
to make a sound.

Camille looked at the window, the sheet pulled over her. She had
left the window open as usual, despite the cold, the coming of the autumn mists. Soon they would have to go home. Why didn't her parents
stay at Villeneuve? She loved this village with its little square. The lin-
den trees lining every lane. The chiming of the church bells, hanging in
the belltower. That sense of the diagonal, as if time stopped for a moment. That moment before falling. That moment before rising again.
The aura of a silent world – around her, the stones down there would
soon awaken, warmed by the rising sun. She arose gently, slipped on
her socks, her shoes in her hand. She was ready. The kitchen was still
sleepy. Bread, cheese, coffee – everything at hand.

Sitting down, she savored this solitude. She loved to live outside
the family's regular routine. To take advantage of the calm, of the

clock, as if objects had spoken to her. Dawn of mists, dawn of faces. Suddenly he was there.

"Camille." That slightly raspy voice. It seemed she'd gotten that from him. Tall and thin, with his shining eyes.

"Come with me. Let's walk a bit." She held out a big bowl of coffee. "No, wait." He took her by the arms. "Sit down a moment." She wanted to escape. She didn't like explanations. He had to understand. "You never stop drawing, modeling with our good old earth. Do you really believe what Alfred Boucher said?"

She raised her head abruptly. Their eyes met.

"I want to be a sculptor!" She stood up. His arms encircled her waist. She was already tall for thirteen. Overcome by tenderness, he stood up and held her against him. "My daughter, my daughter." He felt her budding woman's body. He took her head between his two hands. "How beautiful she will be!" He looked at her large, disdainful mouth. Her cheeks were on fire. They were terribly aware of the silence in the kitchen. The two of them looked at each other. She reached his chest. He wanted to crush her, this little slip of a woman who was too much like him, with her uncombed mop of hair. Then he passed a hand, still trembling, through her hair and kissed her forehead, delicately, as if to wish her bon voyage.

"I will help you. You will be a sculptor."

She threw herself into his arms.

"Come on, let's go before your mother wakes up, we'll walk as far as the field."

"Oh, where is Camille? That child is driving me crazy!"

"Mama, there they are, both of them, Papa-a . . ."

"Keep quiet." Louise kept quiet, sulking in a corner, soaking her buttered bread. Paul was swaying back and forth. He annoyed her, that closed boy who observed her with his two stupid blue eyes.

Their mother said nothing. She was tidying up, cleaning. It hardly mattered what Louis-Prosper did. They no longer had much to say to each other, husband and wife. Yet she could have loved him if not for his violent rages and his books always lying around. And then, she felt he had contempt for her. She was not tall, she was not slim. Oh, she was not like Camille! Neither was Louise . . . She turned tenderly toward that peevish little girl who looked so much prettier when she smiled. All the sadness of the world. She too would have loved to go out early in the morning with her father, but she always caught cold. Every time she wanted to get into some mischief, she got hurt or came down with another illness.

"Go on, children, clear out." The crumbs, the spoons, the drops of coffee or milk, the broom. What a lot of work, but why was Louis-Prosper just sitting there? He annoyed her.

"Listen, I think that Camille is an artist."

"What!"

"I think that Camille will be a great sculptor."

She didn't respond directly. "But what you're saying is dreadful! And it's all your doing . . . She already ruins our life with her earth, her clay. The other day Victoire was covered with red mud. Her apron is always soaked, but just because of this to agree that she should have a profession! My God, a profession . . . You want to turn her into a slut!"

"Camille will be a sculptor, I tell you."

They argued violently. Upstairs, the children kept quiet, unhappy. Camille suddenly stood up again. She threw a jacket over her shoulders and rushed down the stairs. Escape, get as far away as possible from the shouting. Her brother Paul ran after her, Louise wanted to hold him back: "Stay with me, Paul." Paul pulled, Louise pulled, Camille turned around and shot them a disdainful look. Paul was furious and kicked Louise. Shocked, she let go and Paul came hurtling down the stairs. Cries, shouts. Their mother came out, looked at Camille at the bottom of the stairs. "That child is the devil himself!"

Paul got up, pushed past his mother and set off at a run to join Camille, who had already escaped. The last days of vacation, the last green leaves. Tomorrow they would all be at Nogent. He did not like Nogent. "Camille, Camille!"

She waited for him. "You didn't hurt yourself, did you?" The boy shook his head, but blood was trickling down his knee. "Come on, let's go." She led him to the fountain.

The boy looked at her and suddenly burst out laughing. *"Cacha-Diablo. I am going to call you Cacha-Diablo."*

Camille shrugged her shoulders, the blood had stopped. "Come on, let's go to the quarry – let's see who gets there first!"

Madame Berthier shook her head as she watched them pass by.

"When are they going to leave off their galloping, those two? Always gadding about. Not like little Louise, so quiet, so charming with her curls. Always so clean! That wild one, she'll come to a bad end."

Camille and Paul were already far away. Down on that part of the road the path broke up, the little wood . . . Suddenly, there it was: the sunrise, so good, it warmed the earth. "Where shall we put the earth?" In their haste the children had not brought anything with them. Camille wrapped it in her cloak. By knotting the sleeves she made it work as a bucket. Heavy. At least twenty kilos. The children staggered under the heavy load. Paul was exhausted. One sleeve had split, the earth ran out. "It looks like a human body."

"Shut up!"

"The red earth under the jacket, a broken arm."

"Shut up!"

"But Paul, look, it's beautiful, the earth is like a human body. Look!" She emptied out the other sleeve and began to knead. The earth, still damp from last night's storm, took shape. Little by little a bust emerged, violent, heavy. Paul sat watching silently. Her hair was full of red earth. Several times she put her hands in it to push it back.

"You look like an Inca," Paul said. A few red marks on her face were like ancient wounds.

She gave a big kick and trampled what she'd just made. "That's not it, that's not it!"

"Camille, stop!"

"Shut up and help me."

"Are you angry?" They started off again, walking as best they could, swinging their heavy load toward the house.

"Miss Camille! Oh, no! Not today! You're leaving tomorrow!" Victoire broke down. Poor old Victoire, who had just polished everything, made everything shine, folded up the rugs. Order, order! Camille hated that furniture, like a bunch of huge cadavers under their white coverings. She loved life too much. She looked at Victoire and pouted.

"Come on, Victoire!"

"Okay, but not here . . . in the studio."

"The shed."

"The studio, I told you, the studio. That's what it's called."

"Oh, look!"

"Those are the devil's own footsteps." Camille's shoes had made great red marks everywhere. Paul wanted to laugh, he stood a bit apart. "Okay, come on, help me, don't just stand there like an idiot." So the three of them went out again.

Suddenly Victoire stopped at the sound of the piano. "That's pretty."

Camille, too, would have loved to slide her fingers over the piano keys, but her mother had forbidden it once and for all: "The piano's for good little girls. You get everything dirty and you aren't refined enough." So when she was alone outside she sang at the top of her lungs. Anyway, she had too much work to do on her sculpture. She had to put all of herself into it. Besides, Louise played well. Her sister stopped a moment. Victoire looked at Camille. What would become of this child? She was tall, and still growing. But her eyes made Victoire cringe: a will of iron, nothing could break her. She would die before changing her mind.

"Come on, Victoire, hurry up!" The trio crossed the garden to the studio. "Hey, sit down there." She looked at the young girl. "Come on, Paul, pass me the water bucket, move! What are you dreaming about now?"

"I'm tired of helping you."

"Brat, shut up! shut up!" Paul threw the red earth at his sister's head. The young girl continued, unperturbed. "Don't move, Victoire."

"But the sun's in my eyes!"

Camille did not answer. The sun on Victoire's profile was like a knife plunging to the bone, carving her anatomy. The young girl gathered up the earth . . . "You are not going to start in again today. What good will that do?"

"But I'm going to take it with me."

"Oh?" Victoire had jumped up. She imagined Madame Louise confronted with that earth. At the same time, Camille would not give in. She knew it.

The old housekeeper had trouble keeping still. It hardly mattered to the girl, she was becoming utterly self-absorbed, almost mean. When she worked, everything else was forgotten. There was only the desire to grasp her model – the quality of the gaze, especially the gaze.

Victoire tried to reach into her apron discreetly and get out the nuts she had put there – fresh nuts – and her little nutcracker, but Camille was already shouting: "Victoire, what do you want me to do! You're always moving!" And suddenly the girl laughed her big, open laugh. "Okay, come on, a little break. I love nuts."

Camille crouched at Victoire's feet. "Tell me a story, Victoire. What happened with my uncle Paul? You know, the young man who drowned – they found him near the little bridge."

"No, not this time."

"Tell why my father and mother hardly every speak to each other anymore? You knew my mother before?"

"You know, you musn't hold it against her. She was a happy girl when she was young. Your father came and impressed her, he was from another part of the country, intelligent. I think she loved him in her way, but did she know where she was going? She had lived in the shadow of her father, the doctor. Her mother had died young. And then, of course, there was the tragedy with Charles-Henri . . ."

Camille looked away. Victoire hesitated to go on. This poor girl was often reproached for taking the place of her elder brother, Charles-Henri. *Usurper!* her mother would say when she was very angry.

"Poor Camille, you surely weren't any such thing. He wasn't strong enough. Barely fifteen days. Your mother thought she would go mad. Your father would go off by himself at nightfall. He walked for hours to forget, as if he were carrying death inside him. Your mother held it against him. You know, that often happens with us. A firstborn child does not always survive . . . Then they began to argue. Your mother was afraid. Your father became violent. And then you were born – magnificent, wild, strong! Your father was crazy with joy and he showed you off everywhere. On the sixth of December 1864, Camille Rosalie Claudel was born. I can still see you. I wrapped you in my shawl because I was afraid you were cold. The blinds were drawn in the room. Your mother wanted a boy. She did not want to accept you. Your uncle the priest rang the church bells. Ding, dong, Camille Rosalie – a rose was born. I looked at you . . .

"Your mother turned her head away and said nothing for several hours. She was crying, that's all. She didn't even thank the Good Lord. You would think she'd pledged you to the devil himself."

Camille laughed, a little brokenly, sadly.

"Paul, you know, he called me *Cacha-Diablo* this morning."

Victoire tousled the girl's hair.

"My little *Cacha-Diablo.*"

Tomorrow they would have to return to Nogent. She did not like Nogent.

Letter *from the Asylum*

I received them hobbling along, wearing an old, threadbare coat, and an old hat from Samaritaine that came down to my nose. Anyway, it was me. They will remember their crazy old aunt. That is how I'll appear when they remember me in the next century . . .

I would so like to have a little place by the fire at Villeneuve, but alas, I don't think I'll ever leave Montdevergues at the rate things are going! It does not look good!

Sunday, 4 April 1932.

Birth:　　　　Claudel, Charles-Henri, born 1 August 1863 at Fère.
Witness Alphonse de Massary, notary, age 39, resident
of Fère.

Death:　　　　Claudel, Charles-Henri, deceased on 16 August 1863,
age 16 days.

Birth:　　　　Claudel, Camille, born at Fère, 8 December 1864. Deceased at Avignon (Department of Montfavet) on 19
October 1943 at 2:00 P.M.

The list from the civic register. A poor copy. I look at it; held between
my two fingers, it dances to the right, to the left, right, left. A thin
sheet, so flimsy, torn by the slightest breeze.

Is this how the century will remember you? I'm afraid so.

And you took too much time to die. Your poor life that swung continually between two landings: 1864–1943, 1943–1864! And then that handful of earth thrown upon you – the crumbling earth. That's all.

> And as for me, I have absolutely no demands.
> Let it rest with God, and let Him leave us our own
>
> > nothingness . . .
>
> He in his place and we in ours forever!

No! I look at her. I see those hands. She wants to say something. Closer. We must come closer. She is sixty-eight years old. Her hands shake a little now. She is murmuring something under the big hat. She watches them leave and they have not understood. Who will teach them? Who will tell them? She is not only their crazy old aunt! No, not only that, but much more.

The faint smell of earth caught on the heels of shoes. Cinder footsteps marking the floor of the kitchen, there at Villeneuve.

We must look for the sculptures. Her sculptures are somewhere out there in the world.

> The miserly earth that never lies.

That is what she has left us forever.

She goes back toward her cell. I watch her disappear down the endless corridor. The little beggar who sways, smaller and smaller. She turns around.

A tip of the hat. A clown's wink. Blue. Holy *"Cacha-Diablo."* Was it you the old poet was dreaming of? Camille the Moor, the Renegade, the elusive "winning smile" of *Cacha-Diablo?* It doesn't matter!

Camille Claudel. Sculptor. Time without end. Amen.

David and Goliath

You are not able to go against this Philistine to fight with him, for you are but a youth, and he has been a man of war from his youth.

1 Samuel 17:33

SHE WAS EXHAUSTED. All alone she'd carried her twenty kilos of earth. Almost as heavy as she was. But if she'd said something, her mother would have seen what she was doing. The packages, the suitcases, the fishing rods. The mother had said nothing. Her father helped her as much as he could, a little. The official Registrar of Mortgages was thinking of other things. Here, they'll heap everything in Monsieur Favet's old cart. But what's this? Her mother had waited for her to come to the house before shouting. She opened the jute sack. "My god! Red earth, you're crazy, my girl!" Unfortunately, the father was still busy talking with Monsieur Favet.

"Throw that away immediately." Camille stood firm. Paul was afraid. He knew her when she began tapping her foot and arching her back. Now she was shouting, clinging to her sacks, which her mother had had the temerity to touch. Her mother had deliberately waited until the last moment. People turned around to look at them. Louise, frightened and embarrassed, squeezed against Paul, Paul kept quiet. He awaited the adults' decision. He knew that Camille would not change her mind. Her face was red. She cried, "I won't leave my sacks! I'll sit down right here, I won't move. I'll sleep here!"

Her mother gave her a couple of slaps. Camille did not move. She did not cry. Obstinate. Hidden behind her hair. Fortunately, Louis-Prosper arrived. In a single glance he understood. "Come on, let's get into the cart. These sacks are too heavy. We are going to take one of them, and we will come back to fetch the other tomorrow."

"I'll take it, if you like." Monsieur Colin came forward. Camille smiled at him, she jumped on his neck. "I was watching you," he said. "Camille looked like Malquiant, mounting an assault on enemy troops: 'All embroidered with gold was he, facing the sun, he shines . . .'"

She was happy. Her mother threw her a withering glance. Once more Camille had found an ally. How did she do it? She never sacrificed herself. She did what she wanted to do. And that energy prompted a certain affection in those around her. People bent over backward to help her.

Camille now turned back toward Monsieur Colin: "Can I ride with you?"

"Camille, stay here!"

But Camille preferred to be next to this man rather than piled into the family cart. The weather was lovely. A fine, warm autumn afternoon like a velvet dress, a bit heavy. Red.

"Please do let her, the child doesn't disturb me in the least."

Camille won. She took her other sack of earth. Provided that Paul did not come too!

"Can I go up there?"

"No, Paul, stay here, please, you will help us." Paul was sulky.

Monsieur Colin was a journalist; occasionally he worked as a teacher. Hired as the children's tutor, he and Camille understood each other perfectly. He was intelligent, rather bohemian. Camille loved the way he dressed. At Villeneuve his clothes provoked many remarks. And a Republican to boot!

The cart started off. The man was forty-five years old. He began to recite some poetry and Camille took up the refrain.

Count Roland sees Samson dead – imagine the pain he feels. He spurs his horse as hard as he can and gallops off to the pagan. He holds Durandal, who is worth more than all the gold at stake. There is an African from Africa. This is Malquiant, son of King Maloud. His clothes are embroidered with gold; facing the sun, he shines among all the others. He mounts his horse, whom he calls Saut-Perdu.

Camille had stood up in the cart. "He is not a fool who would challenge Roland to a race!" Colin was amused. He gave the horse a flick of the whip. Off they went at a rapid trot. At the turning, Camille laughed: "Go, Monsieur Colin! Down with the Christians, I like the pagans better. That Roland is a stupid boy. I'd have fixed him!"

Colin looked at the little girl. The young girl, rather . . . Was he right to talk of all those heroes? He had read her *The Song of Roland*, *Ninety-Three*, *The Romance of Renart*. Her younger brother listened, too, but said nothing. He seemed to be judging, keeping his distance. She got carried away, as she was doing at this very moment. If he let her, she would even grab the reins and imagine she was on the field of battle, even Count Roland's . . .

Colin smiled, imagining how the people of Nogent would stare at them going by at full gallop! She read everything she got her hands on, but she was not capable of analyzing. She immediately took sides. She was Malquiant against Roland. She was Renart slipping into Ysengrin's house. Why did she love this passage in particular? He remembered the numerous drawings she made in her child's hand. She had illustrated Renart at Ysengrin's. Renart "kissing Dame Ysengrin and pissing, defecating on the children of Ysengrin." Curious child.

But why was she laughing? Suddenly Colin, abruptly yanked from his reflections, saw that they had passed the house in rue Saint-Epoingt.

"You've carried me off, Monsieur Colin!" He had to make a half-turn with the carriage. The horse was tired. They would certainly arrive after the Claudels. "I have a new idea, Monsieur Colin. I am going to illustrate *David and Goliath*. You know, you told me the story."

The young girl clearly had a gift for mimicry. She was never boring. There, they had arrived. The big staircase . . . The packages already deposited in the vestibule. Everyone was busy, Louis-Prosper had disappeared.

"Come," he whispered to Camille. They went through the corridor, to reach the garden behind. Colin carried the sacks. Camille arrogantly disdained her porter-servant. She opened the shed. They were fine out there. A swathed Bismarck looked at a swaddled Napoleon. Cracking slightly, they had withstood the vacation. The young girl immediately busied herself, dampening the earth and setting to work.

"Wait, Monsieur Colin. David will be here, then hanging onto him, Goliath, without his head. I love cutting off heads!"

"Good. I'm off. If not, you'll see, I'll lose mine, too." Camille waved to him distractedly. She was already absorbed in her work. Surrounded by heroes, she had decided to show how the weak triumph over the strong. The idea had come to her the other morning. One of the stones on the Geyn, the tiny clown . . .

"Come on, tell me a story!" What was it she'd done there, lost in the forest? The gray little girl next door.

Once upon a time there was a little clown who had secretly slipped on the big shoes of life. But he had put them on the wrong way. The right shoe on the left foot and the left shoe on the right.

He set off, pigheaded as they come, and fell on his face. But his heart was still bigger than the shoes – you could put two feet in it. And people did not hold back. They slipped into his heart and strolled around.

As the little clown could see no farther than his nose, he put the big shoes on his hands so as to feel life better, and his feet in his heart. Then he set off running. But wherever he put his feet, his heart was crushed, and when he opened his arms, he lost his shoes.

He thought for a while, but his great eyes opened and he lost his nose.

She was standing there, behind "the gossips," forgotten, droll as a clown in a sprawling circus. The cloak had fallen at her feet, and Camille suddenly felt a great tenderness for this little figure. The Geyn was upright, but she was so small, she had a place in her heart. The big, important people . . . she had to fight, she had to show that force does not so easily win out against tenderness, big feet against imagination. Camille thought of big clown shoes. Her head was full of voices, her hands murmuring. "Once upon a time there was a clown, who . . ." She wanted to make him seem both funny and courageous.

"Camille, hurry up."

My God, dinner time! She had forgotten the time. She stood back.

Little David was already astride the huge body of the giant, who was trying to protect himself. He had no head. Had David just cut it off? She would make the head later. The head by itself, without a body. Heads without bodies.

"Camille." Her father was there, standing in the door in the shadow. "Camille, come quickly." He took her hand, pulling her from the dark, damp studio. "Don't work so hard. I will ask Alfred Boucher for his advice. He is coming back in a week."

"Look at that child, Louis." She had dirtied her dress again. Camille lowered her eyes to verify the mess. It was true, her dress was nearly covered with big red flowers. In a way it was beautiful. Everyone was staring at her. "At least go wash your hands before eating, and change your clothes." Camille hurried – her mother had said nothing – she went up to her room, in the dark, she reached the basin and rinsed her fingers. Suddenly she felt a tenderness for her mother – that closed, austere woman, who must love Camille in her way. She was only thirty-four years old now, and already she'd grown heavy, her big eyes often distant, lost. What shattered dreams they must have seen!

Married at eighteen. How had she survived the death of her first child? Who was she, really, and why was there such an implacable hatred between them, giving Camille the feeling that someday one of them would kill the other? Mother, brother, family, marriage . . . Camille was thirteen years old, but all that stifled her. She did not understand how anyone could be close to someone else.

She came down quickly. They were all seated at the table. Her mother looked at her sadly. Camille suddenly felt a great weariness. She wanted to cry for help, to make some sign, a sign of distress, so they would rescue her. But who would believe a child of thirteen calling for help? They would say, "Calm down, don't dramatize." And yet she was suddenly seized by a fierce vertigo, as if she were being devoured by some hidden disease, as if she were dying there, at the table. She could not swallow; she wanted to vomit. "Eat, Camille." She would have liked to please them, and the more she wanted to, the more paralyzed she became. Like a great cry rising, like a tree catching fire in a gust of wind, Camille sat transfixed, looking at them all. They were far away, she heard them as if she had cotton in her ears. To the rescue, help her! Her parents, her sister, her brother continued to gesticulate. She was

37

thinking only that her legs were too short. Slow motion. She would have liked them to pay attention to her and at the same time to be alone, alone with herself. "Marionettes, marionettes!" she began to shout.

"Camille!" She was on the ground. In pieces, lifeless. "The child has had nothing to eat all day. Not surprising with all the effort she expends on those cursed sacks."

CAMILLE ENTERS her four white walls. Hard and bitter suffering. Suffering that wrings your heart. Camille knocks on the wall with her two hands, she cries the name into the mirrors, as if they could conjure her beloved, the light she is waiting for, the struggle she wants to take up all over again. Weariness and a burst of energy, denial, when she is forced to give up defeated, and yet she already knows that in the eyes of the world she will be the endless sad echo of the one she loved . . .

She

*The day has come to prove
To you and your friends the folly of your thoughts —
A woman's weapons are proof.*

VIRGIL, *The Aeneid*, Book XI
Camilla, queen of the Volsci

THE SUN HAD RISEN early this morning. Camille kept her routine from Villeneuve, but here a stroll was impossible. The milkman was leaving the bottles of milk. They clanked like big cracked bells. For a moment Camille remembered the big cows at Bresse. Under the heavy bedspread she stretched her body like a big stomach. She stretched out, kicking. Camille felt with her hand down the length of her leg. She liked to confirm the shapes of her own body. She began to run her hand along her leg a little below the knee. Leaning over as if to pick a flower, she even managed to touch her foot and tickle it; she came up along her leg, skimming it with a finger, then making circles on the smooth surface of her thighs. She pulled up her nightdress a little. There, a thick buttock. She grabbed it, trying to understand its contours, going back to the knee, up again, and slowly slipped her hand into the hollow of her groin. The other morning she had made a curious discovery, what great pleasure it gave her to caress herself that way.

She lifted her nightdress higher, without looking. With her eyes on the ceiling she felt her budding breasts, already forming. She was gripped by a strange reticence and didn't let her hands linger there. One day she would like to sculpt a nude. But who would pose for her? She would not dare look at herself naked. As much as she loved to feel the bones rolling beneath her fingers, the flesh, the ligaments, all the parts of her body that she reproduced from memory in her drawings. She stretched in the bed and reached with one hand to grab her cotton shirt, then the wool one underneath. It was cold this morning. Winter was coming. Soon the days would be too short. She would have to draw by the light of the family lamp. The little shed at the bottom of the garden would be light for only a few hours, it would get colder and colder, and little by little the frozen earth would begin to resist. Her fingers would get clumsy. Camille did not like this long winter sleep, this death of shapes and light. Quickly she got up, pulled on her woolen stockings, underskirt, woolen dress, cape, and shawl. She took her shoes in her hand and tiptoed down the stairs. The door to her parents' room was closed. She suddenly felt nauseous at the idea that one day she would be deprived of the pleasure of waking alone. How can anyone wake up beside someone else all the days of her life? When you open your eyes, the most important thing is solitude.

Camille reached the kitchen, quietly brought in the bottles of milk, and poured herself a big bowl. She went outside. The shawl around her throat. The milk refreshed her, she was cold, but gradually her body relaxed, unclenched. Camille softly breathed in the garden air. Nature, like her, began to warm up. She would never forget the vigorous blood of the modest earth. She slowly crossed the garden, softly opened the door to the studio. The sun's rays were striking the side of the *David and Goliath* she was going to finish. She stopped, as if she did not want to disturb the concluding battle. David seemed about to cut off Goliath's head. How could she make him sweat? Perhaps by the material she used, something shining, ivory – to create life, better than life! A hard material with nothing inside . . . She was happy she'd managed to make a group.

Now she knew she could do it. She did not want to stop sculpting anymore. The sun shone more strongly on her work. Camille had learned nothing yet – she was thirsty for knowledge. She could see Alfred Boucher as he had been yesterday, in the early afternoon. He had come after lunch. Coffee, liqueur, the girl couldn't stand it anymore. She despised him, this man who took time to be polite. She would have liked to drag him off to the garden shed immediately. But at the same time it was her father who had convinced him to come, her father who was discussing, deciding. Her father was seated in the big armchair in the salon that looked out on the garden; her mother, discreet, all in black, never sat down when she had visitors . . . And then Louise had to play her little tune on the piano. Paul had quickly disappeared. He knew Camille was inclined to be violent and dreaded the fallout from Monsieur Alfred Boucher's expert opinion. And he was afraid. How would Camille react?

Paul did not like Monsieur Alfred Boucher, sculptor from Nogent. If he was an artist like his sister, he would have understood her impatience to know the verdict. Camille had remained standing with her back to the buffet. Tall as she was, she behaved like a child who dared not let go of a coveted object. Her father was asking for news from the capital. But when would they go to the studio? Her shed! "Get up," Camille muttered to herself. "I beg you! Even Paris doesn't interest me now. Come see my sculpture." But this is what she heard . . .

A certain Auguste Rodin, a total unknown, had caused a scandal. He had returned from Belgium. Two years earlier he had exhibited *The Age of Bronze* at the Salon of 1877. His first great sculpture. He was thirty-seven years old. It seemed so perfect that the jury accused him of *surmoulure*. Her father asked what this meant. Alfred Boucher explained: "Oh, it's common practice nowadays. The sculptors make molds of the body parts directly from the living model. It goes much faster!"

"But that's fraud!" Camille had cried. Or she had thought it, for her lips had not even moved. How could you call yourself a sculptor using such methods? That would be as easy as making a cake, just let the batter run into a preformed mold. Wait a little, and out it comes, the form served up on a platter! But what about the direct cut, the clay mock-up? She would never make cakes. And furthermore, he was already too old! Thirty-seven! They really had time to lose. When she . . . she waited with all the power of her fourteen years.

"Well," Boucher went on, "this is still a source of gossip among the philistines. They're so refined! Sculpture interests so few people . . ." And off they went discussing the capital again: "Madame Edmond Adam just created *La Nouvelle Revue*. Everyone is dying to visit her salon. Léon Gambetta was invited for dinner there . . . ." And they talked and talked. "The Commune? . . . You know, it's already been eight years ago . . . Well, it depends on what circles . . . "

Camille looked at the glasses of liqueur on the table in front on them – one, two, three, four. Don't throw them at their heads. My God! Her hands behind her back against the sideboard. Well-behaved, her hands. "Well-behaved . . . " Today.

Finally they rose, looking at the young girl tenderly. "And if we want to talk about art with artists . . . " Camille blushed, violently. There, they were going out, Camille, Monsieur Alfred Boucher, her father. They had crossed the garden.

All the details of their route stood out for Camille, the little path, the flowers, the rusty door handle. She opened the door and stood aside. He came in, ran his hand through his hair, as if he were removing a hat as a sign of respect, and gazed a long time at *David and Goliath,* a long time, saying nothing. Camille was soaking wet, as if someone had poured a basin of water over her head. Then he had slowly approached, walked around the sculpture, stopped. Camille had stopped seeing it. Louis-Prosper looked at Camille. Her magnificent dark blue eyes seemed completely dilated. She looked like a seer, ready to predict a dreadful future in the offing. Suddenly he was afraid for his daughter. She had gathered her hair in a kind of chignon, but she still looked like a little girl. She had put a ribbon on, too. She stood up straight, terribly straight. Her proud mouth was pinched. But it was her eyes especially that threw him into a panic.

"This is really astonishing. The contrasts of light and shade, the power. She has the gift of life. That is the most important thing for a sculptor. It almost looks like she's taken lessons with Rodin . . . She must go to Paris. Quickly. Well, it's up to you . . . It is a difficult profession if you are alone. Besides, one has to be able to exhibit in the salons, to be introduced. I will be able to help, but so little. I myself have great trouble . . . not to mention Rodin! It's too soon! I know, she's courageous, but for a woman, I would say no instantly, despite this child's genius. Perhaps even because of it. Colin told me that she bolted for no reason. Earlier I was observing her in the salon. She was fidgeting. And this is a profession that requires patience. And then," he added, caressing the young girl's cheek, "she will marry one day."

Louis-Prosper and Alfred Boucher went out. Camille followed

them. She turned back from the door. So she was a woman, she would marry. It was the first time she'd heard that. A woman! And what about sculpture? Those men didn't always marry, after all. She and her sculpture – they would see!

Letter *from the Asylum*

A fine thing! all the millionaires who threw themselves upon a defenseless artist! For the gentlemen who conspired in this fine act are all millionaires forty times over.

Now the philistines gathered together their armies to battle. . . . And there went a champion out of the camp of the Philistines, named Goliath of Gath, whose size was six cubits and a span. And he had a helmet of brass upon his head and he was armed with a coat of mail. . . . And he had greaves of brass upon his legs and a target of brass between his shoulders. And the staff of his spear was like a weaver's beam; and his spear's head weighed six hundred shekels of iron: and one bearing a shield went before him. . . .

"And [David] took his staff in his hand, and chose him five smooth stones out of the brook, and put them in a shepherd's bag. . . .

"And when the Philistine looked about and saw David, he disdained him: for he was but a youth. . . . "

She has held on a long time. Without weapons, without guile, without substitutes. Her hands empty. There. She has no more chisel, mallet, or sculpture. They have taken everything. She looks again at the old worn Bible. She wanted to sculpt. The weak against the strong, the great. There were still so many others – so many epics she would have liked to hold in her dusty fingers and reread.

She is there, without books, without earth, without arms. Just a camisole.

The Burning Bush

"Why did you leave, unhappy one?"
The boiled meat was tired of being eaten all around.

PAUL CLAUDEL, *Tête d'Or*

THE HOUSE was deserted. Camille drifted from one room to
the next. She was doing nothing. She was wandering alone. Her
parents and Louise were at Monsieur and Madame Chapoulis's. Louise
continued to play the piano. She played remarkably well. Madame
Chapoulis came twice a week, but Louise tired easily. She was only thirteen years old and preferred to chat with her mother in the kitchen.
Camille was surprised at her sister's stories. She sometimes heard the
child's light song. She looked at her. Her delicate little face reminded
her of a weasel's. She had something of her father's laughing eyes, her
nose slightly turned up, as if it were telling you, "All right, you've seen
me," and the pretty curls around her forehead. Camille felt a certain
tenderness for this fragile sister of hers. Louise had also left a bouquet
lying on her bed and her embroidery. How could she spend hours
stitching such insipid flowers?

Camille drifted from room to room. She had not lit the lamps.
Camille wandered through the halls and into the empty rooms. Tired,
she felt tired. It was two years since they'd left Nogent. She was sad

when she remembered Colin, Alfred Boucher. Here, everything was inimical, Paul and Louise no longer studied with her. Paul was at the secondary school. The house was beautiful, with a balcony on the upper floor, a grand front door above a sweeping flight of steps, and beyond that the double staircase. She was sixteen years old and suffocating in this little town of Wassy.

Camille came to her parents' large bedroom. She sat in the armchair and looked at the bed. She wondered. If her mother could see her, she would say, "Don't stare so. It is impolite." But Camille stared. Double beds fascinated her. The couple. What did that mean?

The bed was pale, worn out. The rose-colored cushions slept under their lace. The cross and the palm hung above her mother's writing table. Did her father still embrace her mother, or did they sleep side by side, silently, like funerary statues with no hope of resurrection? Yet her father was so lively, full of secret, wild adventure. But her mother, what did she think about? How she bustled around the kitchen!

Camille wandered into the bedrooms. Walls – a refuge – walls. The stairs. Camille went up and sat down on her bed, resting her eyes, looking off in the distance. She was happy with this solitude, and at the same time she would have liked to escape from this house, from this room. The silence. Yesterday there was a ruckus – one she'd provoked. Yesterday – she saw it again, her father mad with rage, her mother on the verge of tears, Paul terrified . . .

"Camille will make sculpture, Louise is a virtuoso pianist, Paul will go to the *École normale.** After vacation I am going to settle you in Paris and try to find myself a place nearby. I will live alone, I will take my meals at the hotel, and I will come to see you on Sundays."

Her mother had raised her head. Was he going crazy? Her sister, Louise, was smiling. She had wanted to go to the capital. She despised this town, the constant drizzle, the walks, the absence of shops. Paul had said nothing. Curiously, he showed nothing, but then he didn't look happy either. She had not stood quietly. Her father had proudly raised his head, his fine head. He had made his decision. No one would contradict him.

"But Louis . . ."

---

* The elite college in Paris.

"Yes."

"How am I going to manage alone with these three children in that huge city where I don't know anyone?"

"You will do fine. You are not a child . . . and Camille will help you." Her mother had shrunken a bit more. There, it was decided: on 26 April 1881. Paul would enter the Louis-le-Grand secondary school.

Camille knew that she had won. Her father acknowledged that she would be an artist, a sculptor. Suddenly she was afraid. Who was going to take her on? What studio? Were there other women sculptors? Happily, Alfred Boucher would be in Paris. He would help her out. Camille got up. She heard an unruly group of children and shouting. She leaned out the window and saw her brother Paul being chased by kids in the street. Camille wanted to laugh. What had happened? There he was on all fours, frightened, climbing the steps. The door slammed. Camille heard Paul gallop up the stairs.

"Paul, Paul, what happened to you?"

He looked at her, he stopped short. She was there, huge in the half-light . . . He stared at her wildly.

"Why were those kids chasing you?"

"They were *not* chasing me. We were playing. Don't butt in." He went off, but suddenly came back, beside himself: "I will not go to Paris! I will not go to Paris!" And he went downstairs again.

Camille sat there on the stairs, sad. He was unhappy down there in his room. The house was empty. Paul was afraid, afraid of this town. The other kids had made fun of him right away. What would it be like when there were dozens of them? He hated speaking to them. They were dirty, noisy . . .

"My little Paul." The child was curled up on his bed. His little sailor suit was ruined. Why was he so dressed up? . . . Oh yes, he was supposed to join his parents at the Chapoulis's. The kids in the street must have laughed at him — so spick-and-span, like the neat coverlet.

Camille approached the child softly, sat down on the bed. The room was dark. He was sobbing softly. "Listen, once upon a time . . ." She gently caressed his forehead. Gradually the child fell asleep. She carefully removed his shoes and his heavy overcoat, then tucked him between the sheets and under the covers.

Back downstairs she lit the oil lamp and adjusted the flame. A dog appeared in the street. He sniffed around the door. At least it was a presence. She let him in. He looked miserable – just as Paul had. She gave him the rest of the roast, the bone she had saved. She took a pencil and began to draw: the dog, busy gnawing the bone, showed no more interest in her. Gradually Camille forgot her sadness. Head bent, legs folded under her, she drew without stopping. She had forgotten the cold, the time. Suddenly she saw her brother standing in front of her, still sleepy but hungry. The dog barked.

"I'm hungry."

Reluctantly, Camille abandoned her drawing. But the child looked so lost. He had awakened to an unfriendly world, too dark, and he was cold.

"Look, Cam, the drawing behind you on the wall. Papa brought it back from the auction one day. You know what it is? . . . The Great Wall, in China. Why don't we get that magazine *Le Tour au monde* anymore? I loved to read the travel stories."

In the half-light he was dreaming, a fragile boy, and his pale blue eyes glimpsed a gigantic world beyond the high wall.

"You should paint countries, Cam. One day *I* am going to China. I will take a boat."

Paul had forgotten his hunger. The dog barked, turning from one of them to the other. Camille went to the kitchen. There was soup to heat up. Turnips, potatoes, carrots.

"You talk and talk . . . Talk more slowly. It's like pigs running out of the barnyard."

"And you, you don't even know how to cook soup. You draw, but anyone can draw. I like it better when you sculpt. But I don't want to go to Paris."

"Shut up. Alfred Boucher will be there. And maybe Monsieur Colin will come to see us."

"Yes, but Papa wants to enroll me in April at the *lycée*. I'm afraid of those closed classes. But anyway, I'm sick of Villeneuve."

"You say you want to go to China, the great adventurer! But you want to stay in your old house with Papa and Mama. Come on, if you're a rooster, show you're a rooster and not some . . . little rabbit who scampers off at the first sign of danger!"

There they were, the two of them at the table, sitting around the casserole. The bread fell into the dish. They torpedoed it with loud cries: "Bang, bang, bang!"

"Remember when you fell into the pond?" Camille laughed her wonderful, throaty laugh. "You were running behind me, and boom! I heard flop-flop." Paul began to laugh too. "Boom! Headfirst."

"Tell me, Cam, can we go back tomorrow at dawn? All alone?"

Camille raised her soupspoon – "First to get to the burning bush!" – and stuck the piece of bread in the soup with a triumphant gesture. The dog barked. "Don't tell anyone. It's our secret. Okay, Paul?"

The boy gravely nodded his head. He so loved to go there with his sister. Beyond Wassy, the cliff of reddish clay. The bridge above the torrential stream – the danger roaring under his feet – she held him by the hand. And then both of them bringing the purple earth – forbidden.

"All right, I'm going to tell you the story of the burning bush.

"One day, Moses was grazing Jethro's flock. An angel appeared to him in a flame, in the middle of a bush. Moses looked: the bush was burning but it was not consumed. He was going to come closer, but he heard a voice say: 'Do not approach here, take your sandals off your feet, for where you stand is holy ground.'

"Then Moses turned his face away because he was afraid to look at God. 'Now go. I am sending you, Moses, to Pharoah. Take my people out of Egypt.' Moses said to God: 'Why should they listen to me? If they ask me who sent me, what will I tell the people? And what if they say: What is his name?'

"God said to Moses: 'I am that I am. This is what you will say: *I am* sent me to you.'"

"Hey, Cam, do you believe there is a Good Lord?"

Camille burst out laughing.

"Don't laugh like that."

"The Good Lord, the Good Lord! Look, you did your first communion because it was expected. You did what everyone does, but that's all. It's all just grimaces and pretense! Doff your hat and it's all over.

"You must live, go to China, never marry, my little Paul! Dress as you like and make sculptures, ride horseback and die. Look out, I'm attacking . . . You remember *The Song of Roland*. Look out! Down with the Christians!"

The dog barked like mad. Suddenly the oil lamp shook and set the tablecloth on fire. "Cam!" Camille jumped up and beat the tablecloth, rolling it up to smother the flames. They looked at each other, crestfallen. "You almost burned us up. You almost burned us up," Paul cried. "I hate your bush."

Camille put the tablecloth to soak. The soup pot and the casserole were overturned. What a mess. Camille tidied up, but she hated doing it. Paul helped her.

"Look, it's just like a map."

"I would like to go there."

"I would go here."

Suddenly the front door opened. Madame Louise, little Louise, and Louis-Prosper had come back.

"It smells like something's burning here." Her mother was already beside them. "What have you done? Oh, no! The tablecloth! These children are crazy. Get out, go to your rooms."

"But Mama – "

"Go to your rooms!"

"Wait, Louise, let's find out what happened."

"Oh, no! You always defend them – you, you're supposed to be the father – "

And they were at it again, arguing. The little girl looked tired. She went up to her room right away. Camille followed her, while Paul stayed downstairs. In the distance she heard her mother crying: "Paul! Paul! What have you two been up to this time! When will you stop listening to your crazy sister. Oh, these wretched children!"

Louis-Prosper said nothing more.

"Anyway," grumbled her tired mother, "that girl will come to a bad end. You've seen her rages, and those eyes, sometimes she has the eyes of a madwoman. You remember Monsieur the Marquis, he was like her. He always wanted to leave! He walked with his eyes bugging out of his head. I wonder if we will see him this summer at Villeneuve. I hope not."

Camille was lying on the stairs. She was petrified. Why did her mother hate her so?

"Listen, Louise, stop. That child has genius."

"Genius! genius! And you know what comes of genius . . . Besides, it's a disgusting profession. Sculpting other beings. Some of them, it seems, even do nudes . . . Anyway, that wouldn't embarrass you, would it? With all your depraved reading. The other day I surprised Paul with the Zola. But you'll pay for it!"

"Listen, Louise, no more of this."

Camille did not want to hear any more.

"When you think that someday she might sculpt a naked man . . ."

Slowly Camille undressed, she undid her hair, her ribbon. The heavy curls fell in front and behind; she shook them as if she wanted to clothe herself in them. Then the dress, slowly, she let it fall . . . The big boots, the woolen stockings . . . the wide shirt . . . Before slipping between the sheets, she wet her face, as if to wash off all that shouting.

She was riding a superb horse, clinging tight to him, on the hill among the stones, up where the Giant lived. But everything around her began to burn. He burst out laughing. She felt like clay burning between his hands. The Giant jeered and held her in his arms. She fought him off. He squeezed her until she almost suffocated, her body consumed. Then she heard, " . . . the burning bush, the burning bush, first to get to the burning bush" – and she awoke drenched in sweat.

What heat! She opened the window. Everything was quiet, dark. This summer they would be at Villeneuve. Soon they would be in Paris.

Letter *from the Asylum*

I can live again when your package arrives, and as a matter of fact I live only on its contents, since the food here makes me horribly sick, I cannot tolerate it anymore.

The Arrival
in Paris

And as we climbed up a steep path, turning back
We perceived a few faint glimmers of Paris.
And the night ended;
And the sun crossed the sky, and disappeared in a
reddish haze . . .
And once again night settled in the vast air.

PAUL CLAUDEL, *La Ville*, I

THEY HAD ARRIVED late one beautiful morning, tired and dusty. For the fourth time the furnishings were piled pell-mell on a cart borrowed from their neighbor. Black with dust, bewildered, still swaying, they disembarked on shaky legs.

Now they looked around. No more little streets, no more little houses, no more hamlets – Paris! A vast dense seething that was already engulfing them in the flow of their fellow beings. Madame Louis-Prosper shrank back, suddenly aged, Louise tiny, Paul overwhelmed. Only Eugénie and Camille, feisty as they were, faced the enemy. The father had already disappeared, snatched into the huge door of the building where he had rented an apartment. The jolt of the wheels, the paving stones, the shouts, all made Camille tremble with joy. Here something was happening. Here she would make them take notice. It was worth getting dirty, leaving everything behind, the silence, the forest, even the Geyn and his butte. Here another giant would rise up. She would raise him herself, before these men walking along in such a hurry, their heads down. Here, before the great ear-shattering monster, she would raise her work, silent and menacing . . .

Madame Louise all in black, her old hat, her tight chignon. Louise, her curls neatly arranged – how did she manage to look almost proper in the midst of such a swarm of odors, dust, and noise? Cauliflower rolled up in newspapers, trollies bumping across the cobblestones, children losing their balls under the heels of muddy shoes.

Louise, in her little striped dress, pressed against Camille. Eugénie did not know what she should attend to first: the packages, the suitcases, the furnishings, the children . . . "Just remember, don't get lost! Stay calm!" she cried to them. Eugénie was happy. Thanks to this somewhat disorderly family, she could leave Wassy and come to Paris at last. She was very close to Camille, who was only a few years younger than she. Yet the girl intimidated her. Hard, straight-backed, she gazed unblinkingly at the bustle of Paris, rising like a tide around her. Camille thought of the sea that transforms wild tempests into a caress nibbling gently at your feet. Paris lovingly encircled the young girl's legs. She let it happen, queen of this city she'd already tamed; she did not say a word, she learned, she watched, she took it all in. Sometimes a curious sadness gripped her: she had to hurry to know, to understand before being punished, torn from her vision of things. So she concentrated: this detail, that way of walking, this person who smiled a certain way, and that person whose hand was delicately turned, as if in silent apology. In this late morning light, her chignon made her look serious and distant. Her dark, curly bangs set off her gaze, which hit you full in the stomach if you were unlucky enough to catch her eye. A gaze that could kill . . . With her dark clothes, she might have been one of those harsh young widows in some remote, still-pagan village. Only her white shirt with its high collar made her look a bit like a musketeer.

"Ah, at last! Your father . . ." Louis came toward them, a bit stooped. "What do you mean, leaving us here in full view of everyone, like a vulgar spectacle?"

Louis did not answer. He gently took his wife by the arm. "You will see, you will do fine up there." Madame Louise had stopped.

"Mama, I'm tired." Louise's voice held her mother back on the verge of anger.

"Let's go, it's fine! Come on!"

They climbed up the stairs. The father, the mother, Louise, Paul, Eugénie, and Camille. A long climb up stairs that were dirt-worn but scrubbed each day. Camille roused herself: where were they going up so many steps? Madame Louise, pulled by the younger girl, slowed down for a moment. Paul's look was inscrutable. Suddenly he stopped, disdainfully let Eugénie pass, and turned toward Camille. What could he be thinking? Camille looked at him. "So?"

"The Geyn."

"Huh?"

"The Geyn."

"What do you mean! Oh! So?"

"It's the same thing."

"What a child!" Just when everything seemed desperately dull, he found words to transform the landscape. Camille smiled at him and they continued, side by side, to scale the difficult staircase. "The others aren't used to it." Boom! Paul, who wasn't paying attention, had just run into Eugénie, who had jostled Louise and her mother.

"Oh, excuse me, Madame."

"Eugénie, you must look where you're going! We are not going to paradise, and yet even paradise must have a ceiling."

Camille waited quietly. Between the legs and heads she caught a glimpse of the apartment, which she inspected a bit anxiously. The hallway. The dining room to the left, then the salon. There it was — the balcony, a big balcony. Her father had opened the windows: "Look, Camille. Paris is yours!"

Camille gazed at her father. An image lit from behind, silhouetted by darkness, thin against the light. She came toward him as if struck by vertigo before this man who stood between her and the void.

She leaned over. Her father had gone back to help his wife, who was still toiling up the stairs. For a few moments Camille savored the slight breeze. She was in Paris. Here people made sculpture and paid no heed to their neighbors.

"Camille, help us instead of mooning like an animal."

The room was small. Her sister had to sleep beside her. Only Paul had a room to himself. Camille was enraged: she would not be able to stay up late reading. Louise would complain that she couldn't sleep. Oh, never mind, she was in Paris! Eugénie would sleep upstairs in a separate room. Camille envied the girl. Camille scolded herself for her silliness: "Idiot, you are the lucky one. You aren't anyone's servant. You should complain!"

"Children, we are going to sit down at the table." Madame Louise had thought to provide bread and cheese. They would heat up the coffee. "And this evening perhaps we will eat a real meal. With what's here, though, I have my doubts. Have you seen the kitchen, Eugénie? It's like a closet. Well, what don't we do for our children! And how are you going to eat, Prosper?"

"Don't concern yourself about it, I will manage, we have friends at Wassy. And then, I will soon be transferred to Rambouillet, and why not to Paris?"

"We will all be dead by then."

"Okay, that's enough! Don't start."

"Oh, Mama, can I go out after dinner?"

"No, you're not going to start that. You'll just get into trouble."

"Come, Louise, it will be better for them to get used to things as soon as possible. And after all, Camille is quite big. I'll go with them. That way you will have some peace and quiet to set up the house." Louise shrugged her shoulders. "I'll leave Eugénie with you."

"I can certainly use her. Camille might help me, too."

Louis-Prosper did not answer. He wanted to show his eldest daughter Paris. He had brought her here and he wanted to be the first to help her discover the great city.

So they went out, all four of them. Louis linked his arm through Camille's and took Louise by the other hand. Paul walked behind, and sometimes in front. They walked along the boulevard, then through little streets toward the Luxembourg Gardens. Louise pulled her father's hand: "Papa, I can't go any farther." She was pale, about to faint.

"Wait, we'll stop for something." So they sat down at a café.

"Oh, Papa, can I go just to the end of the street, down there, just to that house?"

"Yes, but no further."

"Let's go, Paul! Come see!"

"What?"

"Paris, you little brat!"

The two children ran off. Louis watched the tall girl and the little fellow disappear under the trees. She walked with a long stride, throwing back her shoulders like a man. His Camille. Paul trotted beside her. Louis was proud. He so much wanted to be a success! Fortunately, there were these children, and the other one sat quietly beside him. He had finally managed to take them to Paris.

Suddenly a rather raucous song could be heard not far from where the children were walking. Camille, almost reaching a stone balustrade connecting two stairways, leaned over. She heard the words but did not understand them.

"Tell me, Camille, what song is that?"

"Hush!"

"She has a terrible voice."

Camille went down several stairs and saw a hideous, hollow-eyed woman in rags, a bottle in her hand. Paul stopped beside her, flabbergasted. "She looks like old lady Bault in Villeneuve. Here, too . . ."

But what was she doing, she was stopping men! They shrugged their shoulders and pushed her away. There was even one who showed her his fly, shouting with laughter. Now Paul was quite terrified. The woman was fat, fat and ugly. "Let's go, come on, Cam."

A man had emerged from the stairway, he caught Camille by the chin.

"And the kid, she tickles you, eh! . . . That'll be free."

Camille did not understand. Paul cried out. They both ran away.

Paul remembered. Camille, too, could see the scene all over again. It was dusk, just the two of them. That fat Bault woman was there, under the moon. Several drunken men surrounded her, and slowly, slowly she had lifted her skirts. The men had given her something to drink; Camille saw the two white legs shaking, the thighs smeared with dirt, filth, and suddenly an obscene tangle of gray-black bushy hair. Camille had grabbed Paul and fled, far away, but she knew that the child next to her had been shocked, like her. Camille could not forget the two eyes they'd just seen. Two drowning eyes that seemed to say, "Get out, quickly. Get away from all this."

No, Camille would stay. She knew what she had come to find. Here or elsewhere, she would never run away, even if other old women stood in front of her laughing derisively, other old women with scowling eyes, and men's hands ready to grab you by the throat . . .

Panting, Camille and Paul reached the top of the stairs and stopped a moment to catch their breath. They had not even noticed the steps beneath their feet. "Don't have to run like that, Miss! Sure is pretty, that kid!" Camille was in a panic, *she* was what he wanted. Walking beside her father, she had already caught men looking at her. Perhaps she stared at people too much? Oh, that bad habit of hers. But she so loved to grasp a detail, a fold there, a certain gait . . .

Now they were hurrying. Quickly. Her father was there. Camille rushed to him and sat down. Red with shame. Visibly upset. Louis looked at her. "What happened?"

"There was a man – "

"Shut up, Paul!" Her voice was stinging. She looked her father straight in the eyes. It was his turn to lower his gaze. The child was beautiful, with that haughty look and her swollen mouth. He was suddenly afraid. Afraid of that will, afraid of that demand he read in her eyes. Everything, right away! Instantly. Everything! No holds barred.

"Oh, Papa, look at that!"

At a certain distance, tiny silhouettes were moving behind a little house. The marionette theater! They went off, Louise had drunk a good hot chocolate and she was happy. For once she had been part of the adventure.

Louis-Prosper was sad. Nostalgia dragged on his shoulders. Like a black coat thrown over him. He felt dull, old. His children! He would not see them until the end of the week, and again . . . provided Louise could manage! Would she know how to meet Camille's demands? There was a wall between mother and daughter. Camille! Suddenly he leaned toward her. "Camille, write to me. If you need to ask for something, don't annoy your mother with petty details."

Camille had not turned her head. And yet, it was as if her father could see into her heart. She was overwhelmed by this attention. She would have liked to tell him. She understood his solitude, his modesty, this man who was going to leave without a kind word, without a smile from his family; he lived for her. She knew he was proud of her. Without moving, looking away, she reached out her hand, lightly touching her father's thin fingers, and quickly put her two hands back on her knees.

The marionettes hopped about. Pow! Pow! The children laughed. Only Paul remained cool. Camille tried to understand what could be going on inside him. Paul looked closed up, disgusted. Strange child!

Perhaps he was still dwelling on the recent incident. The curtain came down on the little wooden actors. It was almost the end of the afternoon.

"Let's go, just a little longer! I am going to show you the cathedral of Notre-Dame."

Letter *from the Asylum*

I'm in a hurry to leave this place . . . I don't know if you mean to leave me here, but it is very cruel for me! . . . To think you're so happy in Paris and to have to renounce it for a few fancies you have in your head . . . Don't leave me here all alone.

Old Hélène

When day is done and the shoe kicked off
Here is the darkness, here is the star and the evening,
Here the old people's heart has yielded.

PAUL CLAUDEL, *Larmes sur la joue vieille*

THE END OF the afternoon. Already. The girls had all gone out. Camille was there, seated at the worktable. She sat quite still, her eyes fixed on the bust in front of her. The young girl gazed at the old woman. Both of them terribly cut off; Camille seemed to be withdrawn, as if in prayer. Her eyes, two black slits cut through the whiteness of her face. Camille had lost her amber cheeks, her sun-washed color. Pale, her cheeks a bit hollow, her hair covered with fine plaster dust, in her white smock she looked almost like the old woman in front of her. The old woman was smiling at her, her laughing eyes were full of generosity.

The afternoon had just ended at the sculptor's feet. Beside her, scattered around the room, sculptures covered with damp cloths. The girls had all gone out. Laughing, adjusting their ribbons, darting hands, they had left her. Her friends, most of them English girls, were preparing for Madame Adam's grand soiree. Despite her friends' entreaties, Camille had not wanted to leave her bust, to make old Hélène wait, since she seemed to be growing impatient sitting on the worktable. Camille had not yet finished it the way she wanted. And yet the soiree was being given in honor of the next Salon, set for May 1882. Surely they would all come, painters, sculptors, society men. Nelly, Jane, and Virginia had all advised her to make an appearance. Before disappearing in her characteristic cascade of rosy laughter, Jane had come back to the studio one last time to try to persuade her: "Look out, Camille, you have to leave your sculpture some of the time. If the others haven't heard of you, and never see you, your sculpture will be ignored. You know, most of them don't care two hoots about your bust. They would rather know the beauty of the sculptor herself. I am sure that would do you much more good. You are very beautiful, really fascinating."

Camille had shrugged her shoulders. She could already see the soiree, the pointless chatter, the stupid young bigshots, and the men's looks. And besides, she didn't have anything to wear. Once she had gone with them. Blue, pink, green, dazzling, powdered, laughing, her friends were cooing. Real fireworks! Next to them, almost too thin, all in black with her white collar, she looked like an old governess – she could have been their chaperon. She had been ashamed. Only her unruly hair made her stand out. The men had looked at this adolescent, half chaperon, half widow, the young face drowning in rough, dark curls. Camille had begun to talk about sculpture with one or two people. The other artists clearly preferred to dance that evening. Camille had fled into the night. A dark phantom, bearing her solitary dreams.

The light was still fine. It was springtime outside. Seventeen, almost eighteen years old. And already the studio was deserted. Camille looked around her: the sculptures covered with damp cloths once more . . . She remembered the cocoons in the magnificent book her uncle had given her for her tenth birthday. Multicolored butterflies that concealed their rainbow dreams until emerging from their sleep. Those great white masses upside down, all the same . . . Camille compared the sculptures to the swaddled pupae. She dreamt for a moment of the varied destinies of men . . .

From all over the wall, old Hélène smiled at her or scolded her gently. Camille had been trying for weeks to capture the gaze of the old Alsatian housekeeper who had helped her mother. She had made dozens and dozens of sketches. Sometimes the good-humored old woman had agreed to hold still for a few moments. "What d'you want of me now! I've got work to do!"

A ray of sunlight struck the mirror. Almost eighteen years old.

In a few weeks the first May Salon would open. Camille would take part in it.

How could she capture this stubborn old woman's extraordinary gaze? Suddenly she saw her as she'd been the other day, her broom in her hand, in the same ray of sunlight. Her wrinkled forehead and the slightly pointed chin. Sometimes Camille would gently tease her: "You look like my Melusina."

"Who's that?"

"An old friend who guards the entrance to the forest down at Ville-neuve. But at least she stays still. She was so impossible that a vengeful god must have petrified her." Good Hélène had shrugged her shoulders and continued to sweep, murmuring old sayings, proverbs, or fragments of hymns.

Suddenly they had both heard weeping. Her mother and sister were away. Paul was supposed to be doing his homework. Paul's face was filled with distress. Once more he was prey to nightmares, anguish. Why had his mother taken him to witness that ghastly death? He had changed since then. He hardly laughed anymore. Camille held it against their mother. Of course, she had been resigned in advance – doing her daily duty like a donkey yoked to its buckets – but there is death and death. This one had been a slow agony, ghastly, sordid. On 5 September 1881, their grandfather, Doctor Athanase Théodore Cerveaux, had expired after weeks of suffering. Cancer of the stomach. The mother had not understood how wounding it might be for a young child. Since witnessing his grandfather's death, Paul was anguished, panic-stricken, overwhelmed. From month to month Camille had seen him sink into the obsessional memory of that agonizing death. The vertigo of the void. Nothingness.

But Camille knew about that. The old Bault woman, lying across the path one evening – her toothless mouth wide open, as if she wanted to lap up the moonlight one last time – the old woman, flaccid in her oversized clothes, had finally collapsed for good. Camille had not been afraid. She had only wanted to model her, to render the silence of her two eyes, the stillness of her twisted limbs – like an old sketch that had just been turned on its side. She was almost enchanting in the white light of the young night . . .

But Paul had experienced something else. A horrible death that seemed to go on forever. Day after day, night after night, wrenching cries, gasps, groans, filth . . . The old man had finally gone, emptied out like a pot of excrement, after Paul had watched him during the long hours, his stomach swollen like a drowned man left in the water for several days. Beneath the dirty sheet, the enormous mass was like the belly of a pregnant woman, the waxy, yellowish complexion, the feverish eyes. A physician himself, Athanase Théodore had explained the progress of the disease to the child, as if to reassure him. His hands were shaking, and Paul had thought of the spiderwebs that fell on him when he foraged in forgotten places. Would there be granaries and barns there, too? Where was he going, this beloved grandfather? This grandfather who had taught him the dialects of the wind and the sky, and the old language of the earth. Paul had wanted to go with him. Yes, the old man put one hand on his forehead as if he'd forgotten something important. "Grandfather! Grandfather! Are you looking for something?"

The hand had slipped down and Paul had discovered two distant eyes, white and horror-stricken.

Paul had told all this to his sister in great gulping sobs, broken sentences, images replayed, forgotten. And suddenly the last great vomiting up of life that had so shocked the child. The mother clinging to her father, and the forgotten child, the child who had seen too much, the child who would never forget. Never . . . "What did he see? Tell me, Cam, what did he see?"

Camille had looked at old Hélène bent attentively over the adolescent. She wore just the expression Camille had been trying to capture for weeks in her sculpture. A gaze that lit up the old round cheeks.

"Master Paul, don't be afraid. Your grandfather was judging how far he had to jump to reach the other life. On the other side he had seen such a beautiful countryside, so welcoming, full of friends waiting for him . . . He didn't want to miss his great leap."

Paul had given the hint of a smile.

"Go to bed, now. You are working too hard. They say your father is making you skip a grade! That's unreasonable. Come, eat a little of my cherry tart."

They had stuck their fingers in the still-warm crust. Paul was drowsy . . .

> To everything there is a season
> And a time to every purpose under heaven:
> A time to be born, and a time to die.

Camille had looked at the old servant stroking the boy's hair. "Tell me, dear Hélène, tell me where does that come from?"

"It's in my old Bible . . . I will lend it to you."

Camille looked at the bust. The studio was dark. Camille couldn't work anymore. The drowned light of dusk muddied all the contours. Too dangerous for modeling. The changes she made might be grotesque. Now the mist. Camille was reflected alone in the mirror, oddly doubled . . .

"The studio, the models, the materials, you will never succeed!" She heard her mother's scolding voice. "What a useless expense! Your father helps us, but if you stopped all that, we would live much better. I have not even bought a spring dress for Louise."

Camille wanted to work in a real studio. She would never make progress in this place. Alfred Boucher came regularly to give her advice, but my God! how she wanted to see what it was like in a real sculptor's studio. She couldn't do it alone. They would take her for a model or a "low woman," as old Hélène said. "Watch out, Mademoiselle Camille, button your collar properly. People are quick to take you for what you're not. Your own conscience isn't enough in this bad world."

As if she had time to lose! Another model had quit today. Camille had been working on his torso for several weeks. Now she had to begin all over again. Jane advised her to continue with someone else. Camille was angry when she thought about her friend's suggestion. She would not compromise. If she started paying the models more when they sulked, she and her friends would never manage to pay for the studio. It's true that her friends had much more money than she. As for continuing with the same sculpture using a different model, you would have to be a pitiful sort of artist, a disgusting copier, a scoundrel, a swindler to do such a thing!

"Now stop, Camille, stop! All right, if you want to start all over again . . . but you'll never finish it. Look. Each of us has three sculptures already finished for the Salon, and you have nothing but that bust of your old Hélène that you're so stuck on. The only model who's been faithful to you!" And they all went off laughing. They were not mean. Camille felt incapable of adding a new model's arm to the old one's torso.

How tired she felt! To think how she exhausted herself. If it hadn't been for the bust of old Hélène, she would have had to get notoriety at the Salon by covering herself with clay. Camille smiled and put some of the gray earth on her face, then covered herself with gauze: *Bust of an Artist without Models.*

At that very moment, Jane, Nelly, and Virginia were getting into a carriage to go to Madame Adam's. They might even meet Carrier-Belleuse – if Monsieur Alfred Boucher was there, he would introduce them. Alfred Boucher! The girl cried out. But she had forgotten! Alfred Boucher had promised to introduce her to Monsieur Paul Dubois, director of the national Academy of Fine Arts, who had agreed to see her.

Camille quickly recovered her good spirits. She kissed her old Hélène's damp forehead. Tomorrow she would come to work at dawn. She draped the bust with the damp gauze. She wanted her old friend to triumph at the Salon. Camille fixed her hair. What did it matter, missing this soiree! She was right. Her bust would be the most lifelike of all their submissions.

"My old Hélène! See you tomorrow! Get up early. I will be here before the sun!"

Letter *from the Asylum*

At this holiday time I always think of our dear mother. I never saw her again after the day you took the fateful decision to send me to a lunatic asylum! I think of that lovely portrait I did of her in the shade of our beautiful garden. The large eyes that spoke of some secret sadness, the spirit of resignation written on her features, her hands crossed on her knees in utter abnegation — all suggesting a modesty, a sense of duty pushed to the extreme, that's how she was, our poor mother. I never saw the portrait again (no more than I saw her). If ever you hear about it, let me know.

I doubt whether that hateful person I often mention to you would have the audacity to attribute it to himself, like my other works — that would be too much, the portrait of my mother!

We are only poor women, weak and frail,
But guests on this day among eternal things . . .
How many women before us have sung the same song
in this place!

PAUL CLAUDEL, *La Cantate à trois voix*

VICTOIRE, the old housekeeper. Old Hélène. Her own mother. And now herself.

Four old women. May they rest in peace!

Was she dead? She never quite understood. She had not seen her mother again. Sometimes a package or a letter arrived.

Camille found the writing again, fleetingly – her hand when she was gathering up the crumbs scattered by them, the children. Nothing was lost to her. Except her eldest daughter, Camille, the bad one . . .

If only they had been able to speak to each other! All four of them beside the hearth. To explain themselves without men present. Huddled up, crammed together, they felt confused, superimposed.

And what of her old peasant mother? Camille sees her throwing sticks at the cat, poking at the fire. Camille leaned against the fireplace. Like her, their worn hands spun out the same gestures, perhaps the only language left to them.

The simple woman leaned over the paper. Her mother wrote well. Who had left her time to dream? The stern pen ran along the old notebooks: the household accounts, family letters, announcements, condolences.

All four reunited. Camille imagines their talk. The words they'll never hear again.

Once she had discovered her mother laughing, happy, beautiful. Only once. She was folding the sheets and Victoire was helping her.

Then everything closed up, just as the water had closed over Uncle Paul.

Only once Camille had called for her: "Mama!"

Camille and her child in the solitary room. "Mama!"

The cry had echoed. Louise-Athanaïse Cerveaux never heard it.

If only they had been able to talk with each other, all four of them. What secrets their hearts might have shared!

Why were they all paying such heavy tribute?

"Hélène, why do you cry silently when evening comes? . . . My good Victoire, sometimes you stick your fist in your mouth, as if to prevent yourself from crying out – then you crack nuts. But I see your hands still trembling . . ."

Her mother's sad eyes near the huge flowering acacia.

Mama, put your head in my lap and tell me.

We have time.

Jacopo Quercia

I believe that this man truly incarnates the idea
Of sculpture and of architecture.

BERNI, Poem to Michelangelo

Y OU HAVE STUDIED with Monsieur Rodin!"
Camille raised her huge questioning eyes toward Monsieur Alfred Boucher. Who was this Monsieur Rodin whom Paul Dubois was invoking?

The office of the director of the national Academy of Fine Arts was particularly stuffy that morning. Camille was drenched with sweat. Her camisole, the cuffs and collar of her shirtwaist were almost stuck to her skin, her dress was heavy. She did not dare ask her mother for a new outfit. She wore the only proper suit she had. This striped ensemble of rough cloth, with its matching jacket and skirt, made her seem a bit masculine. Her chignon was beginning to come undone. She could never manage to keep it neat for more than half an hour. Her mother had repeated dozens of times that she must make the part in the middle, pull back the hair, then dampen it. But nothing helped! Camille hated her mother's flat, smoothly parted hair. And besides, the more she dampened her hair, the more unmanageable it became.

"Monsieur Rodin?" Camille was overcome with shame. Monsieur

Alfred Boucher smiled. It had struck him, too. When he had seen the *David and Goliath* at Wassy.

"You must be introduced to him. He himself will be surprised. What do you think, old friend? I am seeing Mathias Morhardt soon. I will arrange it sometime!

"You have some talent. Unquestionably. But many have the idea at the beginning of their career. The knack is to persist. As for accepting you here, I don't see how we could do it. I don't intend to start a revolution in my studios. No, continue at your studio for young ladies."

Camille would willingly have slapped him. Alfred Boucher sensed the girl was ready to jump up.

"Don't worry, Camille. Monsieur Rodin never set foot in the academy. It is not the only way, is it, my dear Director? Come on, let's go. Tomorrow we will meet at Dalou's, with Carrier-Belleuse?"

Camille started to take her *David and Goliath.*

"No, leave it here, young lady. I will keep it for a while. I find it quite beautiful and would like to show it to people."

Camille was afraid. She did not want to leave her two companions. And besides, she did not like this gentleman. But what should she do?

They were going down the long hall. Camille heard the noises of the big building, the bursts of laughter, the sounds of hammers wielded by clumsy technicians. She could recognize at a distance the hesitant hand, the firm wrist, cracking stone, stone bursting apart, stone resistant and stubborn.

"You don't know who Monsieur Auguste Rodin is, do you?" Suddenly Alfred Boucher's voice woke her. Camille shook her head.

She despised him already. She did not need to know who he was. Why should he be allowed to make the same sculpture she did? She had begun before him, surely. She was already modeling clay at the age of six.

"How can I describe him to you? He is forty-two years old. His life has been very hard."

Camille wanted to laugh. An old man! Obviously, even if he'd begun laboriously at the age of eighteen, he had been sculpting longer then she. Eighteen! She wasn't that age yet. Not till the end of the year.

"They are starting to talk a lot about him in knowledgeable circles.

Madame Edmond Adam – by the way, why don't you ever come to her house? I've seen Jane, Virginia, and my other students there. You should visit. She receives the most fashionable writers. Three years ago she created *La Nouvelle Revue*. This Madame Edmond Adam introduced Rodin to Gambetta one evening. And Monsieur Antonin Proust, you know, the minister of fine arts, recommended Rodin to do the huge sculpture on the monumental door of the Museum of Decorative Arts."

Camille listened quietly to the remonstrances of her old teacher.

"Many defend poor Rodin. He has been widely attacked. His first great sculpture, *The Age of Bronze*, was very controversial. Many members of the jury thought that he had done it by applying the plaster directly on his model. The poor man! He'd worked on it more than a year and a half. He had spent all his meager resources on it. What a ghastly suspicion! He wept over it."

Camille thought tenderly of this old sculptor who had been so brutally attacked. The worst of insults! A sculptor who would work directly on the model he had in front of him!

"It must have been quite perfect for the public and the jury to have thought that he had copied it directly to the cast."

"It is an admirable work. I must show it to you. I remember – he was thirty-seven years old and often came to me completely discouraged. 'I am at the end of my rope,' he would say, 'I am exhausted, I have no money.' I defended him vigorously because I had seen him sculpt figures directly, without any model, with fascinating precision. We got together, Paul Dubois, Carrier-Belleuse, and I, a group of friends, and made the undersecretary of the Department of Fine Arts come to verify the honesty and good faith of this little redheaded man who sculpted like a god."

Camille imagined a little gnome now. Rather sad, hobbling along, perhaps, like her. And she found him, finally, quite sympathetic, even if he was a little simpleminded . . .

"This trumped-up scandal was disproven completely. At a recent Salon he showed an admirable *Saint John the Baptist,* and *The Age of Bronze* is now cast in bronze. That was just two years ago. Now we're all waiting for that gigantic door . . ."

They strolled silently along the quays of the Seine. Camille thought about this sculptor with whom they dared to compare her. She would not wait thirty-seven years to begin. She wanted to move quickly.

"By the way, Camille, I wanted to tell you. I am going to leave for Italy. Now that I have my *Prix de Rome,* I must go. It is an unexpected opportunity for me to work, to find peace and quiet. And besides, it's the country of Michelangelo. I shall certainly go to Florence. Your Rodin, he rather resembles Michelangelo . . ."

Camille was scarcely listening. She was overcome with sadness. Not only wasn't she accepted at the academy, but her old friend – poor thing, he was only thirty-two! – was going to leave her. Camille was discouraged; she scarcely heard what Alfred Boucher was saying to her.

"I am going to ask him to take over my lessons. Are you listening to me, Camille?"

"Pardon me."

"I was saying that I was going to ask Rodin himself to take my place with you girls. In my opinion he is the only one who has any genius, even if at first he may seem unprepossessing or timid. He is one of the greatest of us. Still relatively unknown! But I have every confidence in him."

Camille was in a bad mood. If he was doing the same sculpture she was, what good would it do! The girl's lips pursed. That was it! Her chignon had just come undone.

"Camille! Hey, Camille! What's got into you? I can't keep up with you. If you go on, you'll get to the studio before me!"

Camille apologized and slowed down.

The girls cried out: "Mr. Alfred Boucher, come in." They surrounded him, teasing.

"You are too red in the face. You've been running! And Camille, what a face! Boo!"

"Monsieur Alfred Boucher is leaving us."

"What?"

Camille had spit out the news mechanically, without any prelude.

"No, I am not leaving you! I am leaving for Italy soon. I've asked Auguste Rodin to take my place. He has agreed."

The girls clapped their hands. "It's a pleasure! He is delicious, very charming! He's like Vulcan. You know Vulcan!"

Camille thought of Michelangelo. How dare he compare Rodin to Michelangelo, the Florentine genius. It's true that he was not very attractive either. Sickly even, they said. And then Pietro Torrigiano's fist had made him uglier still. His nose broken at the age of seventeen, humiliated in the gardens of Lorenzo the Magnificent, he must not have been much to look at. Nearly deformed. But to compare him to that nonentity. Auguste Rodin compared to the god of sculpture. No!

"What a character, Mademoiselle Claudel!" Alfred Boucher tried to calm her. "Camille, come on! I will think of you. I will send you news, postcards of your Michelangelo. And besides, I have great confidence in you. You have something. Don't spoil it with your violence. Don't behave like a pampered society woman, act like a real artist. It takes a lot of time, patience, and even humility to approach your vision. Beauty, like death, requires long acquaintance. My young ladies, I will come to say good-bye before I go."

"Monsieur Boucher, Monsieur Boucher, Camille! Sorry, we forgot – Camille's in the newspaper!"

They all rushed around, some to show the article, others to look at it.

"Come on, come on, a little air!" Everyone bumped heads trying to read the article at the same time. Bursts of laughter!

"Salon of May 1882. Bust of an old woman. A bust in plaster, by Mademoiselle Camille Claudel. A serious, thoughtful work."

Camille had her name in the paper for the first time – and she was not thirty-seven years old!

Alfred Boucher looked at her. He had not wanted to tell her how much her bust of old Hélène revealed a great sculptor in the making. She was hurtling along so fast. She had spent so many hours on it, making so many sketches and plaster models, but now she was triumphant.

He liked Jane, Virginia, and Nelly, but Camille would become one of the great artists of her era. Unless . . . Sometimes he was afraid. Afraid of her darkening blue-black eyes, afraid of her social ineptitude. Afraid of her difficult family, who did not understand her. Afraid of that absent father. Afraid of that fascinated, ever-present younger brother. What would become of her? And how would his timid friend Auguste deal with such a violent and independent young girl?

"Mr. Alfred Boucher, will you have a cup of coffee?"

"Gladly." He liked them very much, he appreciated the studio bustling with feminine cheer, but most of all, he now confessed to himself, he'd gone there to find Camille again. Her admirable studies, her confident sketches, the revelations to be found in her way of doing this hand or that foot. Without knowing it, she had taught him something. Today, when he was leaving, why not admit that delicate passion he felt for the young girl, his emotion at seeing her large hands caressing, remaking, working the earth . . . and more than all that, her fine face and eyes – looking out at the world with the most extraordinary gaze. He was glad to be getting away from her. He would have fallen in love with her! She was too violent, too strong, a tremendous personality. She alone existed. The desert, the negation of the self . . . until death. And yet here in this dying spring light she was smiling at him. A timid, tender smile, as if to say, "I beg your pardon, I would like you to forgive me." A coaxing, unbearable, delicious smile. He had wanted to hold her in his arms, devour that virgin mouth, disdainful as an exquisite fruit dripping with juice.

"You are so distracted, Monsieur Boucher." And in her beautiful, slightly raspy voice: "Jacopo Quercia, he was almost nineteen years old when he met Michelangelo, wasn't he?"

Why did she suddenly bring up that story?

"Yes, he almost went crazy with impatience waiting for the old master's advice, and Michelangelo complimented him."

Camille remained thoughtful. She was scarcely listening to her friends' chatter.

"Camille, Cam! If you went out more, you would know Auguste Rodin. He is charming but shy, shy! He's tongue-tied. Yes, but he's got blue eyes. He can't see anything. He's nearsighted. What . . . but what marvelous hands . . . "

Camille abruptly set down her cup. She slipped on her smock.

"Rest a while, Camille."

"Camille, known as the poor man's Jacopo Quercia. Come in please, Monsieur Rodin."

Alfred Boucher looked at the girl, mocking, insolent, implacable. He had to warn his friend. This student was not like the others. A bit difficult to bring round. A savage beast when she didn't trust you, but afterward, what a treasure of generosity, of tenderness. If she valued you, she would give you everything.

"Dear Camille . . ."

Alfred Boucher rose, saluted the young girls. Suddenly he came back quickly and stood before Camille. *"Io so . . . Michelangelo! Sei Jacopo Quercia. Ma sei una bella . . . "* He traced a few dance steps around her and exited amidst the laughter of the girls.

Camille retorted: *"Au revoir, M'sieur Angelo!"*

Monsieur Rodin

"We are too much alike; nothing new could issue from us."

"Then who will carry on our line?"

"Someone will come . . . Some handsome officer with a red beard . . . And he will take away my cousin of many moods, my laurel bush of Dormant, my 'virgo admirabilis.'"

PAUL CLAUDEL, *L'Otage*

MICHELANGELO'S *Moses*. The coiled, ringletted beard, the powerful head, the thick, massive torso. Camille looked at the man standing near the door. She had just lowered the scarf Virginia had put on her. The girls were playing blindman's bluff. A luminous morning. The studio was full of light, Camille in a good mood. The girls were amusing themselves by identifying faces and bodies with their hands. A burst of laughter, a song. They had made her turn, pivot, whirl around.

"With pretty maids all in a row," they had sung.

Camille stopped abruptly, Monsieur Rodin was there. With Alfred Boucher slightly in front of him. Monsieur Rodin was there.

He had seen the blindfolded girl. He had seen the two dark eyes, just unmasked. He looked at the immensity of those eyes looking straight at him, observing him, drawing him. He contemplated the infinity of the iris. His own myopic eyes squinted. Camille thought he looked like an old gnome with his red beard.

"Come in, Auguste." Alfred Boucher moved aside. Monsieur Rodin stepped inside the studio. He felt stared at, scrutinized by those pairs of mocking, questioning eyes. Camille had moved back. The young girl in the shadow had just revealed the sculpture she was working on. A bust of a child, powerful. The bare neck, the shoulders covered by a sort of toga. A "male" sculpture. Monsieur Rodin stopped abruptly. He had forgotten the girls, the studio, his friend Alfred. Only this cast demanded his attention. The angle of the face was almost abnormally open. That is what he was looking for, too. The power of the gaze. Monsieur Rodin sensed a sure, intelligent hand, reality exploding in every detail, revealed, explained, monumental. Monsieur Rodin was disturbed. He seemed to have created this bust himself; yet he knew he hadn't touched it. He did not know the model. Boucher had just given him a friendly tap on the shoulder. "Wake up, dear friend, or else these young ladies will doubt your competence. You are behaving strangely. I know you are shy, but to stand transfixed like someone mentally deficient . . . are you under a spell?"

"Who posed?" Monsieur Rodin had an odd, muted voice.

"My brother, Paul Claudel. He is fourteen now." The voice was husky but incisive.

"Pardon me, I was surprised by the quality of your cast. The profile is clear. I always say, model only profiles. It's all that matters. The human face is not symmetrical."

"I wanted you to be surprised. Anyone might think Mademoiselle Claudel had already worked with you."

Monsieur Rodin looked at Camille. So that's who she was! The other evening at Madame Adam's salon, someone had mentioned her name. Oh, yes, he remembered. It was one of the English girls that Madame Adam had invited. It dawned on Monsieur Rodin that he was in the presence of these same young English girls. They burst out laughing. "You are not very gallant, Monsieur Rodin. We already know each other from the other evening, and you don't even greet us!"

Poor Auguste stammered, distressed. He was not at ease in company. His voice took a while to find its pitch – a serious inflection followed by an explosion of dental sounds and head shaking – his companion, Rose, often chided him for it. He knew he wasn't very seductive.

"Come see, Monsieur Rodin, here." Each young girl asked his advice. The sculptor gave his brief, specific recommendations. Camille listened, somewhat withdrawn. This awkward, uncertain man became deft and serious when he talked about sculpture. He seemed larger. An authority, an unexpected energy. His hands revealed, caressed, reworked the damp earth. Suddenly he grabbed the pencil and drew a detail on a piece of paper. Camille could not take her eyes off the sculptor's hands. The bust was "powerful" . . . She had never heard such advice. Nothing was left to chance. A formidable practitioner. Before her stood an admirable craftsman who reworked, refined, completed the material. His suggestions were a revelation. He was handling life. He saw it everywhere and reconstituted it with passion, with power.

Now he suddenly turned toward her. "The bust of your young brother is nearly complete. I am astonished at the modeling of the ears, the shell of the ears, very delicate. The eyelids are nicely cleaved . . . the gaze . . . Life is everywhere. The difficulty is to see it. And life is beautiful everywhere. Model only for the profiles; always test your profiles by a predetermined and constant principle. You need only look, understand, and love. On the other hand, your *David and Goliath* contains too much contrast. Modeling requires gentleness, lightness. Here there is too much contrast, it is violent, knotted . . . "

Camille did not take criticism easily. Her heart beat violently. She wanted to break the cast on his head. He was not right. At least, not altogether. She loved those blacks and whites, those modeled contrasts. "Look at the drawings of Leonardo da Vinci, of Michelangelo. Between black and white there is an infinity of gray, of dark gray, light gray, beige . . . " Camille knew Monsieur Rodin was right. But she did not like those thousand nuances that sometimes muddied the sculpture's line. She dreamt of a singular line. She would have liked to do a sculpture that was a single point, a single diagonal. Something so pure it would be only the husk of the movement. But Monsieur Rodin was not wrong to speak of the modeling. How many sculptors betrayed themselves in a raw detail? The moment the general aspect was there, they were satisfied. They were hardly bothered by the infelicities of the finisher or the technician, even when the marble was so scratched up that the modeling had entirely disappeared. She still angrily recalled that wretched Eugène, who had ruined the only block of marble she'd ever had. He was scratching away, thinking of something else, and the wrist had disappeared. She could have killed him! He had destroyed the result of long months of labor. She would never again let anyone touch her marbles. She would be the technician herself. No, instead of streamlining the details, making the sculpture as a whole, she wanted to find a way to render the "idea," even in the initial study.

"Excuse me, Mademoiselle. It's my turn. Would you accept an invitation to work in my studio?" Camille was trying to think how she might . . .

"Camille, Camille . . . Monsieur Rodin is speaking to you, and you aren't listening. You two will never get on, clearly. When one speaks, the other is in a dream world!"

Camille blushed violently, stammered, withdrew, advanced . . . "Monsieur Rodin, I . . ." She retreated again, knocking over the bucket of water, splashing the floor. Monsieur Rodin stood with his feet in the water. Camille was abashed. He seemed truly bewildered. The girls hurried to him. Beside herself, Camille went out, slamming the door. This man embarrassed her. Outside it was raining hard; why did such things happen only to her? But why was he looking at her with his little, nearsighted eyes? She hated him. And his criticisms – what right did he have? She strode along vigorously. Maybe she liked to work violent contrasts. She was a woman. So he enjoyed making things nice, gentle, and tender! Speaking to her about lightness, beautiful harmonies, elegance, why not? "Hold on, now." "Camille, you're a woman." "Camille, look at your hands." But she liked to turn things upside down, carve directly from life . . .

"Hey, look out, my little miss, you are going to get yourself run down!"

Camille had not seen the cart and the heavy horses. She drew back. What was she doing there, drenched, idiotic, ridiculous? She remembered, but what was it he had said? Oh yes, to come and work at his studio. My God, it was what she'd always hoped for. To be part of a studio for sculptors, *men* sculptors, male artists – as they say – who were taken *seriously*. She made a sudden half turn, bumping into a fat lady, who went away grumbling. A dog ran between her legs. She hated dogs. They always came to rub themselves against her, they smelled of piss. Now she ran in the other direction. "Lightness, lightness, I'll give you lightness all right." She was black-hearted, Camille the black, as her mother said, she was swarthy, a moor. *"Cacha-Diablo."* She went up the few steps between her and the studio on rue Notre-Dame-des-Champs.

Monsieur Rodin was not there. Monsieur Rodin was no longer there. No one was there. Only a few awkward, trembling lines written on a piece of paper: "Come to my studio when you like. Studio J, rue de l'Université – or Studio H at the marble depository. I like contrast, too."

There was no *s* on the word *contrast*. She looked at the writing. Someone had mopped up the water on the floor. Now she was dripping wet. Hair plastered down, eyes burning, her body trembled. She looked in the mirror: her curls had become limp twists running down her neck, her dress was like a crumpled scarf, a rag. She looked like a beggar, like Donatello's *Magdalen*. She did not look like a beautiful young girl.

She made a face, grabbed a cloth, and vigorously rubbed her head. She undid her dress and shook it the way she shook the lettuce at Ville-neuve. The sun came out again. A moment in the sun and everything would be set right. Everyone must have gone to lunch. Camille wrapped herself in a shawl to wait. She sat down and looked at her group. Monsieur Rodin was not altogether wrong. There was too much contrast. It was ugly. The knee, there, the leg was pointed, un-articulated. Camille got up and began to destroy the cast. Useless to keep mistakes. She destroyed everything, seized by an irrepressible rage. She would never achieve her vision. So much dust. She was going to start again. The girl was quite warm now. The dress was dry. Camille did up her hair, arranging it in a chignon. Camille was once again strict, impeccable. She had forgotten. Her cousins were waiting for her, they had come from Villeneuve.

In any case, she felt only a moment's hesitation. She had to go forward. Only bad artists were afraid of losing their personality.

She would go to work for this Monsieur Rodin, who set so much store by lightness.

Siegmund and Sieglinde

Sieglinde: *If it is Siegmund whom I see here, I am Sieglinde who yearns for you: your own sister, you have conquered her along with the sword!*
Siegmund: *Here you are, wife and sister to your own brother.*

RICHARD WAGNER, *Die Walkyrie*
Act I, scene 3

LOOK, CAMILLE. Monsieur Rodin brought you a gift."
Camille looked at the enormous object wrapped in a cloth that took up the middle of the studio. Resting on a worktable, the bust, which was still hidden under its wrapping, looked like a big bucket.

Camille was twenty years old. Almost twenty. Born in December, she always believed she was older than her real age. When the first of January came, she changed her age, forgetting that she had already gained a year only the month before. The weather was lovely on this autumn afternoon. Camille, slightly out of breath, wearing a light-colored dress and a lace collar, held herself very straight in the sunlight. Virginia looked at her. She had grown again; there was something different about her. She was no longer the young girl of last year, and even if she always burst into her big laugh, during serious moments she seemed shrouded in mystery. Another carnal Camille; rounded in certain places, she was always so thin in her dresses, but her complexion was brighter . . .

"Oh, open it, hurry."

Camille approached the white, luminous package.

"Someone might think a lover had sent a pot of flowers!"

"Oh, your Monsieur Rodin!"

"He isn't *my* Monsieur Rodin!" Camille retorted violently.

"All right, calm down. We all adore him and – "

"We are jealous, that's all."

"You know, the other evening . . . See, another soiree you missed."

"But what do you do during the evenings?"

"I read."

"What an idea!"

"I read. I look for inspiration, for subjects. Look, the other Sunday Paul and I went to hear *Die Walkyrie*. You know, at the concert hall; I went with Paul . . ."

Camille came forward, no longer speaking. She divined what Monsieur Rodin had brought. Quickly she undid the swathes of cloth with ceremonial gravity. Little by little she felt the hardness of baked clay – no, how stupid she was! It was a bronze, impossible! There she was, in bronze, but how had he found the time? How had he done it? And bronze!

The girls were overwhelmed. Impressed by this mass that burst into light in the middle of the studio. Camille was all there, as if petrified in green algae, as if emerging from the water, her hair plastered to her head like a young man, a robust ancient warrior, a young Roman. An androgynous being of long ago, a kind of untouchable Hippolyte. She seemed to have retreated to her fortress, scion of an ancient race, heavy with some inner secret.

Her friends looked at her. How could the sculptor have captured that look she sometimes had? At this very moment, absent, withdrawn inside herself, illuminated by the sun filtering through the trees outside, she seemed to be a replica of the bust looking at her. Her hair, always done badly, damp with perspiration, the bangs stuck to her forehead, gave her that masculine look Monsieur Rodin had emphasized. Camille was overwhelmed. For some months he had been giving them lessons, substituting for Monsieur Boucher. She had often seen him lift his eyes from her work to her, but he had never asked her to pose for him. Oh yes, once. Suddenly the scene came back to her.

Her friends must have gone. It was hot. This was in July. That evening was the Bastille Day celebration in Paris. He had arrived late to give the girl some more suggestions on the bust of her brother. She was not managing to capture Paul's obstinate look, his rather provocative sixteen years. She had listened attentively. Suddenly, silence. Camille remembered: "You must begin with profiles, absolutely." He had taken her by the elbow and sat her down. Very quickly he had drawn a few lines of her profile. Drops of sweat had run down her back. There she was, sitting in the stifling room. She was nineteen, planted motionless on the stool. Silence, the scratch of the pencil. He had looked at her and suddenly, their eyes had met. He had squinted a little, as though blinded by so much light, and dropped the pencil. She had looked at him, with his air of surprise, ready to mock his clumsiness, to tease him the way she did her brother. But she hadn't uttered a sound. A pain held her as if riveted to her seat. A pain without pain, a wrenching in her stomach, very low, as if the stool were entering into her gently, something like desire, a desire to open up. Strangely linked to him, this mad desire. Madness to tell him: "Monsieur Rodin, please, put your hand here, just below my belly." That is what she wanted. That hand she had just seen resting on her brother's head, on the bust she was creating, to have it on her, to feel it. As if he were sculpting inside her, in her belly. The silence continued. She wanted to speak and he, his lips mouthed words she did not hear because he was saying nothing, nothing. The sound of the pencil falling to the ground had broken the spell – no, she had seen the pencil escape from his hands and only now had she heard it. How much time had it taken to fall?

"Camille, your umbrella, there, on the ground. It's broken." Camille shook herself, six pairs of eyes were looking at her somewhat ironically.

"I never open it anyway. So . . . And what's going on with all of you? Anyone would think you'd never seen a bust before. You're like a bunch of toads! And anyway, it's not me."

"Listen, Camille, you're exaggerating."

"No, I'm awful. Look, Nancy, a fat, round-cheeked boy. That's what he's done with me, a dull boy. And anyway, I've had enough of Monsieur Rodin! Why does he need to beat us over the head with his works?"

"Listen, Camille, you're really irritating. You're dreadful!"

"Shut up!"

"You too, you cackling magpie."

"Me, a cackling magpie?" Camille threw herself on Virginia. The two girls went at each other.

"Stop, stop this craziness. You two are crazy." A great cry echoed. Camille had just torn the back of Virginia's dress. With a great clawing blow, like a tigress. Virginia's white underskirt was rent, revealing her thighs. The dress hung on either side. Camille, crushed under her friend's weight, heard the horrible noise; she looked at Virginia, stupefied. Her mouth was bleeding, injured by the English girl's ring.

"And the grapes?"

"What, grapes?"

"We'd put grapes there for refreshment."

"Oh!"

"Excuse me." The man cleared his throat; the girls moved apart – Monsieur Rodin was there. "Excuse me for disturbing you. I wanted to know if Mademoiselle Camille had some comments for me. It's my turn to take a lesson today, but please, I'm not up for a fight. I have a horror of violence, and I would rather turn somersaults any day than tangle with one of you."

They laughed. Camille tried to get up. Her friends gave her a hand. "Have a little patience, Monsieur Rodin, we are going to clean up."

Monsieur Rodin was dazzled. Auguste liked this studio more and more. The youth, the gaiety of these girls made him forget his troubles. A little sunlight in his life. That was what he was missing. A little tenderness. Ah, if only he had a daughter. He thought of his son, Auguste, now more than twenty years old, who had disappeared again. If only he had a Camille.

"There, Monsieur Rodin." The two girls had draped themselves in shawls.

He loved women, Monsieur Rodin. These young women wrapped in their cashmeres, one brunette and proud, the other blond, smaller, perhaps a little plump, how he loved to watch them, to see them walk, bend toward each other. Rose had been like them when he'd met her, nearly thirty years ago now. But why had she aged so quickly? And these continual attacks of jealousy. Happily, he had found this haven of peace, this studio full of young girls . . .

"A cup of tea." Monsieur Rodin was late. He should not have come. But he wanted to know. To know if the gift had been well received. Camille looked at him now, even as he picked up his hat. She looked at him with a slightly hidden smile, modestly holding the slipping shawl. She looked at him and smiled.

"Stay a little, Monsieur Rodin." She took him gently by the arm. "My bust is so beautiful . . . I wanted to tell you . . . I . . . ." That was what distressed her. The tall, timid girl hung her head and leaned it briefly against her teacher's shoulder. "No comment, Monsieur Rodin." And she burst into her great laugh, as if to apologize for her clumsiness. Then, like a child, she added: "Can I keep it?"

"It's you. It's yours. For you." The sculptor's hand displayed the bust as if to put it back in its place, then he stammered a few words.

"Until tomorrow, my dear young ladies." He had already gone. People were waiting for him. Camille stood thinking.

"Hey, Camille . . . what's going on?" Her brother Paul. "Did you forget? I was supposed to come get you. I just met Monsieur Rodin. He's frightful. He would be perfect in the role of Falstaff."

"Oh, shut up, you little goose!" Paul was not comfortable with these girls. He wanted to insult them or knock them around. He found them noisy and pretentious. "Wait, my dress is drying."

Paul stopped short. He was bowled over by the bust he'd just now discovered: "Why, it's me."

"What, you?"

"There, it's me."

"No, you idiot, it's me, Monsieur Rodin sculpted me. If you think I had enough money to cast you in bronze."

"Your brother's right. Listen, go fetch the bust you made of him before the vacation."

Camille shrugged her shoulders and set out the bust of her brother Paul. It was true. They hadn't thought they were so alike. The girls looked at the two busts side by side: how surprising! "Twins! You're like twins!"

Camille was stupefied. It was not so much the resemblance between her and her brother that disturbed her, but rather the similarity of the two busts. She and Monsieur Rodin sculpted the same way. He was her real twin. Already last year – what was his name? Oh yes, Léon Lhermitte, had written to Rodin after the Salon: "It was with infinite pleasure" – Camille still remembered the exact words of the letter Rodin had shown her – "that I have seen Mademoiselle Claudel's face of a child. That achievement rules out any question of her being your disciple."

Camille looked at the two busts. Perhaps it wasn't clear which was Paul, which was Camille, but neither was it clear who had done the sculpting, Monsieur Rodin or Mademoiselle Camille!

"Camille, hurry. We are going to be late."

"Wait, come here." Camille pulled her brother into the little room where her dress was drying. Paul was relieved. He did not like being stared at by all those flighty girls.

"You look sad."

"No."

"Is it Collardeau?"

"Oh no, you're not going to start with Collardeau again!"

"This time you got it, your *baccalaureate.*"

"Yes, but not a single prize – not even an honorable mention. Father is in despair. He wanted me to go to the *École normale* at sixteen. He is back to talking about Collardeau, who swept up all the first places. He says that I'm not cut out for rue d'Ulm." Paul muttered between his teeth.

"Wait, my little Paul, I'm getting dressed, we'll talk about it, you're as green as a pear." Camille threw off her shawl and grabbed her dress. Paul looked at her: her beautiful shoulders in the sun, the white underskirt, the corset, the camisole. Paul looked at her, dazzled but also a little uncomfortable. She pulled her dress over her head. "Come help me." Paul was not good at this, he got into a muddle with the buttons.

"You're acting like a duck who's been eating cherries. Come on, quickly!" Camille carefully covered the two busts again, gave the useless umbrella a furious kick. "See you tomorrow. Good night, Virginia." The girls kissed each other. Paul could not bear all this demonstrative affection. He was already outside.

"You are always so friendly, my dear Paul! You're like a cannonball. Either you rush around with your head lowered, or you hit the ground and stop moving, as if you were stuck there."

"Don't start in on me."

"What's the matter?" The two young people were walking quickly.

"I'm suffocating. I want to go away."

"But you were pleased with your teacher, Burdeau!"

"Yes, he is quite remarkable. The man is remarkable, but all those theories . . . don't amount to anything. No light from that direction. Mama is grim. Louise sulks all day. And you are hardly ever there. Look, you know what they call me at the *lycée?* 'Deaf and Dumb.' Dumb. And they even laugh at my accent. Fortunately there is *Le Tour au monde.* That's my only pleasure, reading *Le Tour au monde,* China."

Camille stopped. She looked at her younger brother. It was true that they resembled each other, but how could she tell him? How could she make him understand that she, too, would go away? That she, too, wanted to go to China, and even farther? They came to the Luxembourg Gardens. The park was magnificent, green and golden. Camille thought vaguely of a tune that kept spinning in her head, a rather repetitious rhyme; Paul took it up:

> I cannot call myself Friedmund [peace]
> I would like to be Frohwalt [joy]
> But I must call myself Wehwalt [sorrow].

Camille teased her brother. She had pulled off a small branch.

> Siegmund.
> That's what I call you.

Paul burst out laughing, pulled the branch away from Camille, and both of them started running. Poor Wagner! "On guard! It's mine. *Notung! Notung!*" Sword of the brother and the sister.

Camille stopped. Paul looked at her. Once more he saw the little girl in the woods at Chinchy. Their escapades.

"You know – you've seen the two busts, yours and the one Monsieur Rodin made of me – you've seen how much alike they are. They say that I sculpt like him."

"That's not very bright. He copied what you did. Anyway, it doesn't look like you. Hang on, it'll come to me – yes, he's like old Hunding! You know, the fat man who takes Sieglinde prisoner and fights against Siegmund. Anyhow, I hate him."

Camille drew herself up, red with suppressed violence. She pulled the branch away from Paul and lashed him on the chest. "He is better than you, you whippersnapper. Besides, I've made up my mind. I will start work at his studio next week. And I have no time to waste on your concerts. Find someone else. You boor. Stinking louse!"

The girl strode rapidly away. Paul was wounded to the quick. At this moment, he hated her. Vulgar, she was vulgar . . .

Camille felt desperately sad. Why was she so mean? Her droll twin. Yet she had shared so many things with him. "My little Paul." They would have time, they had time, one day they would go to China and on Sunday to his concert as usual. But for this evening, no, the soiree at Madame Adam's was ruined. Mallarmé would have been there and Debussy, a young musician, perhaps even Rodin, Monsieur Rodin! Tomorrow she would tell him that she accepted his invitation. Finally, a real studio full of men.

Letter *from the Asylum*

Your sister in exile.

C

The Studio

The most beautiful subjects are there before us: they are
those we know best . . . The chief thing is to be moved,
to love, to hope, to tremble, to live. To be a man before
being an adult!

AUGUSTE RODIN, Testament

I T WAS COLD this morning. Even icy. Camille was twenty years
old. She would never tire of coming to the studio. She woke at daybreak. She did not want to lose a single ray of light. She'd been working
at Monsieur Rodin's studio for several months. Her little hat on her
head. Her mother had not wanted to give her consent: Camille was
twenty years old but she still had to keep her head covered modestly.
Half the time she pulled off the horrid, hated black hat. But this morning it was cold, and Camille wrapped herself in the old coat that was a
bit light for the season. Her mother did not have enough money to buy
her a warmer one. And then: "Camille, you'll have to be satisfied with
that. Louise is delicate and Paul has not stopped growing." So Camille
had kept the old coat she liked well enough.

Few people were in the street. It was snowing lightly, and Camille
took pleasure in feeling the little snowflakes gently nibbling at her, sliding behind her ear, down her neck, off the end of her nose . . .

Perhaps he would be there already? Monsieur Rodin was usually
the first to arrive at the studio. Camille was worried. He often seemed

absent, almost hostile to her, and then suddenly he would ask her opinion, her advice. She had entered his studio in the month of November. She could still remember that first day; she would never forget it.

She had not told anyone, not her mother or her brother. Her father was away, she saw him only on Sundays, and her sister Louise, now eighteen, was engaged in an energetic search for the fiancé who would give her what she dreamed of. So Camille had concealed the fact that she would begin work at Monsieur Rodin's studio that day.

That day . . . The walk, her legs growing stiff, her trembling hands, her beating heart, her thudding heart, shattering her composure. And suppose Monsieur Rodin had changed his mind. And suppose no one wanted her, all those men who worked there with him. She knew them all by name: Antoine Bourdelle, Antonin Mercie, Falguière, Jules Desbois.

Ten times, twenty times, a hundred times, she had gone out of her way to see the marble depository. She hadn't dared go to the studio or enter the courtyard. Often, dozens of times, she had glimpsed the old chestnut trees inside, the thick grass. Door five, door five, how many times had he said it: "Come on Saturday, door five." But no, she did not want to come as a visitor. She wanted to arrive by the front door — like the sculptors the master invited to work with him.

She had decided with her usual directness. Monsieur Rodin was advising her about the bust of her father she was just finishing – or thought she had finished. He had brushed a tired hand across his forehead, moved a stool over, and sat down heavily. Worried, Camille did not say anything. He was looking at her bust and at something else in the distance, she didn't quite know what. Her English friends had left for lunch, he had come earlier than usual. Camille stayed there beside him, wondering if she should speak. She had thought suddenly of her father: she looked at Rodin sitting there, and said to herself that she would have liked to put her hand on his forehead, to tell him that she was there — when she was a child, her father used to take her hands and put them on his forehead. "You soothe me, my little Camille, sometimes I feel so bad. These headaches . . ." Camille observed the pallor of Monsieur Rodin's face. "Your beautiful hands, my Camille, you soothe me with . . ."

"Monsieur Rodin, are you unwell?"

He had abruptly raised his head, his eyes haggard, "My father is dead. My crazy father. My father in the asylum . . ." He had burst out laughing, had stammered: "Excuse me. It's not funny . . . But my son is alcoholic. None of this matters . . . Art is only feeling."

Camille still remembered the date: 26 October 1883. He had risen almost spitefully, then turned toward her: "I would love to know your father. I'm overwhelmed by the bust you've made of him. Excuse me. If you wanted to come work with me, truly, I would be awfully pleased."

"I will come the day after tomorrow."

He had looked at her as if she were mocking him. "Studio J, door five. At the end, door five." Then he had disappeared, overturning a chair as he went.

Now she was there, standing in front of the marble depository. That day, she still remembered, that day, the biting cold of a white sun, the silence of the courtyard. Camille had entered the courtyard and gone inside the depository. A silhouette lost amidst blocks of marble. With her hair falling down her back, she seemed so young. Her hand had rested delicately on a block standing there. One day she would cut directly in marble. Like Michelangelo. That day, Camille remembered – she'd looked twice at the letters on the doors, the letter *L*, the letter *J*, and she'd looked many times, just to be sure. The distant sound of the technicians bruising the stone. The door was opened, the dust, the noisy rush of voices; there seemed to be a multitude of people inside, but she saw nothing more, only the gray studio, the gray cinders, the skylight. She had thought: A cell, a prison cell, the stools, the tables, the upended cases, everywhere works that looked at her with their huge, devouring eyes. There – what was it? That day, the silence. She could still hear the silence. Yet opening the door she had glimpsed many people, had even heard something like an uproar. That silence, and a single rough voice: "A woman!" A few laughs here and there, like flowers thrown at the end of a performance. "And pretty," someone had added, "a fine, strapping girl."

Camille had closed the door, a bit roughly, raising her head, "I am a sculptor." A female model, half-undressed, had stood in front of her, dumbfounded. Camille had thought, "Here is a friend!" She had repeated to her, "I am a sculptor."

The redhead had looked at her, undressed her with her sea-green eyes. She had repeated a bit stupidly: "A sculptor! You, you're a sculptor? A woman?" Now she'd burst into a resounding laugh: "Hear that, boys! Madame is a sculptor!"

Camille could still hear the echo of that raucous laughter. Several models, several men had followed suit; they were all laughing heartily. A gentle hand had taken the elbow of the sensual beauty, the mocking model, and led her out. Monsieur Rodin was there. His rather timid voice had restored the silence: "Let me introduce you to Mademoiselle Camille Claudel. I have asked her to come and work here. She is a sculptor. Perhaps a great sculptor."

Jules Turcan and Antonin Mercie had been charming. In no time she had her little chair, the stool, everything she needed. She would never forget that day. When she had begun to work, kneading the clay, the other sculptors kept glancing at her. It didn't take them long to see that they were in the presence of a fine artist. And beautiful besides.

Curiously, the men kept their distance, anxious, not daring to joke with her. She was another species. She frightened them. Neither Jules nor even Falguière ever invited her conversation. Curiously, despite the esteem and admiration she evoked, Camille felt very much alone, as if they begrudged her either her beauty or her talent, which together placed them on difficult ground. Virginia, for example, who was not beautiful, had an instant court of admirers around her when she came to visit Camille. The sculptors showed her their works, asked her where her sculptures were. Jane, by contrast, tall and blond, got invitations for the week each time she visited. Neither Camille's sculpture nor her beauty attracted any sign of friendship. She was there, Monsieur Rodin had asked her to come, they congratulated her, they admired her, they envied her, but when the studio was closed, Camille was left alone. It didn't matter to her – she read, visited museums and exhibitions alone, or made drawings in search of some elusive detail.

The attitude of the models was more difficult to bear. In this studio full of men, the female models seemed humiliated by her presence. Yvette, who had at first greeted her so good-naturedly, particularly despised her. With her drawling voice she never missed the chance to say: "Undress in front of Madame, oh no I don't!" It often took all of Monsieur Rodin's patience and determination to avoid an outright brawl. "You've seen the sculptress! Got more than she does, any day! Mam'zelle Camille this . . ." That day, no. Camille would never forget it. Her deep blue eyes had darkened.

She could find no place – neither among the men nor among the women. Even her English friends no longer laughed with her as they had done before. So Camille set to work doubly hard. Silent on her little chair. She was one of the first to arrive, barely listening to the chatter of the studio, deaf to the obscene jokes that had made her blush at first. The models had tried to goad her, but her obstinacy had quickly shut them up. Now her presence at the studio seemed to be taken for granted. Only Yvette would not be mollified.

Even Camille's father had not understood her decision: "You are a great sculptor. Why are you going to work for him? It is a renunciation." Camille thought quite the contrary. For several months she had been going to Monsieur Rodin's Studio J. He alone shared her ideal of beauty and truth. He alone was making art, the others were good only for castings after nature. They were servile copiers. He alone transfigured reality.

This morning, as so often happened, Camille was in a hurry. "You are going to sacrifice your originality." The first big dispute with her father. He had rapped on the table: "Watch out, Cam, you are going to lose everything. Your personality . . . He has a very bad reputation. His first sculpture, I don't know which . . ."

"The walking man, Papa, *The Age of Bronze.*"

"Yes, what a scandal! He copied it."

"Cast directly, you mean. But listen, Papa, they were all wrong, the sculpture was so fine they all thought he'd made the cast directly on the body of the soldier who had posed for him. But you know better, Boucher even told you about it. Boucher went to find Dubois, the director of the academy, and along with his friend Henri-Antoine Chapu, a colleague, they verified that Rodin had managed to sculpt from memory. Without models. There was a petition: Carrier-Belleuse, the sculptor, Falguière, Chaplain, they all attested to it. The minister for fine arts got involved. Rodin was officially rehabilitated at the time. So don't keep spreading around the same idiotic nonsense."

"Listen, Camille, that's enough. I tell you that you have enough talent to work alone."

"Only mediocrities are afraid of learning something and shut themselves up alone. Time erases all signatures."

"What are you going to learn from that red-beard?"

"My God, you are completely limited. Naturally, you never come to Paris. Your provincialism – "

Camille had slammed the door, furious. Their first big fight. At the same time she felt remorseful. Why had she made that stupid remark about his provincialism? He had sacrificed everything for her. Louise was disappointing him, gradually abandoning her music. Paul was renouncing the *École normale*. He was her father and she loved him blindly, sometimes spitefully, but she loved him with his sad face, his wrinkles, and the smile at the corner of his lips that he'd passed on to her.

This morning Camille was hurrying to reach the studio. Her father's face stayed with her. She would write to him, tell him to come. They would have lunch together, just the two of them. She would tell him how full of joy, how happy she was to be a sculptor, and all thanks to him, to this man who – how old was he now? Fifty-eight years old – fifty-eight already.

Monsieur Rodin was there. Alone in the studio in his sculptor's smock, he was already at work. His blue eyes rested on Camille. How dare they speak of his myopia? Camille was struck each time by the unbearable directness of that gaze, which made her think of a compass that clasped persons and things in its span – a formidable device set to annotate, compare, specify, measure . . . two pincers that defined you, examined you, pierced you through, before the gaze was suddenly veiled, it disappeared, withdrew inside itself. At moments he seemed to have been dragged from sleep, slowly returning from that distant country where no one could follow.

"Camille, I am happy to see you. Look." Monsieur Rodin drew back. Camille approached the work. He often asked her for advice. Despite the envious looks, Camille felt no glory in it. Intimidated, she tried each time to give him the exact measure of her thought, to make some progress with him. This morning there was no one else present. The two sculptors stood silently in front of a statue. Camille recoiled in horror: an old woman sat there, dugs drooping, head heavy, dressed in rags, her hair sparse. She sat there as if she were going to die on this icy morning. A last pose, a last station . . .

Camille looked at Rodin, tears in her eyes. The statue seemed seconds from death. Camille had noticed for some time that Monsieur

Rodin had been absorbed in a study of some human form, but as he worked on several pieces at the same time, she had forgotten this one.

Camille turned again toward the statue. Rodin looked at her. Camille, terribly young, almost fragile in the face of this old woman. The two women confronted each other, and the great question posed itself – on one side, life, Camille's blossoming young body demanding joy without end; and on the other, this old woman in the process of decay, annihilation. Rodin looked at the girl standing at his side, ready to give everything – the tense young body facing the cadaverous old woman, his friend Baudelaire's great corpse lying in the sun:

> When I think, weary, of the old days,
> Of what was, what became,
> When I look at my naked self
> And see myself so changed,
> Poor, dry, thin, diminished,
> I could choke with rage!
> What happened to that shining forehead,
> Those blond locks . . .

Camille listened to her master's low voice reciting Villon's lines. She knew them. He had recited them to her before, when he was beginning to model *The Beautiful Helmet-Maker's Wife*. She had not yet known what he was trying to create.

"I think she's beautiful, frighteningly beautiful. Only the soul remains. I think she is saying something else. Something more serious than the loss of her beauty. There is an appeal, a prayer, as if she were saying, 'Stop, I'm not playing the game anymore. Let me gather myself together a moment, keep silent while I let my immortal dream pass away. My heart is tormented, but I am beyond that. Give me a moment to get there, before I find a great happiness.' She reminds me of Donatello's *Magdalen*, she . . ."

Camille turned her gaze toward him again. He nearly staggered before the light, his soul burning behind his pupils; she alone knew how to see beyond the form, she knew how to penetrate the very meaning of the work.

"You are right. I thought again of something Octave Mirbeau told me. I should introduce you to my friend Mirbeau. It's a story that haunts me. The mother of an Italian model had come here on foot, to see him before she died, and he told her: 'Mama, I'll leave you at the door unless you agree to pose.' He introduced her to me without telling me she was his mother. I learned a few days ago that she was dead. I began to rework in a frenzy. What could this woman have been thinking as she posed for me? The humiliation, the shame. I had asked her to undress. All the time she said nothing. She lowered her head. Does art excuse everything? I was furious when he told me the truth. I kicked him out. And yet I will never regret having made this figure. The strange paradox of artists. Until death, Camille. Until you make someone die to find it. Until you die yourself in the search."

"M'sieur Rodin! M'sieur Rodin!" The bantering voice behind them, Yvette was joking. "So, always in the saddle, M'sieur Rodin . . . *Come on, if you want . . .*" Yvette proceeded to undress in front of Monsieur Rodin. He burst out laughing, she threw him one of her garments. Camille was red with anger. How could he change so quickly? Suddenly she saw him slap Yvette's bottom as she held her two fleshy globes toward him. "Hurry up and do me, M'sieur Rodin, before I get like that one. Your ugly old woman."

The sun began to warm the room. "I'll get a coffee to keep me going. It'll go on for hours today!" Yvette's milky skin rippled. Monsieur Rodin blinked his eyes, the door slammed. One by one the sculptors arrived, the models . . . The whole studio was sparkling with light, with noise, with joyful greetings. Camille had gone back to her little chair, still disturbed by Monsieur Rodin's story.

He was there, already working with sweeping, precise gestures, on a bust, a face that was emerging from the stone. At moments he looked at her as if she were posing. He rested his eyes on her boldly, fixedly, as though he were a vision machine . . .

"You've seen, children! Eyes only for Mam'zelle the sculptor! He's even doing her now! Just told me so. Me, I'm waiting for her to pose naked!"

Camille struggled to stay calm. She raised her head to Yvette. "Why not?"

The studio was quiet. Monsieur Rodin was absorbed in his work. He had not heard.

"Hey! M'sieur Rodin! It's Mam'zelle Camille you're sculpting there! What're you going to call it? *Bust of Mam'zelle Rodin?*"

Monsieur Rodin stepped back, looked at his work. The sun was mounting; the skylight was illuminated by a winter sun still wrapped in a reddish haze.

"No! It will be called *Dawn.*"

Letter *from the Asylum*

It seemed that my poor studio – a few poor furnishings, a few tools I made myself – even my poor little household excited their greed!

Dawn

In the dazzling light of autumn
We left in the morning.
The magnificence of autumn
Thundered in the distant sky.
The melancholy sound of the horn, inconsolable
Because of the time that is no more,
That is no more because of that single glorious day
It is no more.

PAUL CLAUDEL, *Chanson d'automne*

SEPTEMBER 1885. The autumn crackling like pine needles on the Chinchy butte. But she was not there in the little village. Back in Paris. The year had begun again. For several weeks Camille had been back at Monsieur Rodin's studio. The air was heavy with rain. The Claudels had just eaten dinner. Old Hélène was there, faithful. The storm raged outside, but also inside. Old Hélène felt it coming; her habit of reading the sky had given her the gift of reading the soul's weather as well. Camille was drawing her brother. Paul was reading. Louise was tapping on the table with a distracted air. Only Madame Claudel was conscientiously tidying up the dining room. Camille was using her pencil too nervously. She tore up the piece of paper and crushed it in a ball, taking another.

"Make less noise, Cam, I can't read."

Camille said nothing. Camille broke the lead of her pencil. She looked at her mother.

"She doesn't stop for a moment, my God, she doesn't stop!"

Camille wanted to leave, to go walking in the streets of Paris.

Camille took another sheet of paper. She said nothing. Old Hélène swept the crumbs and watched. Something was going to happen. She knew Camille by heart. And Paul! Paul was in a state! He cracked his knuckles, one after the other.

"Paul, stop!"

Paul was seventeen years old. He was enrolled at the *École normale* in political science; he was studying law. Paul gave his sister a vicious look, full of hatred. He would have liked to drive her away. Far away from him, in particular. Oh, if she would only piss off! Paul kept quiet and continued to read. Louise tapped her fingers. Their mother had taken out her old account book and begun her never-ending calculations. Louise hated it when she did her additions. Of course, they didn't have much money, but this mother who never stopped counting! Night after night . . . Louise said nothing and kept drumming on the table. She would have liked to go for a walk. Madame Louise was thinking of her house at Villeneuve. How happy she'd been there with her father the doctor. She could see the little village square, peaceful in autumn, Monsieur Athanaïse Cerveaux, medical doctor, "His honor the mayor," greeted by everyone. There they were respected. She was eighteen years old, on her father's arm, and how the boys looked at her! Oh, why had she married Louis-Prosper? Was it Paris she hated? Madame Louise said nothing. She could see the wild races with her brother, the old forest, the sibyl's fountain. Madame Louise counted the sous. The sun on the river, the pieces of gold. Her brother in the river. Why had he thrown himself into the river at twenty-three? Madame Claudel counted the remaining sous yet again. Madame Claudel said nothing. Old Hélène waited. The storm grew more menacing.

Paul began to read aloud. Camille hated that. It was as though he were forcing everyone to listen. And besides, he read badly. His lips moved like the lips of a marionette. But what was he reading? To Hélène's great amazement, Camille was listening. Normally she got up and went out, she always found a way of interrupting or else she would look like a virgin being led to the slaughter. She knew her Camille. When she was obstinate, hypocritical, closed up, she looked as though she couldn't sit still. Paul continued to read:

You tear me, my brown beauty
With a mocking laugh

And then you cast your eye
Gentle as the moon, on my heart.

Under your satin shoes
Under your charming silken feet
I put my greatest joy
My genius and my fate.

You've healed my soul . . .

Louise violently scraped her chair as she rose. "You're so tiresome,
all of you! Thank goodness tomorrow I'm invited to the Fleurys'."
Louise opened the piano.
"No, Louise, it's late." Bang! Louise had closed the piano, even
locked it. Now she slammed the door behind her with all her strength.
They were no longer listening to Paul. But he kept on reading. Instead
of being released by Louise's outburst, the tension in the room only in-
creased. Hélène waited.

I am beautiful, O mortals, like a dream of stone!
And my breast, where each in his turn has been broken . . .

"God, what garbage you're reading, children!"
Madame Louise had said one word too many. Camille leaped up.
"It's worth more than your cringing in front of the cross. Besides, you
don't believe in anything. You only do it because you're afraid."
Madame Claudel got up, slowly. She was scarcely twenty years
older than her elder daughter. "It's not cringing."
"You go to church because Papa isn't here. So you'll have company. You just do what everyone else does. And I brought back the
palm on Palm Sunday. And I feel reassured by the old man who recites
the prayers. Why not get on with him? Go on, take off your hat and
he's happy."
"Camille, stop." Paul got up too.
"Oh, you too! You'd do better to read Mama *The Life of Jesus* from
your old teacher, the teacher who congratulated you on your prize two
years ago. Monsieur Renan!"

"Camille, that's enough. In the first place, he smelled bad. He has a pig's head, with his thick hide and his yellow eyelids."

Madame Claudel went up to bed. Camille continued: "Nonsense, all that's just nonsense."

Paul was annoyed. "Stop now. I'm not a believer, so stop. Let me read. Go find your old man."

"My old man!"

"Monsieur Rodin!"

"Right, Monsieur Rodin, he reads the same things you do. *Les Fleurs du mal.* Even the poem you were reading, he's doing a magnificent statue of it. *The Abduction*, it's called, or *The Cat!*"

"Well, he'll abduct you one fine day and then we won't have any more talk of your Monsieur Rodin. We've all had it up to here with him."

Camille overturned the chair, she was mad with rage. Paul threw the book at her head. Camille got it right in the face. Paul slipped off. The doorbell rang. Hélène went to open it.

"Monsieur Paul, it's Messieurs Chavannes and Schwob. They've come for you."

"Good-bye, charming tigress!" Paul made a face at his sister and disappeared.

Flee! Where to? Escape far away! Flee from this hateful family and her brother, who got to leave after dinner just like that and stroll around Paris.

The storm had grown worse. Camille took up the book. Oh, yes. She had promised to find Monsieur Rodin the passage in *The Divine Comedy* on the damned struck by lightning. Camille went to look for the big red book with its dark, gilded pages. She sat at the table and began to search. Hélène sat down beside her. The two heads leaned over the thick book. The storm shattered the night with streaks of lightning. The sky went violet, crackling. Hélène was afraid. "What are you reading there, Mam'zelle Camille?" Hélène forced her tired eyes. "*The Divine Comedy*, Dante. What is it?"

Camille suddenly read aloud: "The nine circles where the damned must dwell . . ." Camille followed her finger. "And I said: 'Master, what is it that is so grievous to them, making them lament so sorely?' He replied: 'I will tell thee in a few words. They have no hope of death, and so abject is their blind life that they are envious of every other lot. The world suffers no report of them to live. Pity and justice despise them. Let us not talk of them; but look thou and pass.'"

Hélène listened, her eyes round with horror, like a terrified child. Camille got up. "It's for Monsieur Rodin. 'The Gate of Hell.'"

"Hell." Hélène nodded her head. Camille closed the book once more, slipped it under her arm, grabbed a cloak.

"Where are you going, Mam'zelle Camille?

"To Monsieur Rodin's." And she went out.

"At this hour?" Hélène was dumbfounded, devastated. Suddenly she realized. She had to intervene, to warn Madame, follow her. She got up. No, she would go herself, she would follow Camille. She went to take her old shawl. The wrinkled, bony hand fell at her side.

To what good!

> To every thing there is a season,
> And a time to every purpose under heaven:
> A time to be born, and a time to die.

Hélène thought of her Camille. May God protect her. Besides, there was no avoiding anything, and especially not life here below. Fortunately! She would not want to deprive Camille of life, of her life, for anything in the world. Hélène sat down again, she looked at the plate of fruit left on the table, the juicy peaches . . .

"Oh, my old Jean." She could see the barn, his fine teeth biting into the peach, the juice running down, Jean's large hands. Jean . . . a tear ran down her wrinkled cheek. She felt his hands as if he were there. She was seventy-two years old now, she still wanted Jean. Her Jean, who had died ten years, twenty years ago. Her belly still burned. She could feel her Jean's rough hands, the sun was setting, the odor of the peach. Camille running in the street – Camille. Mam'zelle Camille, the peach, wait . . .

She ran the length of the street. It was almost night. Yet the autumn was like ripe fruit ready to burst. She was warm. She hoped he would be there. She did not know why she had just left the house so abruptly. The way she used to do when she would leave for the grotto of the Geyn. Her giant, if only he were there!

She arrived at rue de l'Université. She reached the door to the studio. In a last ray of sunlight he was pondering his clay study. He looked at her. Not a word. Not a gesture. She stared at his hands smeared with earth, she could not take her eyes off those hard hands. Slowly, slowly she closed the door, or rather she leaned her whole body against it. He still hadn't moved, he still looked at her. Slowly, slowly he took the cloth, the dampened cloth, and covered the clay he'd been kneading. The sun had just set. Dusk suffused the studio. He was far away but she felt him. She knew what she wanted. She had chosen him, and her belly burned like a stiffened member. She wanted it to be quick, she had seen the village animals, she had read stories, and anyway, she knew, her body drew her on. Then he came toward her, calling her name: "Camille," so softly it might have been a child's moan. He came to her. They were nearly the same height.

"Camille, why?" But he rested his two hands on the door and leaned against her — like two relatives saying good-bye. His cheek was against hers, as if he were resting there a moment, "Child, child . . ." He stood back, softly stroking her cheek.

She was beside herself, utterly torn by longing. Her heavy coat, her skirts, her woolen stockings, her bodice squeezing her breasts. She felt like she'd suddenly grown larger. Then he fell on her, violently kissed her lips, his two hands like a vise around her neck. She attacked, almost fought him. She herself pulled off his clothes, she wanted to understand, she wanted to know, she wanted to see, she had crossed over and never wanted to turn back, never mind the others, never mind the rest.

She kept standing against the door, her coat fallen, she turned, her cheek touching the wood panel. She felt him loosening her bodice, breaking her corset, she felt her breasts freed, she felt him, his fingers on the skin of her back, tearing her undergarments. She no longer knew where she was. He had taken her around the waist, led her, pulled her like his prey. She wanted to see, she kept her great eyes open. Her woolen stockings were hanging over her shoes. He threw her on the couch used for the models, kneading her, and she wanted to feel his fingers inside, she opened her mouth, she opened herself, she couldn't wait anymore, he left her a second and she began to knead herself, she took her breasts . . . he grabbed her hands, lifted them from her body. He was there, his hands crushed her clitoris, took it between two fingers, she loved, she tensed again . . . he parted her legs, every unfamiliar gesture engraved on her brain, she was lucid as she had never been, she saw her body in memory, she saw the swollen vulva, the man's member, she saw the curve, the button above the lips, he caressed her there, she felt his sex against her beating, striking. Then she opened up still more. She knew this was more eloquent than hands. She had never learned and already she understood his language, she wanted him, let him lay waste to everything inside her. She had heard such horrors, girls injured. She had never believed that, she had such desire to grasp him between her two lips. And suddenly he was there inside her, driving in. She was afraid of a single blow, of being disemboweled, but no, a mad sensation seized her, as if she wanted him to drive into her still more. She plunged willingly, wound herself around him, and she felt everything sliding, flowing . . . then she turned against him, as he supported her. She was now entirely turned inward, and she tore herself away and threw herself into this quartering. If only he could cleave her heart and her head forever. Not to think anymore. Her body was tensed, and suddenly he touched a sensitive spot, deep inside her, so deep, she had not said a word, her eyes were dilated to the point of madness, she felt a pocket emptying, an easing, and she yielded to it . . .

She was lying naked, the moon had risen. He was there, she saw his attentive eyes, a kind of fear in his eyes, like an homage, like a rising prayer. She had no regrets, she knew that she had done what she had chosen to do. No thought of turning back, only a power multiplied tenfold and such joy, as if she had defied the gods. Then he smiled for the first time, softly caressing her hip. "*L'Aurore.* My own Dawn." A lunar landscape. A child sleeping. The butte of Chinchy, my little Paul. The children of the moon were dead.

Letter *from the Asylum*

They've reproached me (oh dreadful crime) for living all alone.

25 February 1917.

The Gates of Hell

And if desire should cease with God,
Ah, I would rather be in hell.

PAUL CLAUDEL, *La Cantate à trois voix*

THE SUN had set. Monsieur Rodin lit some candles. Now and then he would sit alone, looking at his statues in the flicker of the flames. And they would come to life, a kind of dim, other life. He would never rework any detail in this uncertain light, but he loved to see them shimmer, turning toward him, burning in that trembling, treacherous light. But this evening he was contemplating a living body, rich flesh cast of white gold, his student Camille.

Auguste stood there before her, unmoving, drunk with this moment, with the fire that after nearly forty-five years was scorching him for the first time. His life was forever wedded to this moment. He was utterly vulnerable, almost threatened by this young woman who had just staked all she had with such triumphant force. And he felt her arms around him awkward, too light, too slender, slow to grasp the torrent sweeping away his heart, and his head. Camille still distant – Camille turned inward, her absent smile, his student Camille, there in all her splendor. Monsieur Rodin was afraid – with a mute fear that tinged his joy mounting in dark, red waves. She was teaching him something new. Yet he understood, he had known love, lovers, sensuality – no, it wasn't true, he knew nothing, and he was struck repeatedly by his ignorance. Never mind the scandal, never mind what people would say. Rose, his old companion, was far away. Camille's parents . . . And if it were madness, death, yes, even hell on earth. As for the other kind, the hell hereafter, he didn't know, he no longer knew what that was. And suddenly he was afraid, afraid of losing her. He couldn't do without her, the marvelous limbs he gripped with his two hands, that open gaze.

Camille looked at him. With no thought for the future, she thought only of peace, everything was now resolved. There was no more fear, she knew that all was well. She had done what she had to do. She felt fully resolved, like a mathematical equation, entirely in proportion. Everything was miraculously balanced. She was the golden mean – her head, her heart, her soul. Now she believed. And the soul within her swelled, animating her, and whispered that she had arrived. Camille was no longer afraid.

If only she might stay, now that he had uncovered her, discovered her. He knelt beside the couch, bent his head toward the smooth belly glistening with small pools of semen. The center of his potency, she smiled at him, he slipped down toward her groin, and she laughed, joyous, vibrant, free. She knelt on the couch, like those good little girls crouched beside the Christmas tree. Then he needed to possess her again, this new, younger self. He embraced her, gently licking below her belly. He spread her knees, and she let him, turning up her stiffened torso, her breasts pointing toward the bluish transepts. Slowly he buried his face between the two muscular, almost masculine thighs. Now she slowly unfolded her legs and turning, threw herself face down across the couch; she held out her buttocks, bringing them against him, then spread her two arms.

A quartered animal, she did not know her body but she understood it. She accepted even the tearing – but no, the man was lashing her with his tongue. Camille felt emptiness inside her, vertigo, as if he were drinking her in, sucking her up. The pools of her childhood where she had gravitated so reluctantly. The desire to know, to let herself be swallowed up. Then she refreshed him, devoured, drunk with thirst; burning herself, she let him quench his thirst to the last drop. She gave everything once again; at the end of her strength, feverish, inflamed, she slipped to the floor along the couch, desiring, seeking to appease her own thirst, that endless desire. The two of them lay together on the ground. He stood up, leaned over her, raised her, held himself against her face. She felt his sex against her, in her hair, then he leaned delicately toward her, looking at her with a strange yearning. Camille did not understand, she saw his eyes, black, charred, sorrowful. So imperious was his demand, she appeased him, at last she understood! She was no longer afraid, and if this meant death, she would drain it to the dregs. He took her face between his hands and brought his sex to her cheeks, her lips. Camille kissed it. Camille took what he gave her with such intensity.

"Camille, Camille!" She heard the distant call in the forest of Tardenois. "Camille, don't go on, no more." Monsieur Rodin looked at her tenderly. He had just covered her with a sheet so she wouldn't catch cold. She sat there on the floor, overcome. When had he gotten up? He held out a big glass of cold water and made her drink. Camille's pupils were dilated. Now she put the glass against her forehead. She had no regrets, she was beyond life, beyond death.

She got up and sat on the couch without saying a word. She saw the thick red book there, on the ground. When had she dropped it? She no longer remembered. *The Divine Comedy* . . . like a child who is going to sleep and asks for someone to tell her a story.

"It was for you . . ." Camille stayed there, seated, wrapped in her sheet, almost timid now. Monsieur Rodin was naked; he looked at her with great feeling.

"I've just understood – my figures, they're you multiplied, begun anew, saved, damned, but calling each time, your flesh forever resurgent, the resurrection of the flesh, you are the young girl and death, the martyr, the damned, but you are also *Fugit Amor*, the cat, the crouching woman, the falling man, earthly illusions, eternal springtime. I see it all now. An infinite night of love, you, the eternal idol . . ."

She was standing up, she listened to Monsieur Rodin, who was kneeling and kissed her gently between her breasts – "My eternal idol."

Camille looked at him. He was happy, joyful: "*The Gates of Hell* will soon open. My two hundred figures – a single figure exploding in space, an elusive meteor, you, hurled out into space and forever reborn – the phoenix."

Now she laughed. "But I would never pose naked in front of everyone, I would be ashamed!"

"No, only for me."

Monsieur Rodin had found his model, the perfect Eve, but she belonged to him. Not like the other one, his Italian model who had hidden her heaviness from him. She belonged to him, with him, the model who completed the creator: his creature.

"I have to go home." Camille threw off her sheet, dressed quickly, Monsieur Rodin contemplated her long legs. She jumped into her skirt, pulled her blouse on inside out. He had never seen a woman get dressed this way. Everything thrown on like that, haphazardly, and then in the blink of an eye, there she was, dressed and ready. She had more or less fixed her chignon, thrown the cloak over her shoulders. A woman dressed once more, even more beautiful. Monsieur Rodin looked at her. He felt old now, now that she was leaving. No, she came toward him: "Monsieur Rodin, don't forget me. Monsieur Rodin, you're not mad at me?"

He felt dull, stupid, "See you tomorrow, Camille."

And suddenly she put her arms around his neck and kissed him. He felt her entire body in this kiss that stirred him deeply, she clung, seized him, gave him eternity – and fled.

Monsieur Rodin remained, immobile, in the studio that still glowed in the candle flames, the high doors of the unfinished *Gates of Hell* before him. He felt small, devastated. He turned around: a man, there, below the menacing gates, *The Gates of Hell*, which he had proudly wanted to defy. He had already been working on them nearly four years, he had to finish them . . . *The Gates of Hell*, gigantic, monstrous waiting . . .

Camille walked in the rain. The storm had abated. Curiously, Camille felt happy to be alone. She would not have wanted to stay. She had drained everything from life; now she could die. Camille felt dangerously powerful, she loved, she knew love, everything else paled. She deliberately splashed through the puddles. No one could argue with her, no one at home could tell her anything now. She knew man, she was man and woman, she was a sculptor! She would shape great works, as colossal as his. She would know how to learn again and again. One day she would sculpt a gigantic work, like Michelangelo. That night she had understood the intelligence of the flesh, she had grasped what was missing. They said that virgins were invincible – she thought quite the opposite. This evening she was no longer the unformed girl, she was a free woman, who walked in the night and knew where she was going. This evening she was Diana and Aphrodite, she dominated, the world was at her feet. This night she had possessed a man, the man she loved, this evening Monsieur Rodin had loved her for the first time. She was as strong as love itself.

Letter *from the Asylum*

Madhouses are houses . . . [illegible].

Giganti

The best of artists can but choose the concept
That the block of marble doth contain
In its excess, and he alone attain
This goal whose hand obeys the intellect.

MICHELANGELO

H OLD STILL."
Paul had had enough. Enough of this stifling studio. April 1885.
The skylight was warm; Paul squirmed in his tight collar, he had other
things to do. "I hope you'll soon find other models."

"Shut up! You're thrilled to pose for me." Camille looked at her
brother. Nearly eighteen years old. She would love to talk with him,
but he was so closed, so secretive. Sometimes she caught a glimpse of
his friends. They rarely came looking for him. Camille would have
liked to confide her great secret to him, only to him, but oddly, she was
frightened of this big rude boy with the violent look. Violent, even
brutal.

From her position she could see the couch behind him. If only he
knew. Had he sensed it? The evening of the storm it had been terrible.
They had never spoken of that episode again.

She had come home around ten o'clock, nearly eleven. The storm had
burst, a torrential rain, the streets dark, Paris black, arrogant, applaud-

ing. She had clambered up the stairs, four at a time. Standing, a dark silhouette, her mother erect, her forty-one-year-old mother, hissing dreadfully, insulting her with every name in the book, the worst, lashing her with her scorn, her hatred, her curses. After sending Hélène to bed, she had waited up for Camille's return. Camille, who had dared to go out alone after dinner without permission. "Where were you?"

Camille had refused to admit that she was at Monsieur Rodin's: "I needed to walk."

"Whore, whore!"

All that had happened. Her mother had come toward her, she wanted to hit her, the sky was torn to pieces with her mute cries. Suddenly Paul was there.

"What's going on?"

Louise was cowering in a corner – how long had she been there? Then the mother had suddenly collapsed, looking despairingly at her son. She had begun to weep, standing there, shriveled, shrunken. "This child will be the death of me. I hate her. I hate her."

Paul had turned toward Camille. He did not understand, saw nothing. Madame Claudel kept quiet, but a murderous light glittered behind her tears. She hated them all. "I forbid you to sculpt, do you hear, I forbid you to continue." She hammered out the words, nodding her head.

Then Camille had thrown it all up, save what she had just experienced. "I'll go away. You won't make me into someone like you. I'm not like you. I want to be free. I'll leave here. I'll go where there is no one."

Madame Louise got up. "Never again, do you hear! Never again like this. You will never go out again. Locked up. I will have you locked up."

"Try . . ."

Paul had begged: "Stop, for pity's sake, stop!"

Madame Louise had left the room, with Louise trailing behind her. "Come on. It's over now, Camille. It's over." And she had left, bent, bowed. Camille would have liked to detain her, to tell her that she loved her. But why hadn't her mother understood, why?

"Why?" Paul had asked, his hand on his sister's arm. "Camille, what is it?"

"Nothing. It's nothing. I went out, that's all."

Paul's gaze had wavered, he had recoiled and bumped into a chair, which he'd grabbed brutally and flung to the ground. It was broken. Camille had sat there all alone amidst the debris, alone in the dark, wounded, disgraced – by everyone. What did that matter? She was outside society, outside their petty judgments, but Paul, she would have liked him . . . Bah!

"Camille, I'm not going to stick around." Oh no, that was too much! Now Monsieur Rodin was there. His buttocks glued to the stool, that was already too much, but then to pose in front of that bearded pot-belly, that pig. No, it was simply too much! "Camille, that's enough." Paul got up.

Rodin had wanted to stammer a few words. The three of them looked at each other in the white studio, hot and humid. Camille did not know what to say. Paul kept quiet. Finally Monsieur Rodin tossed out the words: "And are you all happy in the new apartment, is your mother more comfortable?"

Silence.

"Camille told me it was a little bigger. Thirty-one, boulevard de Port-Royal. Is that right, Cam?"

It had escaped him. Paul looked at him, red-faced, embarrassed. So now he called her Cam – his Camille, his sister. What bad manners! Anyway, he despised Rodin.

"No, it's not better. Anyhow, I hate everything about this city. The City. I will leave as soon as possible. Excuse me . . . I must go."

Paul went out. Camille was annoyed at him – what bad manners, that Paul! It was quite simple, she would destroy his bust, it would serve him right. Paul Claudel was eighteen years old. Okay, there would not be any Paul Claudel at eighteen. Paul Claudel would not have the right to posterity. Paul Claudel would be reduced to rubble.

"Camille, what are you doing?" Rodin caught her arm. She was unnerved. They had hardly seen each other. Since that evening of the storm, she had stooped to lies and tricks to steal an hour here or there, a kiss, a hasty caress. They had a tacit agreement to behave in public as though nothing had happened. And yet everyone knew, they all guessed, guessed that something had passed between them, something dreadful and violent. Everyone wondered. Had she repulsed him? Had he assaulted her? They were no different than before, she on her little chair, attentive, silent, determined, he devouring work, gulping down projects. Curiously, she seemed appeased. Even the sadness that so often cast its shadow on her forehead and traced three folds between her eyes had disappeared. He, entirely absorbed in his work, paid no attention to the life around him. Each of them kept quiet. Monsieur Rodin no longer caressed his models, yes, they had all noticed that. Even Yvette no longer ventured her jokes, as if she felt a higher bond had been forged between the two. Moreover, she sometimes surprised her former lover's gaze turned toward the other woman, the solitary girl. She was not jealous, she did not regret the good times spent with Monsieur Rodin. They had laughed a lot, the two of them. And love with him was never sad. Anything was permissible. He saw beauty everywhere. She thought of the jokes they made, of certain rather crude details . . . No, he couldn't be doing that with little Miss Camille there. Yvette smiled. Bah! one day he would slap her on the bottom and say, "How about a drink, Yvette . . ." She wasn't a bad woman, she quite liked her sculptor. She just needed to wait for the storm to pass. Camille often surprised Yvette's gaze resting on her. Since the evening of the storm, she was so deeply, so secretly fulfilled that she had to steel herself to contain the joy that constantly threatened to fill her to bursting.

Since that evening they were never apart. They took advantage of the slightest thing, an exhibition . . . and they took long walks around Paris on the way home.

Camille could not spend even a single night with Monsieur Rodin. So they snatched fleeting moments here and there. Sometimes Camille would stay a little longer at work. Monsieur Rodin closed the studio, hung out a sign: "Monsieur Rodin is out." No, all that had become too burdensome.

"Camille, come." He was going to close the door.

"No." Camille suddenly felt weary, played out. To go on caressing each other now and then, with endless interruptions – no! Besides, she had heard rumors: Rose Beuret . . . who was this Rose Beuret?

Camille went on with her modeling. There, at least, he belonged entirely to her. The master's face was kneaded and transformed beneath her fingers; she had been working on it for weeks: *Bust of Rodin* by Mademoiselle Camille Claudel. At the beginning of their "cohabitation" – that's what they must have said when she wasn't there – at the beginning, then, of their cohabitation, she hadn't dared. She had often done drawings of him: Rodin supporting himself, leaning over, hoisting himself up, ready to stoop down and add a handful of clay to his study. Her sketchbooks were full of him, mingled with ideas, projects for groups, fantastic evocations, illustrations of great dramas. Would she have the time to realize even a part of this work that sometimes kept her awake at night?

And then one day, in front of the whole studio, he had said aloud: "I would like to pose for you, Mademoiselle Claudel." A general silence had followed this declaration. With a smile he had added: "Yes, if I die, it is perhaps the only bust of myself I would like to represent me for the future. I put my fate in your hands, you see what confidence I have in you. I'm sure you won't let me down. You're the only one who knows me."

She was scarlet. She had taken up the challenge and had been working on it since. Today, once again, she would take advantage of the last light to make some progress.

"Camille, stop a moment! Listen to me."

She raised her head. She was obstinate, but she couldn't bear the idea that he might turn away, that he might love someone else.

"You have made me with the shoulders of an Atlas. Unfortunately, I wouldn't know how to hold up the world!"

She loved his smile that made her heart leap. He walked slowly around the worktable. "The profiles are always right, true. You have listened to me. You must always model by the profile, only by the profile. Constantly exaggerate the profiles in a predetermined and constant proportion."

Monsieur Rodin burst out laughing. "You're sure you haven't embellished me a little? I'm having trouble judging the sculpture because this time I'm not so well acquainted with the model who posed for it."

Camille smiled at him. Those tender lips, those eyes, she was so close. Monsieur Rodin knew that he couldn't go on seeing her like this – as he had done with the models. She would ask for nothing but she would leave or she would refuse, as she had just done.

She turned toward him. "I am not a flirt . . . " Camille felt the silence settle between them. She decided to be quite frank. To try . . . "I will not go on like this. Impossible. I want too much."

Monsieur Rodin knew very well that this wasn't a threat or a claim.

Simply a statement. She was straight, direct. For a moment he thought she was toying with him. But no, he had been her first lover. And yet she escaped him, always eluded him.

"Never dilute the ugliness, the deterioration of old age. If you re-arrange nature, if you gloss over it, disguise it, you create ugliness because you are afraid of the truth."

She had just made an abrupt gesture, as if she wanted to speak. Camille listened to Rodin, the evening behind him, the studio still tinged with a golden light . . .

"I am not afraid of the truth, whatever it is, Monsieur Rodin. I am lucid, too lucid. It's as if I were seeing beings drawn with the knife, souls unsheathed!" She had cried out, at least almost cried out. "What are you thinking of, standing there in front of me like that?"

"You are made for a Michelangelo. And I am not Michelangelo."

Camille stopped, dumbfounded. What was he saying? What was he muttering in his beard? Wait, she noticed a few white threads in that red beard. Suddenly she wanted to embrace him, to snuggle in his arms. She threw herself against him.

"Camille, forgive me. I am worried . . . My life is over. And besides, I am always thinking about sculpture, I see you there, wounded, angry. Instead of listening to you I am thinking that your body is all contrasts, tormented like the figures of Michelangelo. That is how he's different from Phidias."

"How's that?" Camille had forgotten. Her anger had vanished. She wanted to know.

He sat on the stool, Camille against him, a little girl listening to a story . . . "Wait a minute." Monsieur Rodin got up. He pulled two worktables near the window. "Look, there in the last light. I am going to model two figurines. Here I'll make a first figure in the style of Phidias. In fact, following the Greek conception . . ."

Camille admired the sculptor's quick, nervous hands. The large palms, the thumb hollowing the clay, the fingers shaping it. With incredible speed, Monsieur Rodin made a figurine. "Look, it isn't as beautiful as an antique, but it's good enough."

Monsieur Rodin's voice became clear, clean. Camille was fascinated, she remembered the day of her arrival in Paris. The puppet theater with her father, then the juggler, and especially the magician, who had made a dove appear in his hands.

"Look, Camille. From head to foot the statuette is composed of four planes in opposite directions, but alternating, four directions that result in a very gentle undulation across the entire body . . . An impression of charm given by the very balance of the figure. The line of balance crossing the middle of the neck falls on the instep of the left foot, which bears the entire weight of the body. The other foot, by contrast, is free. It does not provide any supplementary support, it does not compromise the equilibrium. A posture full of abandon and grace . . . The double balancing of the shoulders and the hips again adds elegance to the whole. Look at it in profile, it is arched behind; the back is hollow and the thorax bulges slightly toward the sky. It is convex. And catches the light straight on. The art of antiquity or the joy of life, equilibrium, grace, reason . . ." Monsieur Rodin bowed, exactly like the magician. What would he pull out of his black box now?

"Let's go on to Michelangelo." Rodin took the clay and twisted it. Rodin firmly planted the figurine on its legs, torso flexed forward, then he stuck one arm against the body and placed the other behind the head. Effort, torture, Camille loved his way of sculpting, that violence, that near-madness . . .

"Here, instead of four planes we have only two. One for the height of the statuette, another in the opposite direction pulling downward. This provides a striking contrast. We are far removed from the calm of antiquity. The two legs are bent. The weight of the body is distributed evenly on both. No more repose, the two lower limbs must work, the hip rises out of them, the body's own momentum is in the process of self-creation, in a way. And the torso . . . follows the hip. The concentrated effort flattens the arms and legs against the body, the head; no more openness, no more freedom. The statue is a block."

Camille rose.

"And the profile, look, Camille, by way of support the torso is arched forward, so the shadows are accentuated in the hollow of the chest, the legs. Michelangelo sang the hymn of the shadow. The most powerful genius of modern times expressed his troubled spirituality in this way, his unreachable ambitions, his will to act with no hope of success . . ."

Monsieur Rodin tenderly approached Camille. With his hands full of earth he gently parted the dark veil that covered her eyes – her eyes, two huge, devastated chasms. She stood against the lingering daylight, he saw her silhouette.

"My black stone of love, you know what Michelangelo said: the only good works are the ones that can be rolled from the top of a mountain without breaking; anything that breaks in such a fall is superfluous. You are one of that race! Nothing will break you. No matter how high the mountain. You are cut from eternal stuff."

Shrugging her beautiful shoulders, Camille murmured: "I am not classical, Monsieur Rodin. Don't forget that I limp." She laughed her broken, heart-wrenching laugh.

Rodin took her head between his two hands.

"Don't leave me . . ." He showed her another bust in the fading light. "Look, your bandit *Giganti*, he looks like you. You are a law unto yourself. Stay like that. The thought of great artists is so vivid and profound that it comes through, whatever the particular subject. In any fragment of a masterpiece you can recognize the author's soul. In any scrap you'll find the complete vision of the artist, if he is great. My *giganti . . .*"

Camille was disturbed. Hadn't he bared his soul to her? She had wanted to speak of mundane matters, of Rose, and here he had just offered her one of the greatest moments of love. Just like that, so simply, he had just raised the level of debate. What did it matter, all the lost hours of love, their separate lives, what did it matter that he might love a wife, models, women, a child!

"My God, I've forgotten the time." Camille frantically straightened her chignon, grabbed her shawl.

"Camille!"

She left. Monsieur Rodin was alone. He turned around. The sculpted couple were undressing each other. *Fugit Amor.*

That was when Rodin decided to rent a place for himself and Camille. He would never again have to watch her leave. Never again. He would tell Rose about her.

Slowly he took his old hat; he felt old and tired. He was almost forty-six years old.

He still had to finish *The Gates of Hell.*

Thought

Adieu! Thus do parricides embrace
When they part before fleeing on the vast sea!
Thus
Do I part from you, sister
Once of a name
Named by me, ungodly!

PAUL CLAUDEL, *Une Mort prématurée*

CAMILLE, CAMILLE, sing with me. Do you still know it?

Do you want to eat some cress
Do you want to eat some flan
When we're going to Lièsse,
When we're going to Laon?
On the feast days, ding, dong.

Paul hung cherries on his sister's ears. He laughed, he was happy. Camille wondered what was going on. For several weeks Paul had seemed revived. They were both in the kitchen, one fine Sunday in May. Camille thought sadly of Monsieur Rodin: where was he at this very moment? He had left for a few days in the country. Since the other evening they had done so much work; she absolutely wanted to finish her four busts, especially his, *Monsieur Rodin*. She had even been afraid for a moment that she would have to start over. The clay was not hardening properly. Everything was threatening to crumble, to crack. Rodin had joked in front of everyone: "I am going to lose my dignity.

Little pellets, Roger Marx, a crumbling heap of dust, that's what I'm going to become."

Roger Marx, his old friend, art critic and administrator of the Beaux-Arts, was coming to the studio more and more frequently now, too. He had looked at Camille's work – "the great and very interesting artist," he always called her. Camille thought he had the face of a horse.

> Do you want to eat some cress?
> Do you want to eat some flan?

Paul was relaxed. They had the whole Sunday to themselves. Madame Louise and Louise, accompanied by Hélène, had gone to see Monsieur Claudel. Camille had been able to escape the family meal and Paul too. He was preparing for his exams. He had to work. As for Camille, the less her mother saw of her the better it was for everyone. When Camille suggested staying home, her mother agreed. In any case, she had lost interest once and for all in her older daughter. Let her do as she liked!

> When we're going to Lièsse
> Do you want to eat some cress?

They were free today. But Camille was not entirely content. She could have spent the day with Monsieur Rodin. They'd had so much work in the last month. Why hadn't he asked her to go with him? Rose, no doubt . . . It had all turned out fine in the end. Camille had been able to show the bust of the master, along with three others, *Louise, Paul,* and *Giganti.* Once again she could see Paul's anger when he saw himself beside Monsieur Rodin. He was furious, fuming, the words tumbling from his lips. That had made Camille laugh, seeing him in such a state.

"You think it's funny. A bunch of heads. A fairground. Decapitated. Ready for someone to throw balls at them." Camille had remembered the celebration at Château-Thierry, the little silk balls they'd thrown at the wooden heads that fell when they were hit. Paul had left, slamming the door of the studio.

At this time he used to walk alone for hours on end. Camille had surprised him one day. He was walking with his head down, she had followed him, first for fun, then out of fascination. He was walking, that's all, at random. They had crossed Paris like that, all the way to rue de Tolbiac, at the Pont d'Ivry. There Camille had left him. Hélène also knew about it. One evening the adolescent had told her about his long, solitary walks across Paris, those fatiguing, pointless walks. Since then, Camille had been worried. As long as he didn't go mad. They used to say that the uncle who'd thrown himself into the Marne . . . And now, for several weeks he'd been happy.

Do you want to eat some cress
Do you want . . .

Auguste's sculptures. She would have liked him to be here. They would have stayed in the studio or gone out for a stroll. Everyone had noticed Monsieur Rodin's sculptures. Everybody had something to say about them: "It's her?"

"Oh yes, it's her!"

Monsieur Rodin did not exhibit, but on Saturday mornings he received visitors who all wanted to know what had become of *The Gates of Hell.* They stopped in front of other works: *Fugit Amor, Thought,* and *The Kiss.* "It's her?"

"Yes."

"She looks so young. How old is she?"

"Barely twenty."

"And she is a sculptor?"

"Yes, look at the bust she made of him."

"A model and sculptor?"

"No, a sculptor."

"But she inspires him . . . He asked her to pose for him."

"What vulgarity, that kiss!"

All of Paris was talking about it.

"Have you seen *The Kiss?*"

Do you want to eat Lièsse?

But why had he done *Thought?* Camille bit into a cherry.

"Paul, why *Thought?*"

"What?"

"Why *Thought?*"

"Listen, eat your cherry and talk later."

Camille spit the pit at her brother.

"Disgusting! You don't know how to behave. What were you saying?"

"Why *Thought?*"

"Oh! Your bust with the coif that the great man made. Why *Thought?* Because you will become the abbess of a convent – and mend your ways too!" Paul burst out laughing; he was quite pleased.

> Do you want, dear mother abbess,
> Do you want to eat some cress?

Camille was amused. She preferred a joking Paul to a Paul who was gloomy and withdrawn.

"'O my Good! O my Beautiful! Hideous fanfare where yet I do not stumble. O rack of enchantments! Hurrah for the unheard-of work and for the marvelous body, for the first time! It began with the laughter of children, and there it will end. This poison will remain in all our veins when, even as the fanfares subside, we return to the old disharmony. Oh now we, so worthy of these tortures, let us fervently take up that superhuman promise made to our created bodies and souls – that promise, that madness!'"

"Who wrote that?"

"My comrade."

"You have a friend!"

"A son, a father, a brother."

Camille had never known Paul in such a state. Even in his excitement at hearing Wagner for the first time.

"Look." Camille took the issue of *La Vogue.* "Read."

"*Les . . .*"

"No, further on."

"There?"

"Yes."

"*Illuminations* by Arthur Rimbaud. Who is he?"

"A young poet. He is only thirty-two years old. I've tried to find out about him. I would love to meet him. Verlaine knew him well. Through friends maybe I could . . . He's a young man. He left everything one fine day. He's a vagabond. Apparently Verlaine shot him. He would be in Harrar now."

Camille raised her head. "In Abyssinia?"

Camille had already been dreaming of going there. She could see the map, the imaginary journeys with her brother, leaning their young heads over the red, green, and blue drawings. Camille's eyes were tinged with gold today, a bit feverish.

"You're sure you're not working too much?" Paul had noticed the weariness of her gaze. His sister had seemed less happy for awhile now. "Come on, let's go out, it's a beautiful day. But take off your earrings or eat them. You are beautiful, like Galaxaure."

"Who's that?"

"I'll explain."

"No, I don't want to go out. All those people, it's Sunday. Those families, I hate them. And all of them out strolling, stinking. They are everywhere. As if Paris were being raped. And anyway it's too hot! Perhaps this evening . . . Mama won't be here. Let's go out this evening, Paul. When there's no more crowd of people in the streets. They make me suffocate. All those bodies pressing against each other."

"Don't drink ice water on top of cherries. You're going to be sick."

"*You* are going to be sick!"

Camille winked at her brother. She chided him for his advice and knew just how to annoy him. But Paul was in a good mood. She would not make him angry. He loved this good, mild warmth. He felt fine. For some time now he seemed to be waking from a long nightmare. If only he could meet this Rimbaud. How much older was he, twelve, fourteen years? That was nothing. There was also Verlaine. He had met him several times at rue Gay-Lussac. Two cripples, one with his little beard, his lorgnette, the other disheveled, his leg swinging to the side, and a great dream in his eyes. Often he saw them going to the François I café, near the Luxembourg. The other man was someone called Pasteur.

"You know, Cam . . . " Paul stopped, terrified.

Camille turned: "What?"

He had been about to mention Verlaine with his crippled, limping walk, like a great wounded bird, and there she was, with the same gait, the same insistent dream, one beat behind, always a beat behind, with an effort defying harmony. Paul babbled: "I know Verlaine. In fact, I've met him several times near the Luxembourg."

"Ask him, then. He must know the whereabouts of your Arthur Rimbaud."

"He's a drunk, he looks like an old bum, he drinks all the time."

Camille leaned on her elbows next to Paul. "So, he won't bite you, will he?"

"You're so brutal!"

"Listen, Paul, when you want something, you don't just sit there on your ass. Your Rimbaud won't come here."

Camille sat down and began drawing. Paul watched her. She would have known how to do it. She would not have been afraid. They had something in common, she and Rimbaud, curiously: that ambiguous air of menace and childish innocence behind an untroubled brow – he had seen a portrait of this Rimbaud. And Verlaine – how old was he now? He looked worn-out, so dreadful, sitting in front of his glass of absinthe and the spoon he used for stirring, as if he saw nothing but a naked white wall. Forty-two years old, yes, someone had told him the other day. Paul looked at Camille. She was drawing, pale and absorbed; she had become thinner, in some ways she seemed younger, completely absorbed in her search. Paul had been making fun of her, but in the transparent air, seated before him in the gloom, concentrated, self-contained, she resembled one of those young nuns who enter the convent at the age of seventeen.

Camille was drawing a hand. For several months, when she had a moment, she would work on hands. She had always studied the hands of the people around her. From the time she was quite young. Her mother's hand, the play of her fingers on the table, back and forth, back and forth, the index finger, the middle finger, an infernal dance, I take, no I don't take; her father's hands, slim, tapering, transparent, delicate for a man, smaller than normal; Paul's hands folded behind his back, hidden, thick in the palm, yet with rather long fingers, but always on top of each other, sometimes hidden between his crossed legs.

And *his* hands. That was why she had fallen in love with him. He, too, often worked on hands of all kinds. Like a religion, a sort of rite . . . Suddenly Monsieur Rodin would be absorbed for hours and hours sculpting hands: some distinguished, others crude and heavy. He had said: "There are hands that pray and hands that curse, hands that corrupt, hands that heal, hands that refresh, and hands that love." Camille looked at the pencil she was holding, her thumb bent, her fingers squeezed around the tip of wood. The sun had just struck the white paper like a drum roll. The hand of God creating Adam, his finger extended.

"Camille, creation comes from here – from the hand – that's why our art is higher than the rest. We create life from inert matter. Like Him . . ." And he had watched as she kneaded the clay.

"You know that a man dies if he loses his sense of touch. It's the only one of the senses for which there is no substitute – touch. The hands never lie. Observe them constantly and you will know what people are really thinking."

The sun on her work. The white paper. It was unbearable, the memory took shape in her hand, she felt Rodin's hand on her. No, it was Sunday and he was not there. The month of May, he was not there.

"Camille."

The warmth crept along her arms, engulfing her. He was there against her, his hand on hers, the sun caressed them, burned them, enveloped them. With her other hand she had leaned on the worktable. Now she had slipped her whole body backward, leaning against his. He was there, he had just put his other arm around her. Their two hands entwined. A captive, she was a captive of the sculpture, of the man!

"Listen, Camille." His voice against her ear, low, a little rough, as if he had trouble speaking. She saw his hands, muscular, deliberate, powerful. "Maria, her name was Maria."

Camille wanted to escape the confession of this man who held her in his two arms, but she felt his heart beating too quickly against her back, his heart, as if he were going to have an attack. She wondered if she would fall despite his arms around her, despite the worktable.

"Maria." The voice had echoed like a summons. Camille expected to see this Maria suddenly appear.

"Two huge serious blue eyes, a delicate mouth and a smile, a determined chin! She was the one who managed to persuade Father and Mother to let me draw. I wasn't gifted for studies, but I copied all the drawings I found. The pages used to wrap the plums Mama bought . . . Maria pleaded my case. She was so beautiful." Camille had stayed still, still as death.

"Two years older than I, tall, with long hair, and eyes so big, clear." Monsieur Rodin was quiet. Camille had lowered her head. Did he still know that she was there, in his arms? His hands clenched, Camille felt the short nails dig into her skin.

"1862. My friend Barnouvin. His name was Barnouvin. He had left her. She loved him. He went away. Forgotten. She entered the convent, and then they brought her back to us. She took several days to die. With a smile . . . without a word. You must never let someone . . . she is dead, dead! Scarcely twenty years old. My sister, Maria. Maria."

Camille felt the face fall on her shoulder. Monsieur Rodin was heavy. As if she were carrying him on her back, a wounded beast, mortally wounded. "Do what you want with me," he seemed to say. Camille gently turned around. He raised his head, he looked distraught.

"She was there in her bed, with the coif she'd wanted to keep. I will never forget that face. There, as you were just now. Limpid, so young, miraculous. All wrapped in dreams like a great swallow about to fall. But I saw the veins of her neck, and the chin she pulled above the white sheet like a vise that was slowly strangling her. An iron yoke. I was looking at you with your white collar, hard, bent over your sculpture, your forehead lightly furrowed, shining, forcing yourself to conquer matter, and I saw her, her . . . "

Camille leaned on the worktable, she no longer knew whether it was the heat, the sculptor's words, the story of his sister, but she foundered, overcome, felt herself slipping, throwing all caution to the winds. Monsieur Rodin had gone to look for something at the bottom of a drawer.

"Look, Camille. How alike they were . . . " He held out a locket with the portrait of a young man and a young woman exactly alike.

"Then I entered the monastery. Wore the white robe of a novice for one year. I left. It was then that I met Rose. Everyone has told you about her already. I am going . . . Camille."

Camille had swooned, white with a ghastly pallor.

"Camille, Cam-i-i-ille." Quick, the Chinchy butte, to be first, to get up there to the Giant. Camille opened her eyes. Paul was there, distraught. "Camille, what's happened to you?" Camille no longer knew where she was. She was on the ground, beside the table. Paul helped her up.

"You set your pencil down. You were so pale. With your white blouse and skirt, you looked like a dead woman. I called to you. But you were distraught."

Camille felt a little better. Paul helped her to sit down, she breathed more calmly. Seeing him so attentive, she almost forgot the big surly boy. Sometimes he had such delicacy, such sensitivity . . . "I've eaten too many cherries, Paul! It was your song . . . *Do you want to eat some cress. Do you want . . .* ," she sang weakly, her voice broken.

"You know, Camille, you should rest. You seemed so distracted just now. Alien . . . I was looking at you – everything was drawn into your two big eyes staring into the void. You were like those nuns who take the veil . . . You remember the awful ceremony at Villeneuve. Mademoiselle Bargnier all in white, with flowers, taking her vows. Brrrrr! It still makes me shiver. Then the priest came forward. They lifted the girl's veil, a nun came to her with scissors and her hair began to fall. I remember, I was off to the side and I saw her haggard, pale face, like yours just now. A disembodied soul – immaterial, elusive, *Thought!* Hey, just the way Rodin sculpted you. For a change I like that sculpture, it's the one I like best. He managed to capture you . . . You remember, after they'd put on her white headpiece, she turned around, and there was nothing but that face throbbing under the two wings of the coif. Never do that, Cam!"

"*Thought* . . ." Camille felt bloodless. That bust was her favorite too.

"You're not ill, are you?" Paul was worried.

"No, it's nothing. It's the heat, the cherries. The Salon that just finished."

She would have liked to add: "And Rodin, who isn't here. His absence." Rose, she had never known exactly. He had not mentioned her again. No time. They'd had no more time.

"I'm going to lie down for a while. Go out if you like."

"No, I don't want to leave you. This evening, if you feel better, we'll go out for a stroll."

The white bed, the little room. She lay down. No one. She heard no one. Paul must read his Monsieur Arthur Rimbaud. She too was abandoned. Almost twenty-two years old. A little tenderness, someone, Rodin near her . . . His fine head leaning toward her, his hands on her body, his arms. It was all too hard. She was too much alone. Artists, men, women, spouses, her brother, her mother, they were all taken, spoken for, "situated." Sculpture – she would never succeed. Monsieur Rodin's student, yes, but she would never be Michelangelo. In the eyes of the world she was only Rodin's young student.

"Monsieur Rodin, is that what you think of me?"

She closed her eyes.

Clos Payen

T HE WROUGHT-IRON fence was rusty. A For Rent sign
swung back and forth in the spring breeze. Monsieur Rodin had
taken Camille by the hand, for a few moments. They were extremely
discreet when they were not alone. Unconsciously, tacitly, they used a
simple manner with each other, walking side by side, working side by
side, with no misplaced gestures. Camille no longer allowed Monsieur
Rodin to hang out the sign saying, "Monsieur Rodin is out." A sign
like the one swinging back and forth in front of their eyes at this very
moment. The misty spring twilight . . .

"Come." Sometimes Monsieur Rodin addressed her familiarly,
like a friend. They pushed open the gate. Two children entering an enchanted realm. Before closing it again, Monsieur Rodin removed the
sign. Camille burst out laughing, protesting a little. Rodin hushed her
with a mysterious air and put the sign under his arm. The grass had
grown quite high, the shrubs half hid the old house. No one answered
the door. Abandoned, melancholy, the place seemed to be waiting just
for them. Brambles, weeds, wildflowers, Camille thought of the valley
in the fifth circle of Dante's *Inferno*.

They were at the entrance. A heavy lock, a turn of the thick key, they entered. Rooms upon endless rooms. The ceilings crumbling in places, the gilding, the blackened mirrors, they plunged on, the two of them, always going forward, they turned and returned in the silence. Then their steps echoed and again silence. Monsieur Rodin and Camille face to face in the great salon at the back of the house. The tall fireplace, the windows, the windowpanes nearly opaque from neglect, and everywhere mirrors, huge gilded mirrors covered with dust. Monsieur Rodin came toward Camille, who stood with her back against the fireplace. She saw her multiple reflections, she saw him, three times, no four, no three more, all approaching. She did not move, she felt him near, so near with his desire for her. For weeks they had hardly embraced. Since the evening of the storm, *The Kiss*, there had been the May Salon, the exhibitions, the visits from ministers. Since that tempest of love, how often had they really been able to find time for each other? She saw his head, his beautiful head, the thick lips, the straight nose, the flaring nostrils, his scent, her own odor . . . He took her gently. His hand stroked her neck. Slowly he opened her dress and now his two hands unfastened the corset to free her heavy breasts. Camille wanted to help him.

"Don't move. Let me look. Let me do it." He never tired of contemplating her. It was so long, so long since he'd been able to have her to himself. Her magnificent breasts, her violent, domineering, large hips, and her proud head, her two eyes glittering with intelligence. For she was intelligent. Deep inside he was sometimes afraid. She was more intelligent than he, more intuitive. And she had read much more. He sometimes envied her – her youth, her unselfconsciousness, her power. He was afraid that she judged him, that one day she would stop admiring him, stop looking at him with that dazzled, childlike gaze, as she did this very moment. With a total trust involving her entire being. He looked at her because at this moment she was giving him her very soul. Delicately he stroked her breasts, the nipples stiffened toward him. Rarely had he seen a body so eager to love . . .

Rodin had possessed many women, society women or models. Education had not been an issue. Despite the splendor of their flesh, these pleasures had left him with a stale taste, and sad. Caresses required the intelligent gaze – carnal love had surprised him in that, too – demanding a search, a rigor, a glimmer of spirituality. Her belly spoke, responded to his hands because she herself was saying something to him. Her legs were alive because she, Camille, his Camille, had something to say. He leaned over her and took a breast in his mouth. She groaned. "Not here."

"Don't worry. No one will come. What I adore in you, in your body, more than its exquisite form, is its internal flame. That's why I dedicated *Thought* to you."

He slipped off her dress and there she was, naked. "Don't move." On his knees he took off her boots, her stockings. He wanted to see her standing, naked, upright, he wanted to look at her there, nailed to the fireplace, to him, entirely subjected to his gaze, photographed there in his poet's eye, delivered to him alone, posing for him alone, an angel plastered against the block of the fireplace, as if the wind had brutally swept her to earth, her two arms outstretched in a last effort to support her broken wings . . . As if she were going to take off once more – a female Icarus. He would never manage to express the beauty of her body!

"I understand the ancients. Full of respect and love for nature, they bear desperate witness to their respect for the flesh. It is mad to believe that they disdain it. In no people has the beauty of the human body evoked a more sensual tenderness. You are made for all sculptures. If I had the talent for it, I might make an antique sculpture of you: *Venus*. A rapture of ecstasy seems to travel through all the forms they modeled." Rodin followed the modeling of the body. The curve of the hips, the crevices between belly and thigh. He encircled the sides, fingered the small cavities, came back to the belly, imperceptible rises . . . Camille was begging now, imperious, she summoned. The body stirred – he was no longer an artist but only a man.

In the studio, the stove was smoking. Yvette was shivering, naked, Camille had turned away. Yvette on her knees, Monsieur Rodin, crouching, circled around her; Yvette was leaning on the table. Monsieur Rodin and Bourdelle stood back. She on her knees, minute after minute. Camille felt like shouting. Monsieur Rodin hollowed her sides with his hand.

"Hold yourself out more, Yvo, please . . . there, thrust out your nice curves." Yvette stout, shining near the stove. He explaining to the technician: "Look. It's an urn, there. The back growing smaller at the waist and then opening up wonderfully large again, a vase with an exquisite sweep of line, an amphora whose flanks hold the life of the future."

"Monsieur Rodin, I'm shivering. Stop the jawing."

"Get dressed, that's enough for today."

Rodin had a fondness for making his models assume this position. Camille could hardly bear it. The only woman in the studio, she saw her sisters on their knees, sex open, tensed, folding themselves according to the whim of the artists – all of them men. And she herself had been like one of them, shameless, like Yvette. Yvette, who had gotten up and winked at Camille, catching her by surprise: "And so what? You've never been like that?"

But she had not been exposed like that to so many eyes. Suddenly Camille was conscious of her privileged status. She understood Yvette's hatred, the difficult life of the models. Unlike them, she called the shots, she did not submit. She'd had pleasure, there, on the ground, taken like a beast, while the others simply undressed every day, whether it was warm or cold, and they put in hours of work, posing. There were bad models, too; they weren't good just because they posed nude. The male models seemed at ease, even naked they had no problem discussing things with the sculptors. Camille had often noticed the difference. Yvette's proffered buttocks – could she one day put a man in front of her on his knees for hours and draw the exquisite curve of his buttocks? An amused smile played on her lips as she daydreamed. A few lines of verse surged up from memory:

> Woman's flesh, ideal clay, O marvel,
> O sublime penetration in the mud . . .

No, that wasn't it.

"What are you thinking about?" Monsieur Rodin was dressed, Monsieur Rodin leaned toward her. "Get dressed, you look cold."

"Wait, I'm thinking of some lines from a poem by Hugo that I learned with Paul, wait:

> Woman's flesh, ideal clay, O marvel,
> O sublime penetration in the mind,
> In the mud which the ineffable being kneads,

Matter in which the soul shines through its shroud,
Mud, in which we see the fingers of the divine sculptor,
Majestic mire summoning kisses and the heart,
More holy, more holy . . .

"Wait . . . I've got it!"

More holy than one knows, thus is love victorious,
Thus is the soul raised up mysteriously to this bed . . .

"No."

. . . pushed mysteriously to this bed,
If this pleasure is not a thought
And one can, one cannot,
And one cannot at the moment when the senses are on fire,
Embrace beauty without feeling one embraces God.

Rodin had said the last two lines with her.
"You know it?
"Yes, I know it. I think those lines of Hugo's are sublime. I have
not had much of an education, but you know, after Maria's death, I
told you, when I was in the novitiate, Father Eymard – he was a true
saint – saved me from despair, and at the same time he was convinced
of my genius. He's the one who advised me to dedicate myself entirely
to sculpture. 'It's a mistake,' he always repeated, 'you needed a refuge,
that's all! But you must return to your sculpture. That's your vocation.'
He strongly encouraged me to read. 'Read everything you can. Especially the poets.' When I left the monastery, in memory of him, I spent
hours in the public libraries: Hugo, Musset, Lamartine . . . That was
when I discovered Dante. Father Eymard, he was a saint!"
Camille was all dressed. Monsieur Rodin spoke, leaning his forehead against the window. It was still early, even if the tangle of trees
and bushes obscured the garden. Camille got ready, tidying up her
hair. "I'm going to have to go home."
"Wait! Wait a moment. This old place belonged to Jean-Nicolas
Corvisart, surgeon of the Grand Armée, it's called Clos Payen, or
Neubourg Folly. He was Napoleon's physician. You sculpted Napo-

leon when you were twelve – there you are, his doctor's house. Robespierre lived here, then Musset and George Sand. Now we . . ."

"We just spent some time here."

"No, Cam. We are living here. I've rented it."

Camille leaned against the mirror. "What did you say?"

"I've rented it. Here. For us."

Camille came to him. He was looking outside at the garden. She leaned her head on his shoulder. "Is it true, Monsieur Rodin?"

"Yes, it's yours. We shall work here together. Our new studio."

Camille burst into laughter, she began to dance. She was twelve years old, she began to play hopscotch on the parquet floor. She ran through all the rooms and leaped up the stairs at a gallop.

"Camille . . . Cami-ii-iiille . . . Where are you? Cami-ii-iii-lle . . . "

"Monsieur Rodin."

The voice was so far away, nearly stifled. How could he find her in this maze of rooms?

"You are nothing but a naughty child."

"What?"

"Filthy brat!"

Camille was amused. Monsieur Rodin pretended to rage. All this belonged to her, no more family, no more curfew! Monsieur Rodin belonged to her. He would never catch her; from one room to the next she went, climbing up to the eaves.

"Neubourg Folly."

Suddenly she was there. Covered with spiderwebs, dirty, she curtsied: "The princess of Neubourg Folly."

She held out a sovereign hand to him, he clasped it, and picked her up, holding her against him: "Little fool! Little fool!"

He put her down again. She was heavy, all muscle. She looked at him oddly. "I wonder how they posed."

"Who?"

"The models for *The Abduction* . . . I would have liked to see that. Carnal love . . . *I am beautiful, O mortals, like a dream of stone.*"

Rodin remembered. The man held the woman at the end of his arms. "You are too curious, Mademoiselle Sculptor. I will explain it to you. If I give you all my secrets, you will get ahead of me and you will become famous instead. You are already a genius, so no lessons for geniuses. Figure it out yourself!" He burst out laughing. "Go on, we'll go home now. Soon we'll put in some furniture."

Camille took her companion's arm. They closed the wrought-iron gate.

"Until tomorrow, my 'Folly.'"

The couple went away. Camille withdrew her arm. Now they walked together side by side.

Letter *from the Asylum*

It's really madness to spend money like that. As for the room, it's the same thing, there is nothing at all, no eiderdown, no commode, nothing, a nasty chamberpot that's chipped three-quarters of the time, an awful iron bed in which one shivers all night long (I hate iron beds myself, I must see if I [illegible] find myself inside).

Wild Hope

*You, wretched someone in the inspected crowd, nothing
is left! and there is nothing to do about the wild welling
up of hope!*

*Nothing to do about that eruption of Faith like the
world in the pit of my stomach!*

*Everything I was sure of, it's all finished! And it's
all finished, what they taught me at the* lycée.

PAUL CLAUDEL, 25 December 1886

Now what is he up to, that child? The one time we are all here.
It's unbelievable!" Madame Louise protested. Still, on the
twenty-fifth of December, he ought to be there for dinner.

Camille had just turned twenty-two. Fifteen days before, on December eighth, Monsieur Rodin had made her a gift of his work
Thought. Camille had left it at Neubourg Folly. Her mother would have
broken it. Inadvertently, out of clumsiness. But what was her brother
up to?

"Tell me, Camille." Her father looked tired. He hated being so far
away from his children. "Are you making some progress?

"Certainly, she spends her time with Monsieur Rodin."

Louis-Prosper had shrugged his shoulders. "What's this all about?"

"Monsieur Rodin has more and more commissions. He has started
a second studio."

Camille was careful not to mention the address. Young Louise carried on: "All of Paris is talking about it. She poses for him. Go see

The Kiss, Papa. She is dishonoring us. I'll be lucky to find a husband."

"No, I am his inspiration, if you like. He has plenty of models. He doesn't need me for that. I've begun to work in marble."

Louis-Prosper decided to have a talk with Camille – in private. His wife had told him all sorts of tales, but didn't she hate her older daughter?

"Yes, you know, he got the commission for *The Burghers of Calais,* then *The Gates of Hell,* the busts . . . He cannot manage anymore. There are more and more technicians. I do some cutting, too. Marble, he let me start. Now then . . ."

"Camille, wait a minute, please. Explain it a little more clearly. I am not a sculptor. Doesn't Rodin do the cutting himself?"

"No, listen. A sculpture is not like a drawing. You don't take a pencil and whoosh, it's done. I mean, many elements are involved."

"Listen, Louis, we are going to eat supper now, it's late."

"One minute, Louise, Camille is explaining something to me."

"Okay. For example, you decide to do a sculpture. All right . . ."

Paul arrived, out of breath, all red in the face.

"Paul, what is going on?"

"Nothing, Mama."

"It's a woman, it's a woman!"

"Cut it out, Louise, go fuss with your dresses!"

"Oh, no, you're not going to fight on Christmas Eve!"

Louis-Prosper took Camille's arm. "Let's go to supper. You will tell me the rest later." He had whispered in her ear. Like a secret between them.

The company was complete. There was Madame Louise, all dressed in black, serving the soup. Then young Louise, smiling in her new dress, her curls around her face, harmonious – why did she sulk so often? On the other side of the table Paul – but he looked overcome, distracted, as if lightning had struck at his feet. Beside him, Camille, a little pale in her striped dress – but it was the same dress as in past years. She seemed even thinner in this dress, with its fluted white collar, which added to her air of fragility.

"You ought to buy yourself another dress, Cam."

"She spends everything for her tools, her materials, I don't know what else. It's only right that she should do her own hair."

"Listen, Papa . . ." Camille tried to resume her explanations about sculpture.

"Oh no, you're not going to start again. Sculpture, all you do is go on about that wretched art. Tell me, instead, have you seen the Thierrys?"

And so they were going to talk about the family. The children kept quiet. Camille looked at Paul. Between two mouthfuls, she remarked to him: "Paul on the road to Damascus. You've been struck by lightning, or what? Read the Bible I gave you."

Paul looked at her, astounded.

"So Paul, are you eating?"

"Yes, Mama, I'm almost done."

Camille secretly observed her younger brother. He looked as if he'd met someone, it was odd. They paid no more attention to him, but she could see herself again, the evening of the storm. She had been like that. What could have happened?

The turkey arrived, plump . . . the chestnuts. Camille hated these long holiday meals. Happily, her father was there.

"Tell me, Paul, have you read this Arthur Rimbaud? While waiting for you, I leafed through *La Vogue* and I started to read a few of his poems."

Paul was inexhaustible on this subject. Louis listened to him. The mother continued to grumble in her corner, the plates made more noise than usual, ten times she asked if anyone wanted more turkey, more chestnuts, salad; ten times she interrupted the conversation. Young Louise was elsewhere, thinking of young Ferdinand de Massary, whom she'd seen some time before. Their conversations were so boring.

"Rimbaud, Rodin, Rodin, Rimbaud!"

Camille listened to her brother. He had given her *A Season in Hell*. Camille understood his fascination with the poet. He must be mad, somewhere out there in the world. She was sure that Paul had been incapable of tracking him down, as she had told him to do.

Finally the dessert arrived – the *bûche de Noël*. This was the climax of the meal! Camille hated these sticky chocolate logs.

On the other hand, there were no gifts. Their father would probably add a little money to the usual sum, but in this family, no gifts. No, that wasn't quite true. Louise was wearing an old brooch on her blouse. Camille looked at her sister, whose portrait she was doing, but Louise never wanted to pose, always finding a thousand excuses.

"So, Camille, tell me a little about this sculpture business."

They were sitting quietly. Paul was plunged into a book. Camille glanced at him – ah, he had opened the Bible she had given him several months ago. The bell rang. Madame Louise went to open the door. Ferdinand de Massary had come to find Louise. Ah, that's why she was wearing the brooch. Probably a gift from their mother. Introductions, greetings, good-byes. Camille saw her sister leave and thought of the day their mother had barred her way: "You will not go out. I will lock you up!" She smiled to herself. If only they knew what progress she'd made.

"So, Cam!"

"I'll go on. Yes, you have a model. You have to find one first. If it isn't a friend, male or female, they have to be paid, the clay has to be bought, obtained, transported. You know, ten kilos of clay isn't negligible. When you've completed your study, you must quickly bake the clay or else it crumbles, breaking from the effects of cold or heat. You can dampen it with cloths, but at the last moment, everything can dry out. At the beginning of his career, Monsieur Rodin lost dozens of studies that way. Look, one of Rodin's first busts became a mask. His name was Bibi – a poor old man who helped Rodin out now and then . . . At the time, Rodin didn't have the money to make his bust to submit to the Salon. This was in '64, the year I was born. Because of the cold, Rodin was working in an unheated stable, and the bust broke in two. The mask was left: *Man with the Broken Nose.* He submitted it as it was. Furthermore, it was rejected. Several years later, they thought *Man with the Broken Nose* was a superb antiquity. You know how they are, the critics!"

"Yes, but why do you do the cutting?"

"Wait . . . Once you've made your plaster model, it must be enlarged. At that moment, either you do it alone and it takes you five years to make a sculpture, or you hire technicians to do the work. I'm exaggerating slightly. It took Rodin eighteen months to finish *The Age of Bronze.* Still in plaster. Fine, you can make it in plaster, but it's extremely fragile. Afterward you cast your model in bronze, but it's very expensive. You have to find a foundry, and they are often booked up for several months ahead. A bad foundry can ruin a statue forever. You can also shape directly in marble or stone, but while you can ruin clay, you cannot allow yourself to spoil a piece of marble. It costs a fortune. Besides, it takes hours of work to rough out the marble. That's why this work is given to qualified workers, technicians, and the sculptor only finishes it. But before that, there is all that work of roughing out the stone or marble. I love it myself. So I asked Monsieur Rodin to let me cut the marble directly."

"Yes, but what does he do?"

"Listen, when you have made your clay study, if you continue all alone you'll never finish. You have what they call cheap labor for the plaster, the workers who prepare the material for you. Okay, you make your model. And this is nearly the most important thing – here's where a sculptor shows what he knows how to do. Afterward, you have it enlarged by the technicians, the 'finishers.' Monsieur Rodin never works any other way. They make him ten, fifteen, twenty enlargements, and he takes it from there. These mock-ups are executed at one-third or half the final size. Then he asks them to enlarge one of the mock-ups, and only then does he do the final work. Clearly, this requires a master's hand. For marble and stone, the best technicians make the definitive mock-ups. He indicates with a pencil what movement to emphasize – or look, you know what he does? He takes out his handkerchiefs, like you, you know; he puts them on the places to 'excavate.' They end up as dirty as yours when you repair something with them."

Her father smiled. "But you do the cutting."

"Yes, it seems that I've become his best worker. You know, marble is very delicate, if you come upon a 'worm' – yes, that's what they call it, when the chisel suddenly sinks in and it's as if the marble were rotten, if you like – it will be broken, you have to begin all over again. I want to become a great sculptor but also an extraordinary technician. I think I would be furious if I saw someone else ruining my marble. I want my sculpture to come directly out of the block."

"And Monsieur Rodin?"

"Oh, you know, he has too many commissions. And then, he has never done the cutting directly. Well, not really . . . That doesn't interest him. And then, he couldn't live off his profession. He has difficulty managing as it is."

Paul raised his eyes from his book. "He's not so stupid, your Monsieur Rodin. He does the dreaming and you do the work."

"Shut up, Paul, you don't understand anything. I am not alone. There is a crowd of people. Besides, there will soon be three studios: there is Jules Desbois, Danielli, Jean Escoula, the Schneeg brothers, Lefèvre, Fagel."

Monsieur Claudel was worried. "You're sure you're not wearing yourself out?"

"Oh no, Papa, I'm very happy. He's given me the hands and feet of *The Gates of Hell.* You know, he also obtained the commission for the monument of *The Burghers of Calais* and – "

"Very well, Camille. But you, what are you working on just now?"

"I'm doing his bust; you must come to see it. And *Paul at Eighteen.*"

"Not that there's much resemblance . . ."

"You complain, Paul, everyone has asked me who that proud Roman could be. I'm also sculpting Louise."

Louis-Prosper looked at his big daughter with admiration. It was clear that she was deeply engaged in what she was doing. Yet he would like to see this Monsieur Rodin up close. Camille was twenty-two years old now; she said nothing about her private life, she was secretive. Her mother would have had trouble wangling anything out of her. He looked at this tall amazon of a girl, sitting astride the chair, her hands on its back. Would he manage to unlock her heart? Tomorrow he would go to see this studio. "Tell me, Cam, will you let me visit?"

"If you like, but don't be offended by the nude models."

Louis burst out laughing. "Do I look like a priest?"

Louis got up and went to get a little cognac. "Would you like some, Paul?"

Paul growled a refusal. He always seemed so absorbed in his reading.

"Give me a drop, Papa." Camille was annoyed. She didn't really want the alcohol, but it made her furious that her father should suddenly send her to sit by the fire. Louis served her.

"Listen, Louis, don't go getting her drunk now," grumbled their mother.

"Come on, take a glass with us too."

"Not on your life."

"Oh yes, it will do us all good. Come on, Paul!"

Camille had difficulty restraining her laughter. Her mother held the glass as though it were a slug. Her lips puckered.

"I wanted to tell you. I am going to be transferred to Compiègne. I'll finally be closer to you. I'm fed up. My dinners at the hotel, no time with my children . . . and you, my wife."

Camille looked at them. Her father was sixty years old now. He was a bit stooped. His white head, his prominent cheeks, his little skullcap, his beard all made him look curiously like an old sage.

"So, we won't see you anymore." Madame Louise shot back her reply.

"But you will, Louise, and I will be closer, you understand."

Louise tested the drink. Camille noticed the obvious pleasure her mother took in this little glass of alcohol.

"Oh yes, you see, Louise, how good it is!"

"Not at all. It's just to please you."

Camille hated those women who never say what does or doesn't give them pleasure. Eternal victims, they are always sacrificing themselves. Having restrained their joy, they can only submit. They've built such a barrier between themselves and pleasure, they can't even accept a dish, a flower. All of existence is a cross to bear. Camille thanked Monsieur Rodin from the bottom of her heart for giving her the taste of pleasure. Although she would have found it anyway. Even as a small child she had sworn to search for it. There is a certain egotism that is a form of health. One of her father's reflections had remained fixed in her childish memory. "Camille, tell others what gives you pleasure. Sacrifice can drive everyone away. Let others know your true desire. Nothing is worse than someone who sacrifices herself for you. That is not a gift anyone should make. For a man, it is an unbearable form of blackmail."

She remembered. Her father had been angry that day. He and Louise had shouted at each other. Camille didn't remember why. Her mother had left, telling Louis: "I already make such sacrifices for these children."

They had put down their glasses. "Tomorrow we will go to the restaurant."

"Listen, Louis, it's much too expensive."

Louis abruptly got up from his armchair. "Well, you will stay home if you like. I will take Camille and Paul."

The door shut. Monsieur Louis had gone out. It was snowing outside.

Camille thought of Monsieur Rodin. Where was he this evening? It was out of the question that she should stay with him or invite him to dinner with her family. Where could he be? Clos Payen – Neubourg Folly – had become their meeting place. No one else came there. They worked there together. Camille had never been so happy. The concierge had orders to prevent anyone from entering and to give out no information. They were there, just the two of them, hidden by the shrubbery, the trees, the wild flowers. Only the vacations forced them to separate. Camille never tired of going to Villeneuve, as they did each summer. If only she could go there with him – what happiness! He was often in the country. Sometimes Camille felt like questioning him about Rose, but she kept quiet. He would surely speak to Rose about her. She did not want to lower herself by inquiring. Monsieur Rodin now had three studios. Camille knew that he was becoming increasingly famous. Society women, politicians, sculptors, Englishmen, Swedes, even Americans came on Saturdays. They all wanted to see *The Gates of Hell*. Camille saw them jostling each other to speak to Monsieur Rodin. If only they knew!

It was true: her father was right. She was Rodin's worker, his model, his muse, and his companion. Sometimes, at the end of the day, she could hardly stand up for fatigue. Her hair covered with dust, and clay or bits of stone in her clogs, Camille came home reeling with weariness. When she had spent her day roughing out a block of stone or marble, she felt it physically – she, too, worked at all three studios. Sometimes she posed for hours for him at Clos Payen. He wanted to draw her, he wanted to model her. She was secretly happy to be his model, but sometimes, unexpectedly, she would feel an odd twinge of regret, as she had just now, when her father had asked her what she was working on herself. She did not work enough for herself. When she posed, her mind filled with a world peopled by imaginary sculptures. She saw scenes, groups, busts – and then, one day, her monumental work. But how could she refuse to be there for Rodin, to give him what he asked for?

On one occasion he had dedicated *Meditation* to her – and one of his most beautiful pieces, *The Danaïd*. He must have finished it in early spring. She could see it now! She had been sleeping in the studio. It was still warm out. He must have held her, made love to her; she was curled up on the couch asleep. Which had been a stupid thing to do, naturally she had caught cold. He hadn't thought to cover her, he had simply kneaded his clay and calmly sculpted. He had been warm, he was working. She had awakened with an awful stiff neck. First she had suffered her mother's reproaches, and the following day a ghastly inflammation of the throat. She had said nothing but had dragged around for nearly a month, coughing, her throat on fire. Not once had her mother shown any concern. Only Victoire had taken care of her when they had arrived at Villeneuve, as they did each year at the end of July.

"Paul, what exactly is a Danaïd?"

"A butterfly."

"Oh?"

"A beautiful butterfly found in temperate zones."

Camille was thoughtful. A beautiful butterfly. She was anything but a beautiful butterfly. Perhaps she hadn't been the model for this *Danaïd* after all.

"One of the daughters of Danaus."

"Ah! Right. And who were they?"

"They killed everyone, except their husbands, on their wedding nights."

Camille was dumbfounded. "What?"

"They got their punishment in hell: they had to fill a bottomless barrel for eternity. The barrel of the Danaïds is used as an image for a heart whose desires can never be satisfied."

Camille had an aversion to people who were satisfied. She had told this, one day, to Monsieur Rodin. So he had compared her to a Danaïd . . . Suddenly Camille wanted to hurt him, to make him angry. As a matter of fact, she had never seen him angry.

"Listen, Camille." Paul had his nose deep in the Bible.

> Say unto wisdom, "Thou art my sister"; and call
> understanding thy kinswoman:
> That they may keep thee from the strange woman, from
> the stranger which flattereth with her words.

Camille felt weary, and a little drunk. They had drunk wine with dinner, then cognac. Camille had wanted something else.

Doth not wisdom cry? and understanding put forth her voice?
She standeth in the top of high places, by the way in the places
of the paths.

"What is it, Paul?" Camille came to him, staggering a little. Yet she
hadn't drunk much. It was fatigue, and then she had eaten very little
during the long dinner.

"From chapters seven and eight of Proverbs. Wisdom, wisdom is
symbolized by the qualities of a woman. The human soul, the muse."

Camille looked at Paul. They all needed a muse. She saw Paul,
Monsieur Rodin, all those men working around her. She didn't really
know them, after all. The world of men. The world of young boys. But
why was she so excluded from the world of women too? Yes, there was
old Hélène, Victoire, Eugénie, but in general she felt ill at ease. She
was often bored in their company. When she was with her father, or
Rodin, or in the studio, she felt free. But it was true, nonetheless, that
she did not know them. Yes, their desires, their occasional childish-
ness, their figures suddenly diminished, and then suddenly their con-
centration, their will, their inaccessibility, as they became entirely
absorbed in their task.

"Paul, I want to go out, to have some fun." Camille was familiar
with this sudden desire to do something silly, impulsive. She drank
another glass of cognac. "It's burning me up! Down in my throat. See if
I'm not breathing fire!"

She gave her brother another glass too; he drank it absentmind-
edly. And she began to sing a popular song while tracing some dance
steps:

> Listen to me, then, mademoiselle,
> I would offer you a glass of Moselle.
> Listen to me, then, my little doe,
> I would offer you a glass of Pernod.
> No, monsieur, I won't listen for sure,
> I'll have none of all that, I just drink water pure.
> No, monsieur, all your drinks I defy,
> I'm going straight home, for I live right nearby.

Then two steps and a half – and a half. She hiccuped and thrust out
her dangling leg as if she were doing a French cancan, with one shoe.

"Cam, stop!"

"What is it?"

"I don't know. Christmas Day!"

Camille burst into her hearty laugh. "Oh, yes! Christmas! Christmas cakes! Religion, the family, the fatherland, ta-dum, ta-dum, ta-dum!" Suddenly Camille stopped, "But I love life, love, hope! I don't expect any rewards! From day to day. Savage. I'm a savage."

Listen to me, then, mademoiselle . . .

When she let loose like that – Paul knew – nothing could stop her. Louis-Prosper had just come in. There they were, the two of them, waltzing around the room. Camille shouted with laughter. Madame Louise appeared in her nightgown, a shawl around her shoulders. Camille looked at her and started laughing, laughing. Crazy laughter.

"It's nothing, Mama, she's a little drunk."

Paul looked at all of them. And what had just happened to him? He had gone to Notre-Dame today, an atheist, a student of Renan, he'd gone to listen to the *Magnificat* at Notre-Dame. How could he tell them that he'd felt a presence, that he'd been struck by someone's presence? How could he admit this encounter, which had swept everything away? Everything he'd learned at the *lycée* was negated. He could see the Virgin in shadow, her child in her arms, the child's elusive smile, that promise of innocence, that deep joy. Camille was laughing more and more, but he felt like sobbing – tears of joy. He had wanted to cry out, to purge his heart of all the horrors of these last years. For the first time he had been disarmed, utterly overwhelmed. Something was torn out of him. He had wanted to tell them, to shout out the wild hope that churned in his entrails. And he knew it wasn't the alcohol. It had been burning in him before, since the end of that afternoon he had embarked on a terrible adventure. All the vessels were burned, cast off; he, too, rose. Louis had stopped, worn out by this mad dance, and Paul caught his sister and they spun around shouting with laughter, as they had done when they were children. The one returned from Notre-Dame, the other working on *The Gates of Hell*. Neither had given away his secret. Still, this evening they were full of joy.

Rose Beuret

And if this man does not want to harvest the grapes,
And if he wants to continue to play the judge
And if he does not want to lead, he must not be
taken by the hand
And if he does not want to drain the cup, he must
not bring it to his lips.

PAUL CLAUDEL, *La Cantate à trois voix*

IT WAS COLD – even icy. February was ending in storms, showers. Camille felt like stamping her feet, like those powerful horses that walk in step and no longer have the courage to kick over the traces. Camille was dissatisfied with herself. The year 1887 did not interest her. That was how it was. Yet she was seeing Monsieur Rodin more often. She had a magnificent studio. Neubourg Folly covered with snow was more than ever a haven of peace, of sensuality, of work. But curiously she felt the need for something else.

"This is a time of year that doesn't speak to me," old Hélène would say.

Louise had been very busy. She was going to marry Ferdinand de Massary, a fine young man with his little mustache and goatee. Camille had suggested doing a bust of him. Along with the brother, the father, the brother-in-law, the sister, Rodin. She was going round in circles. She would have liked a real model of her own, a couple, a naked woman, a naked man, she would have liked to escape this series of busts that pursued her like phantoms. She wanted naked flesh to fashion, life, and not these busts she was using to refine her technique, like a surgeon preparing for the day when he might perform an actual operation.

Monsieur Rodin had been completely absorbed in the big commission for *The Burghers of Calais*. Failure, criticism, Camille often had to comfort her teacher. The critics were never happy: "the burghers of Calais looked dejected," "they were not elegant enough." When Rodin thought he'd scored on one point, there was always some scribbler who wrote a lot of nonsense and influenced the council. There were moments when Rodin was ready to destroy the whole thing. She knew he was furious. Yet she had closely followed the history of this sculpture, the care Rodin had taken with it. He was overwhelmed by that scene in which the six hostages of Calais offer their life to save their city. He had asked Camille to do the research. Often they were bent for hours doing hands – the hands of Pierre de Wiessant. He was her favorite, Pierre de Wiessant, an insolent man with a proud, haughty soul, who threw himself arrogantly into the supreme sacrifice. And Jean de Fiennes, the youngest, magnificent, almost entirely undressed. That is what she would have loved to sculpt, a human tragedy. Each of them alone, confronting his fate, and yet transported by the same political adventure . . .

Camille had just sat down in front of the bust she was doing. What was the point? She'd been more courageous at the age of twelve; then she'd taken on the story of Antigone, Bismarck, David and Goliath . . . But what was she waiting for? Tomorrow she would go to Monsieur Rodin and ask for two of his models. She would do a group: the tragedy of Oedipus or a scene from the poems of Ossian. A disheveled Salgar calling on the windy heath, discovering the bodies of her brother and her lover.

The storm was raging outside. Rodin had gone out a few moments before to buy some alcohol at the corner grocer's. They would make hot wine, because the studio was freezing. The doors rattled, and the empty rooms echoed with the sound. From time to time pieces of slate or tile fell from the dilapidated roof. They hadn't enough money to repair this huge place.

"My God! the rain is beating down. We'll have leaks again, and now hail . . ." Camille went back to sculpting – with difficulty. She would have to stop. She could hardly distinguish the outline of the nose, the lips. She was trying to capture their sensuality. The clay had already cracked twice. Now Camille attacked the plaster. Perhaps it would be more resistant.

Camille froze, her hands on the bust. Someone was behind her, and it wasn't Rodin. She felt a hostile presence. Camille tried to calm herself. Her heart was beating. This was war. Someone was there. She had to turn around. The devil at Villeneuve . . . This time he was there, lurking in the shadows. Camille took a chisel in her fist, distracted, and turned abruptly, ready to leap. She could barely see it at first, a dark silhouette standing against the wall, dressed in black. A woman was there, soaked, disheveled, an old woman but tall, slim, and straight. Her hat had slipped to one side, hanging on her shoulder. Camille was there, in her white smock, her stockings, her clogs, her hair held back by a childish ribbon. The two women together. Perhaps ready to kill. Camille murmured: "Rose! Rose Beuret!"

"Yes, Rose! His Rose!" Rose came toward her and Camille could now distinguish her hair, still wild and streaked with white, her angular face, her eyes, violet and savage.

"I wanted to see. Whore! Thief! You are not the only one. He's had others . . . Little conniver! Not good enough to kiss my ass! It's easy to have him now!"

"Shut up!"

"No, my girl. Listen. We were dying of hunger. We were living in a stable. I'd worked as a dressmaker to earn money. I was not a kept woman. Never a kept woman . . ." Rose came closer to Camille. Camille, who was holding her chisel and mallet. "I kept his plaster casts from drying, I did his accounts. You don't frighten me, you little tart, I've lived through the Commune, I have! He will never leave me — never, do you hear?"

Rose had cried out, she spit in Camille's face.

"Then what are you afraid of? You are afraid, that's it! Are you afraid?"

"I had him when he was young, he was young when I knew him."

"So what are you complaining about, you old hag?"

Rose recoiled at the insult. Her arms were raised, ready to strike. Camille had anticipated the gesture. She had dropped the tools and grabbed the fists coming at her. The two women grappled with each other.

"Tart! Tart! Wretch, sculpting naked men!"

"Go home to your soup!"

"I put up with the others. I put up with everything. The models, the society women. There's only one thing that matters to him, his work. But with you it's different. I'll kill you. You've become sculpture itself. Everyone has told me about you. I'll crush you! He's under a spell. Look at the house he's paying for. And you have no shame when I'm dying of hunger. Tart! Tart! And our son, filthy kept woman, guttersnipe . . . And you sculpt, you dare to represent him. Just wait!"

Rose threw herself on the bust of Rodin. Then Camille went mad, a cold rage ran through her, a murderous anger. Rose was flung off . . .

"Camiiiiiiilllle!" Monsieur Rodin shouted. The mirror flew into pieces. Rose was on the ground, perhaps injured. At some distance, Camille, too, lay on the ground. The worktable, along with the bust, had fallen on top of her. She was badly hurt.

Horrified, Rodin stood before the two women, not knowing which way to turn. They both kept quiet. Then slowly he went to Rose, who groaned softly. "Rose, you're hurt. My good Rose . . ." He helped her sit up. "There, drink! You're sure there's nothing wrong?"

Rose wept, hiccuped, her shoulders shaking. Rodin took his handkerchief, lifted her veil, and wiped her face. Rose was now sobbing. Rodin cradled her in his arms. "Rose, your heart, how is your heart? Come, I'll take you home. You shouldn't have come here. Why did you come, you're usually so obedient, my poor thing?" Slowly he helped her to her feet.

Camille swept off the debris of the bust that covered her body, and pushed away the worktable that was crushing her stomach; she felt terrible, something had burst inside. On her knees, she painfully pushed herself up and staggered to the fireplace.

"Are you all right, Camille?"

"Yes, Monsieur Rodin." The young girl leaned against the fireplace. Rodin did not see her face, Rodin did not see the two silent tears running down her face, now reaching the corners of her lips.

"Camille, I can't bear violence. Rose has a heart condition. I am going to take her home."

Camille nodded. She felt such pain, she could not speak. She gripped the corner of the mantelpiece, that's all. She heard the footsteps recede, the door close, the creaking of the gate, and a horrible nausea shook her. She was slipping, slipping.

"Auguste!" she called desperately.

What time was it?
How long had she been there?
Dawn.

The Tuesday Group

*Mallarmé is the first to have placed himself in front of
the exterior, not as he would in front of a performance,
or a page of French exercises, but as he would in front
of a text, with the question: What does this mean?*

PAUL CLAUDEL, *Mallarmé*

CROUCHING, powerful, a woman's torso. Her mother would
call it "obscene." Rodin stopped short. In this sunny month of
April, it turned its back on him, provocatively. Turned in on herself, a
squatting woman whose head was not visible. Rodin came toward her.
Camille had made this with her own hands, she had molded this plaster. As powerful as his *Thinker*, as brutal as *The Kiss*, this time she had
deployed all her knowledge of the flesh, of the model.

On the pretext of doing a nude study, the young woman had begun
immediately. The surrounding busts gazed at this powerful figure who
defied them all with her nudity, her naked flesh. Rodin had begun a
similar torso, which he'd called *Head of Lust*. But she had struck hard
and quick. The daring position suddenly troubled him. He could make
such a sculpture, yes, but she – how had she done it, who had posed
for her?

"I posed for myself. Are you surprised, Monsieur Rodin?" She
burst out laughing. "I wanted to do myself in the nude. So there it is."

Despite his admiration, the work frightened him. His sculptures
were already causing scandals; they treated satyrs, leering fauns, licen-

tious old men. But if *she* should produce an erotic, sensual sculpture, she would be crucified! The problem was not that she addressed the genre of the nude; there were nudes that were strictly neutral, that had no sensuality. But she had the gift of flesh. This nude was unbearable. She had dared, and she would dare again. That was not in doubt. But why wasn't she content with busts? She could have continued with nudes as well by working on *The Gates of Hell.* Everyone would have thought they were his work. But she would exhibit this piece alone.

"Camille."

He admired the suppleness of the torso, he touched it, that extended back, the separated buttocks. She had posed for herself. She must have been there, naked, crouching. The other Camille was standing there in her light smock, intact, immaterial. As if she were reading his thoughts, Camille smiled with that ironic smile that made her mouth gather at the corners "in three wrinkles, as if traced by the finest pencil." That's how Paul had described it one day.

Since the other evening, the night she had confronted Rose, Camille had become more dangerous; she warded him off, as if she had been beaten. Rodin thought of that struggle between the two women. Fortunately, it had turned out all right: Rose had finally calmed down.

Rodin was afraid that Camille would ask him: "Monsieur Rodin, do you want to pose for me in the nude?" She stared at him, as if she wanted to humiliate him.

Camille was happy to see him there, before the outrageously crouching woman – herself. She had wanted to insult him. She would never forget the days following Rose's intrusion – no word from him! He hadn't come back to Clos Payen for more than a week. She could have died, disappeared. Not once had he asked for news of her. And she had been chased away by her mother the next morning.

She had come home in the early morning, happy to feel safe, finished with that ghastly night, happy to find herself home again. Her mother had been there, in front of her bowl of café au lait. "I must speak to you."

"I fell asleep. I didn't dare go out into the streets, into the night."

"Follow me."

They went to the parents' bedroom. The double bed, the crucifix. Camille had stared stupidly at the crucifix as her mother spoke. In a low, hissing, choking voice: "Now, you take your things and leave.

Louise is going to be married. There will be no scandal, do you hear? And don't you say a word. You are going to live your way, all right. I've put your things together. I don't want to know who you live with, who you meet. Let us avoid a scandal at all cost. I will tell your father I agree that you should live alone. You go where you wish. There must be plenty of men who will take you in. What will happen will happen. You have chosen. I warned you. Not a word to anyone. You leave now. Eugénie will help you . . ."

Camille had swallowed her tears. She was banished, wounded — she had done nothing, and she had been condemned and judged. Shame clung to her like a burning leprosy. She would keep quiet. Since everyone thought she was guilty, she would leave. Her mother had left the room, Camille had looked at the double bed, the couple's room. "Papa! Papa!" He was not there, perhaps he would be chased away too. The Christ was in front of her, torn, his head bowed. She hated him. No, she would not let herself behave like that. They would see, all of them! She, too, went out of the room, but she left there behind her, once and for all, the overconfident little girl. Camille felt that a part of her lay there, between her father and mother, in the double bed.

Paul had said nothing. He had learned the news that evening. Eugénie had told him at the family dinner. He had paled, gotten up, and locked himself in his room. It was now a cold, merciless struggle between him and his mother — they were no longer on speaking terms. Young Louise, utterly self-absorbed, sensed and saw nothing. Her sister had gone, she had the room all to herself, she was free to dream of Ferdinand.

At the outset, Camille had been a bit disconcerted: making herself something to eat, the silence, Rodin's complete absence. Happily, Eugénie had come every day to encourage her, to help her. She alone knew where Camille was living. But if Monsieur Rodin left her, how would she manage to pay the rent on Clos Payen? She had to find someplace else. And then one morning, near dawn, he had arrived. He had surprised her sleeping; what was she doing there? He had sat on the bed and she'd told him everything. The blow to the stomach, the nausea, the loss of memory . . . How could he have done this? He would take care of her from now on. "Child, poor child!"

The tears Camille had held back for so long finally burst out. Shaken with sobs, she had let herself go, and he had consoled her, cajoled her. Adoringly. That evening, he'd stayed with her. For the first time Monsieur Rodin had stayed, slept near her, held her close. She had been delirious, hardly knowing where she was. In the early morning she had calmed down, and she'd been oddly relieved to see him depart.

Life had resumed. Thanks to her father, Camille could again go home for meals. Paul had never spoken to her about all this, but now he came to see her at Clos Payen. His sister was Rodin's mistress. No one knew what he thought about it. Camille had won her freedom, her independence. Her father also understood. He never spoke about it. Everything was back in order. Camille had a studio of her own.

"Camille, yes? She always works with Monsieur Rodin."

"The famous sculptor?"

"Yes." Her mother almost boasted. "She even has her own studio!"

Their honor was spared, hypocrisy – the fount of lies. Propriety was again clothed in her high-necked dress. Everyone came out a winner.

Only Rodin was worried. He could not spend every night at Clos Payen, and Camille was becoming freer, more independent, more audacious. That figure before him heralded a new style. He was dealing with another sculptor, his student, but for how long? And yet they loved each other to distraction.

She was there, his beloved, solitary disciple, and his lover, still expecting his criticism, his judgment, humble, attentive. Who was she? Bestial, spiritual, slave, dominatrix . . . Saint or whore? In any case, a young woman with whom he was hopelessly in love – his madness. Where would she lead him?

He kissed her neck, nibbled at her. "Watch out, Cam, that they don't destroy you!" He kissed her again and again, there in the hollow between the breasts that he had already bared.

"Paul!"

"What about Paul?"

"I'd forgotten. He's coming by to pick us up. First we're going, remember, to see Puvis de Chavanne's latest painting. And this evening it's Tuesday, we're all dining together with his friend Roger Marx."

Monsieur Rodin had forgotten. A month ago he had introduced them to Mallarmé. He was part of the Group of Twenty that had started in 1883: there was Felicien Rops, Whistler, Catulle Mendes, Odilon Redon, Villiers de l'Isle-Adam. For several years, poets, painters, and writers had met at Stéphane Mallarmé's, 87, rue de Rome. One day he had spoken of Mallarmé to Camille, of his meetings with Puvis de Chavannes, Verlaine, Carrière, Charles Morice . . . "I am going to take you there."

She had asked him: "And Paul? Do you think we can take Paul? Recently he told me he'd sent some poems to Mallarmé. It would give him such pleasure."

"Paul writes?"

"Evidently."

So on Tuesday they had all three gone to 87, rue de Rome.

Camille loved these evenings, that exquisite, affable man surrounded by artists. He had been there, seated, with his grizzled, nearly white beard, his dark, piercing eyes, an old plaid shawl thrown over his shoulders, elegant, strict. She loved to watch them all. Paul had seen Verlaine but hadn't dared to speak to him. What an idiot! He had sat rigidly on the sofa, distant, perhaps embarrassed by his sister's presence. There were few women, many writers. Nor was Rodin very much at ease; Camille loved this refined world, discussing the Symbolist manifesto, Huysmans's book, which was causing such a furor. *Against the Grain.* Joris-Karl Huysmans fascinated her, though she hated his book. She'd kept her opinion to herself, but his vaporizings – "the perfumes, the cypress, the champak, the srianthos" – all offended her stark sense of reality. She thought they were decadent. They were, and even gloried in it. The attraction of an artificial paradise, the taste for the morbid, the charm of unnatural conditions – all this repelled her. Only a dark young man curiously caught her attention. Especially his forehead. She would have liked to sculpt it, with its two large, pointed bumps. Someone had mentioned his name: Claude, Claude Debussy. He was a pianist. Villiers de l'Isle-Adam had terrorized her with his irony and his glaucous eyes. She should read his works. But she had no time. In the evenings at Neubourg Folly, she read by candlelight; she devoured books, but they were expensive. She had so much to learn, so much to read, and then often she drew for hours and hours, late into the night. No one was there to tell her to go to sleep. Rodin did not always stay, contrary to his promises.

"Camille, Rose is ill. I must go home, you understand." What could she do? He had spoken to her of Rose, of how he'd met her just after leaving Father Eymard's monastery. She had given him everything, her twenty years, her joy all those years; she had suffered poverty, his absence during the Commune while she fought against cold, hunger, violence in the streets. When he had gone to work in Belgium she had stayed alone with the child. She had kept his plasters damp, she had taken his father in when his mother died, during that terrible year of 1871. No, he could not, it was too much to ask of him . . .

Camille listened. He had met Rose the year she was born, she sensed her there. She, too, had given him her twenty years, she, too, had loved him. Camille had understood. He was afraid. Afraid to repeat the story of Maria. Maria, who had died a few months after being abandoned. He would never abandon a woman again.

"And then she said nothing. She has never asked for anything. She is there, behind me. She has not asked me to marry her, or even to recognize Auguste. Never anything. She is there. She loves me. That's all."

Yes, but what would become of the two of them? Camille tried to calm down when he looked at his watch, threw off his smock, and took his hat. She often went upstairs quickly to escape under the covers. Not to see him leave, not to hear the gate close behind him. Then began the long hours of solitude . . .

"Get dressed, Cam." Camille buttoned her dress. This evening they would all be together. As it would be over late, he would surely stay with her. Come on, life was good!

"Wait, there's Paul." Camille looked through the glass doors.

"What's so funny?"

"Paul just got caught in some brambles, he stuck his foot in."

"Paul!" She saw him grumble, lift his leg, try to detach the thorny, clinging plant.

"Ha, ha, ha!" Camille began her crazy laughter.

"No, Camille."

When she started that crazy laughter, nothing could stop her. She opened the window: "Paul, do you want some scissors?"

Now he was on the ground in the grass.

"There's our poet with his four paws in the air."

Fortunately Paul was in a good mood: "I'll get my revenge, Cam. I will describe dreadful termagants, and they will be you!"

Camille laughed more pleasantly. She jumped over the little ledge and went to help her brother up. Paul had stopped short. He had just perceived the crouching woman. He was shocked.

"I'm the one who did it. Look, Paul." Camille turned her nude. Paul said nothing. "Come closer. She won't bite. Mallarmé would say that before pronouncing judgment you must question yourself at length. The spectacle is not enough. You need a certain willingness to understand, not to reject the work. That is the principle of science as well as art."

Camille imitated them all: Mallarmé, Villiers de l'Isle-Adam, Huysmans. Paul was "a wet blanket," Camille said to herself.

"Okay, you are not going to spend the day looking at my lines and my curves!"

Paul didn't understand, Camille did two dance steps. "Mademoiselle Camille Claudel, by the great sculptor Camille Claudel! And hop-la boom!" She gave a kick and tapped herself on the behind, like the French cancan dancers.

"Members of the Tuesday group, let's go! " Paul let himself be led away. "That's what they call us, the 'chaps' who go on Tuesdays to visit the Prince of Poets."

Monsieur Rodin followed them. The sister and brother. She might have been a little taller than he. Twenty-two and eighteen. He felt excluded from their intimacy, their childhood games, even their disputes. Where was she going, the tall young woman there, in front of him, disappearing under the trees, with her clear laugh and her serious, mocking voice?

"Watch out, Paul, if you fall, I'll let you fall," and she chanted: "If you fall, I'll let you fall. Are you following us, Monsieur Rodin?" The flash of her eyes. A flash of lightning!

She came back to take his arm, pulling Paul with the other hand.

"Love me with all your heart."

Çacountala

*I sleep, but my heart waketh; it is the voice of my be-
loved that knocketh, saying, Open to me, my sister, my
love, my dove, my undefiled.*

The Song of Solomon 5

CAMILLE was waiting. The Champs-Elysées Salon of 1888.
Camille was anxious to know the results. So she walked and
walked, back and forth in front of the exhibition. Days and days of
strenuous work. She was exhausted. She had worked and reworked the
couple dozens of times – without help, without advice. Even Rodin
had not been allowed to comment – it was her own work! Later she
would tell him what this sculpture was about.

She walked, she was hot, she saw the crowd from a distance. It was
a lovely day, but as she waited in suspense for the announcement of the
judging, no odor, no sound reached her, words were just a babble. She
walked, she circled around the Salon. Still half an hour to go, maybe
an hour. She stood with her back against the wall in the rather empty
little street, a few moments of calm. Time to catch her breath. At the
Salon they were all peering closely at the couple with their monocles,
their decorations, their furrowed brows, as though it were a matter of
life or death. They circled around with their disagreeable pouts, their
pursed lips. And they couldn't even knead a ball of clay. The old, the

insipid, the blasé! She had felt like shouting: "It's my soul, all I hold sacred!" She had wanted to drive them away, to throw them out. They were talking, discussing, and she saw their twisted paws crushing, tearing apart her very life.

"Monsieur, this represents hours of work, hours of scrutiny, hours when my soul was on fire. While you were eating, joking, while you were guzzling life, I was alone with my sculpture, and my very life ran drop by drop into this clay, it's my blood, my youth."

She saw the heads leaning over the man and woman. The man was kneeling, the woman slightly inclined toward him. "Monsieur Rodin." It was cold. They had made a fire to warm themselves – the smell of wood, the smell of the forest.

She had gone back to Villeneuve. Winter was beginning. The year 1887 was coming to an end. She was about to turn twenty-three. And then something dreadful happened.

Six o'clock one winter evening, she was heading to studio J. For several days Monsieur Rodin had asked if she wanted to take one of the studies for *The Gates of Hell*. She had decided to drop in before nightfall to take the rough sketches back to Clos Payen. Then she could study them at leisure. The card was swinging from the door – "Monsieur Rodin is out." Watch out, Camille! The card was there. She didn't see it, she was thinking of the statue he was continually reworking, transformed by turns into *Prayer, The Invocation, The Supreme Summons*. The young child holding out his hands before being swallowed up.

The stout woman, thighs open, was sitting on the man, sunk onto him, screwed on, sitting on him, grotesque. He looked like a satyr to her. One of his arms went under the woman's right thigh. He held her left hand, which was moving up and down on his sex. He was sunk into her. The woman caressed herself and caressed him. Camille was there, as still as the surrounding groups of marble figures. She had to do something. She could only repeat to herself the lines Shakespeare gave Titania to say when she falls in love with Bottom transformed into an ass: "Come, sit thee down upon this flow'ry bed / While I thy amiable cheeks do coy . . . And kiss thy fair large ears, my gentle joy." Monsieur Rodin, you have become an ass. I see your muzzle, Monsieur Rodin, you don't hear it but you're braying now. Monsieur Rodin was panting against the white shoulder.

Camille was lashed by Yvette's laughter, Yvette on Rodin's knees. "What's that! Hey, Auguste, there's the virgin. Monsieur Rodin, do something. No, not you, not you . . . So, are you a sculptor or not? Got to be cold-blooded. Your Rodin isn't interested in a bunch of rotting flesh. He wants life. Come on, M'sieur Rodin, it's not so serious. She is a sculptor, a craftsman like you. Have to know. Whether she's a man or a woman. You don't make such a face when it's Desbois or Escoula."

Yvette had struck home – hard and fast. So Camille came forward, insolent, but said nothing. She was outside, she couldn't. It was him, him. But Yvette was right. She was so much a sculptor that she, too, forgot herself; the jokes had gained currency again in the studio and distracted everyone's attention from her. She wanted to be among men, okay, she had to assume their vulgarity, their tactlessness. She had passed to the other side. They made the law. She couldn't have it both ways. Yvette was right.

A week had passed. They were working side by side, studio J was a bit tense. Camille had looked for the drawings, she had reworked the statue, but everyone felt the hostility between teacher and student. Yvette had said nothing; she was sorry for Camille. She saw her, such a young woman, trying to come to terms with such contradictions. She even found her courageous, and secretly she would have liked to shake her hand.

And then, late one afternoon, Monsieur Rodin had asked Camille to dine with him. After the restaurant, he had gone back with her to Clos Payen. The fire in the fireplace. Camille poked fun at herself. She loved the sculptor, whatever he was. So . . . She had joked with him, their "cohabitation" was a gift, a free gift, she was more generous than Rose, she did not want the gestures of fidelity, did not want to pretend that his liaisons didn't exist, no, she would face them, and she would have her own liaisons . . .

Rodin had violently clutched at her wrists. "Don't do that, Cam. Not you. Don't begin. Or it will be all over. Not you, Cam."

Camille had looked at him, this clutching child. She drew back, and he clung to her as if she were going away, his eyes desperate, imploring. He was a man diminished, on his knees, his face ravaged. If she were going to become like the others, then all of life was filth. He would no longer believe in anything. But Camille had yielded. He was there, on his knees, his arms around her waist, she had her back against the mantelpiece, her back was warm. The smell of the crackling forest . . .

She leaned her head toward him, kissed his temple, delicate, ineffably tender, she gave him everything, even her heart . . . "Monsieur Rodin." She shuddered, gave herself, yielded. She went beyond Yvette, the satyr, the ass, she was ravaged by love. Even unto death.

The logs flamed. She saw herself, she saw him reflected, multiplied in the mirrors, the great blaze behind them. It became the altar for the sacrifice, and she the lamb, she leaned over him, her cheek against his, still standing, her whole self slipping downward, against him, kneeling. He still held her but her head was already sinking. One of her arms hung, lifeless . . . In a final gesture, she pressed her hand against her heart – a mute pain gripped her, the intense joy of finding him again, the second before contact, then she surrendered, dying. He closed his hand on her breast, all of her belonged to him, her heart, her body, he bore her far away . . .

When she awakened she was alone. It was late. He had assumed a strained expression and written in his somewhat shaky script: "Eternal Idol." Desire to sculpt quickly. To realize her couple at long last. She knew what she wanted to do. Swallowing some coffee, she had hastily searched through a collection of Indian legends. There it was, Çacountala, the king intoxicated with the desire to recover his lost beloved, her memory reconquered in a moment of eternity.

My God! What had she done? She hurried toward the Salon. The crowd in motion. She threaded her way through. She heard: "*Çacountala*. Plaster. Sculptor: Mademoiselle Camille Claudel. Honorable mention."

Never mind the others. She had gained recognition as a sculptor. Her eyes filled with tears. The crowd pressed around her, but where was he?

"She will never do anything without Rodin."

"He must have had a hand in it."

The two remarks were like the lash of a whip in her face.

"Well, she's his student. He taught her everything."

"Even the rest, it seems. He would have done better to omit that."

Camille was choking. They'd ruined everything. The bastards –

stench, stench – they defiled everything. They saw only the negative. Incapable of creating anything themselves, they demolished, destroyed.

"You are mistaken, gentlemen." Rodin's voice was furious, glacial. Camille had never seen him like this. A cold, metallic anger. "It is true that Mademoiselle was my student. For a short time. She very quickly became my collaborator, my most gifted technician. I consult her on everything. She is my best colleague. I make my decisions only after getting her consent. To put an end to the debate, I will tell you this: I may have shown her where to find gold, but the gold she finds is her own."

He had seen her. He smiled at her. The crowd parted for the couple. Tomorrow all of Paris would be talking about it. He was proud of her. He took her off to celebrate her success. Artists surrounded them. Monsieur Rodin and Camille Claudel. He beamed, gazing at her; supple, tall, she was silent at the congratulations, smiling a little, with that lopsided smile that was uniquely hers, her impenetrable soul, *"Virgo admirabilis,"* as her brother Paul had called her one day. She listened and answered, but who had access to her proud soul? At the sight of the two sculptors leaving side by side, the others sensed something like fear. A woman and a man entwined in the same sculpture.

Rodin, Rodin, Rodin

IT HAD BEEN SNOWING for days. She'd had enough of the winter of 1890, a dirty mud that left her battered and aching. She managed to sculpt only with difficulty. She could hardly see a thing. Scarcely two hours for sculpting. This light distorted everything. She'd had enough. She had just turned twenty-six. She was old, she was a failure. Almost no commissions, but on the contrary, hatred, envy, slander, or silence, indifference. That was her lot. Even Rodin was in a bad mood. Almost two years had passed since her honorable mention at the Salon, and everything had settled down into a "banal kindness."

The recognition, her once promising future – what was left of all that? Anyway, she hated the start of the new year, as if everything were going to change because the year changed – ridiculous!

Twice she got up and then went back to bed. It was so dark she couldn't do anything. So she stayed there stupidly, useless, with no project and no commission. Who needed her? She visited friends, family. Rodin had Rose, his models, his sculpture. You had to be essential to someone to want to get out of bed on a day like this. Work, she had work! Or more precisely, Monsieur Rodin was besieged by commissions. His technicians could hardly manage. "Rodin & Co." – that was what they called the three studios that roared like forges all day long. They attacked him here, defended him there. Then the artist had to be reassured, consoled. He was bombarded by criticism, apparently victimized, and everyone was worried about him.

There was the scandal of *The Burghers of Calais*. The monument was never erected, the hostility of the committee from Calais continued to be as heated as before. Total incomprehension. A year ago Rodin had obtained the commission for the monument to Victor Hugo that would be erected in Paris, then the unfinished *Gates of Hell*, the monument to Claude Lorrain in Nancy, not to mention politicians and all the rich women who wanted him to do their busts. Oh, those women, if only Camille could have poked their eyes out! They came, fidgeted, implored, ingratiated themselves, swinging their backsides. Yet thanks to them, Camille had found, if not a friend, at least an ally. When they swept through the studio with their perfumes, their jewels, their money, their visiting cards, Camille and Yvette made fun of them. They were vile – they were kept women, the parasites of society. Under the pretext of marriage and money, anything was permitted. They were even privileged to approach the conjuror of human forms. "Oh, oh! Monsieur Rodin . . ."

Auguste Rodin often went to Madame Adam's. There he met Gambetta, Waldeck-Rousseau, Eugène Spuller, minister of fine arts, the all-powerful art critic Castagnary. Camille no longer went with him. First of all, they rarely invited her, and besides she had nothing to wear. She remembered the last big party: Rodin surrounded, assailed; even Castagnary wanted his bust done. Especially him. It may have been his only chance to live for posterity. Camille couldn't bear him. As she stood in the entrance to the room, only Charles Gounod had spoken to her. But she knew nothing about music. She had spoken of Faust, of the myth of youth, of Faust's pact with the devil. Hadn't she ever had a weakness for the old Faust? Gounod, who was going on seventy, had smiled into his great white beard.

Today she understood the pact. Time had flown, the impudence of youth; that was precisely what she was in the process of losing. It would be used up drop by drop.

Rodin had triumphed in the year 1889. He had imposed himself. And Camille was there in her bed, cowering, crouching.

She had met his demand: "You will be there, won't you, Camille? I will wait for you. It's important to me. And after all, you are present in all my sculptures. It's a kind of homage." She had been beautiful, all in white. Passersby had turned to look at her, a tall, luminous silhouette going to meet a lover, surely. Men enjoyed dreaming, women envied this free companion who walked alone – and was surely awaited.

A breeze, the odor of lilacs. Camille approached the Georges Petit Gallery. Such a crowd! Suddenly she was afraid, she didn't recognize anyone. Among the crowd pressing around her she barely glimpsed the canvases of Monet, the sculptures of the "master," as she called him with mingled irony and tenderness. For she always thought of "master" in relation to "mistress." She was his *mistress*, he was her *master*. The double meanings always made her laugh.

He had seen her, gone toward her, taken her by the elbow. "I'm happy. I'm so happy that you're here." A young woman approached: "You know Blanche, don't you? – Camille Claudel."

He had turned slightly toward this young goose, when someone took him by the arm, oh yes, it was Octave Mirbeau, she quite liked him. Mirbeau led Rodin off to introduce him to someone. There he was, snatched up, borne away. She tried to say a few words to Blanche, but Blanche had friends there.

"Excuse me, Mademoiselle what?" Camille had not had the time to say her name, and then what was the point? They had all forgotten her. She saw him looking at her from a distance; he was keeping an eye on her, in fact. And she knew those eyes. She had already had occasion to note his strategy; troubled at seeing her speaking to one of his friends, he was not jealous properly speaking, but he was Rodin – disturbed by any friendship that excluded him, that was displaced onto another, male or female, onto *the other*. Rodin had not even introduced her as a sculptor. She saw nothing, neither the paintings nor the sculptures. She would come back to visit the exhibition later, quietly. Besides, all those people were making a mockery of it, of the exhibition. They were there to be seen, not to see. How could they stand apart and wait for a work to touch them?

A triumph! Seventy canvases by Monet mingled with thirty-six figures by Rodin: "A resounding affirmation."

Eugène Carrière also seemed a bit neglected. He had left with Camille. They had walked, talking of one thing and another. She quite liked Eugène, and it was reciprocal. Both of them had noticed how Rodin had been caught up in the flattery, a court that had spit on him only yesterday, and would very likely do the same tomorrow. "The number one innovator, the liberator of sculpture. . . . The exhibition that just opened . . . was a huge success for the two superb artists. . . . Above all others in this century, they embody most gloriously, most definitively, these two arts." And what place was left for her? To be Rodin's student.

Camille tossed and turned in the bed. It wasn't that she was jealous, but she couldn't see a way out. Success led to success. A few months later, Antonin Proust, special commissioner of fine arts, had put other sites at Rodin's disposal.

And present she certainly was! Everywhere sculpted by him, transformed by him. Everyone dreamed of their mad love, all of fashionable Paris envied it, women were jealous of her. Hadn't he created *The Eternal Idol*, in which everyone had recognized her? – the man delicately kissing a young girl beneath her breasts as she sat on his knees. Camille thought she was seeing her *Çacountala* again. Two people had made the same connection. But so what? Everyone had already forgotten *Çacountala*. The critics were in ecstasy at Monsieur Rodin's couple, "that marvel of tenderness."

Camille turned over on the white pillow. She saw them in the room. The man and woman entwined, lovingly sculpted by her, her only "Honorable Mention." Why had they abandoned it? No one had bought it. No one had wanted it. Her defeat was there before her.

She had to get up. Victoire was always saying, "God helps those who help themselves." Villeneuve! Even Villeneuve repelled her. She hadn't wanted to set foot there this past summer. The mayor's white wine, the innumerable visits, the trips. "You are our native daughter, our artist. And shall we see Monsieur Rodin one day?" And then the news had come, incredible as it seemed.

They had refused to give her a commission to create the monument commemorating the hundredth anniversary of the Revolution. Another sculptor's work would be erected on the little Place de la République, where she had played as a child. They had made excuses: she was a great artist now; and after all, she had been born at Villeneuve, people would gossip. The municipal council did not want to be charged with favoritism. Finally, they would see . . . This business had left her unstrung, wounded to the quick. There was Rodin. Monsieur Rodin. But what about her, who would give her recognition? Better to end it right away.

The rusty iron gate groaned on its hinges. The heels tapped the ground. He set down his umbrella. The heavy steps came up the stairs . . .

"Cam, Cam, are you ill? What's the matter?"

"I won't make it. It's all over. I am forgotten." She wept, shaking with sobs. She resented being like this! There, now she was hiccuping, and in front of him!

"Stop, my Camille. You are going to make yourself sick."

"No one gives me any commissions. I don't exist."

"What are you talking about? Lhermitte has commissioned you to make the bust of his son, Charlot."

"Yes, but he asked you to advise him for the bronze casting. And your recommendation was needed for Liard to do what I asked. The black patina . . . And after all, he is your friend and you don't have the time to do the bust. So he's made do with me."

"You're babbling. And *The Prayer?* I'm not the one who made it. I'm just an old wretch. Your *Prayer*, I could never manage such a piece. And all the work you do with me . . ."

On one hot afternoon, by herself, she had entered a church whose name she did not know. Calm, silence, peace. Camille sat on a straw chair. A young woman was there on her knees, her head back, radiant. Beatitude. One day Camille had read a lament: "the beatitudes." She had looked at that woman; what was she doing, what was she thinking? What was that solitary joy, that light flooding her face, beyond all human comprehension? Camille hadn't taken her eyes off the woman; in the distance a red light flickered – like a heart. Camille felt at peace, sheltered. Ordained. Two hypocrites had entered, babbling on and on, whistling between their teeth the way her mother did when she scolded – spitting out their malice – and they settled themselves noisily on one of the benches. Camille had not taken her eyes off the imploring woman. Not a muscle of her face had moved. She was in another world. That joy! Camille had fled, as if to escape that peace she was denied.

"I'm going away, I'm leaving."

"But where will you go? Listen, Camille, I'm almost fifty-one years old. I've only begun to get on, to get commissions in the last year or so. You have your whole life ahead of you. Sculpture is a long process. You will get there. Just have patience . . ."

But that was precisely the point, Camille didn't have the time. She could feel it. She didn't want to sculpt when she was seventy. Everything and right away! "Right away! While I'm young . . . In ten years I won't do any better."

"Have patience, Camille. Inspiration doesn't exist. We are honest workers, artisans of time. If you're a new talent, you can count on few supporters and a crowd of enemies. Don't be discouraged. Your supporters will triumph because they know why they like you, the others don't understand why you're repugnant to them; they have no lasting enthusiasm, they blow with the wind. Look, it never stops, even for me. You've seen the *Victor Hugo*, it drives them into a frenzy of fire and brimstone because I want to represent him naked. To my mind, you don't dress a god in a frock coat!" Camille smiled. "Listen, Camille, I didn't make my first real sculpture until I was thirty-seven years old. Before that I was a worker, an employee."

She knew all that. But she was different. She did not have the time. She would not have the time.

"You are a child. You will see later. Work. You wanted to sculpt. It's a long, hard road. No one is interested. Who needs your sculptures? They could care less about what you do or don't do, and if you stopped, they wouldn't even celebrate. They would be indifferent. It's up to you every morning to create your desire, your need – your own justification, if you will. But if you stick with it, if you succeed like Michelangelo, then you take all of humanity with you, you make it essential – you make it more beautiful . . ." And Rodin added, as if for himself: "Especially in this time when people chiefly value utility in modern life. Not the spirit, the thought, the dream . . ."

She looked at him, her blue gaze lost; he was there, a bit bent, contemplating something in the distance, he too was lost: "Artists are the enemies. Come on, drink your coffee, Mademoiselle Sculptor. You've made me talk enough nonsense. A rambling old grandfather!"

She laughed. Camille glimpsed him as he would be, with his old coat and a plaid rug over his knees. For he would be famous, idolized, rich, his beautiful beard all white, a shawl or woolen blanket over his shoulders and his old beret, his big beret, on his head.

She knelt before him, "Tell me, Monsieur Rodin, what was she like, this Camille? It seems you loved her very much. She made sculpture, or was she simply some beautiful young girl you loved?"

"Wait, I'm going to explain it to you." Rodin caught Camille, rolled over on her. She pulled his beard. "Wait, we'll just see who's so old!"

He held her firmly. "But you're cold, Mademoiselle, wait." He pulled up her nightdress, turned her over his knees, and vigorously rubbed her bottom. Camille struggled but Rodin clasped her firmly. "You must have muscles, Mademoiselle, to be a sculptor. You have to chisel, to hammer with the mallet."

Camille had her nose in the sheets. Her legs wriggled, but she had lost her balance and had no strength. He slapped her bottom and threw her on the bed, and himself on top of her. She laughed, making no resistance. No, it should not be said that she gave in so easily. She went wild, kicked out, arched her back to unseat him. But he held her down with all his weight, she felt the rough coat, the scarf. Now he wanted her badly. She wanted him. Her struggle was an additional provocation. She felt the man's fingers searching her out. She gave herself a little more. He held her there, folded in his arms as if she were sleeping. She opened a little more . . . remembering Psyche-Springtime . . . she wanted to know and let herself go. Rodin's sculpture appeared to her: he had called it *Psyche-Springtime*. The violence of the gesture fascinated her – and she also wanted him to force her. His finger gently penetrated her from behind, without any embarrassment, then, with her hand she helped to separate her buttocks. Camille saw the shaft on which she sank the great lump of clay, the soft black earth, the pivot that anchored the emerging form as she kneaded, creating anew – Camille was the pivot. And Rodin manipulated her, took her, kept her, "No, not yet . . ." She was crumbling, the earth slipping, the clay was about to escape. No, there he was, against her once more. She was retaken, reassembled. He penetrated her, raised her on his upright sex, plunged into the mire. He flattened her as she deployed herself around the mother stone, the vault key. He buttressed himself, striking front to back. Ogive, circle, rose window, trefoil – the black rose. Prodigious arabesque of life and death. Seed and dung. The cloaca but also the belly. The end and the beginning. The alpha and omega, a whole world suspended in a second, a world – a second – stopped in its course . . . What was that secret playing between their two steaming mouths?

Glistening, luxurious, spent, perfumed, they slept now. Engulfed by each other, absent from the world.

Letter *from the Asylum*

Actually, they are trying to force me to sculpt here, and seeing that they can't they are making all sorts of trouble for me. But that won't convince me, on the contrary.

M UST WE THEN assume that by dint of frequenting sepul-
chres, sculpture today is so dead an art that it has lost its very
reason for being? No indeed . . .

"But henceforth proscribed from the public square and open air,
sculpture, like the other arts, withdraws into that solitary room where
the poet shelters his forbidden dreams." (Paul Claudel, *Camille Claudel,
Statuary,* August 1905.)

The rooms of Neubourg Folly.
She had said: "It's folly!" She had laughed. "It's too expensive, this
old place!" He had taken her in his arms and murmured: "My own
folly." They had run through the fifteen rooms of Clos Payen, losing
each other only to find each other again in their "Neubourg Folly."

She had since learned her lesson – never to use that word. "That was
folly," "They loved each other madly – to the point of folly" . . .
Never, do you understand?

In the depths of that back room where they had left her, her only remaining freedom was to say NO.

With her ten mute fingers, today she had decided to shout his absence.

Forever?

Like Orpheus, she dared to confront the underworld . . .

The Princess

O hands! O arms! I remember!
I am nailed here by those hands!
And broken, I fell to dreaming, unhappy woman!

PAUL CLAUDEL, *Tête d'Or*

H E WAS WRITING.
That was his secret. For months he'd seemed preoccupied, distracted. Paul wrote. One book was finally in print, *his* book. Camille was happy. The first edition. She was going to read all evening. He had left the book for her without a word; that was so like him! She had been out. It was still cold and she had wanted to make herself a good hot soup for the evening. For some time she'd felt chilled, overwhelmed by the desire to sleep. Some afternoons she gave in to it.

Paul had left the book without any explanation.

No commission, no sculpture in sight. Only her prodigious work for Rodin absorbed her. In any event she had no models, nor enough money to pay them, and even after several reminders Rodin had "forgotten" to provide them. She had said nothing, vowing never again to weep in front of him. After their "orgy," as she called it, they had taken coffee together. He had looked at her, almost shyly; she had asked him if something was wrong. He seemed to want to say something to her but he had kept quiet, content to repeat: "You sculpt like a man. Don't worry, you'll get there." He hadn't proposed anything concrete: she simply had to continue, she was sculpture, she *was*, that's all.

The month of February was almost over. They would be able to work longer hours. Rodin was preoccupied. She, too, would have liked to complain of too many commissions!

"We'll have to rework the hands of *Despair*, that little figurine. You looked like that the other evening, you know. And Eustache de Saint-Pierre, I'm not happy with how he's turned out. *The Burghers of Calais* is driving me crazy. I have too many things to do. I will never manage."

"But I love Eustache de Saint-Pierre. He is the most dignified, he has understood that there is no more to say, that now they must simply comply. He goes toward death directly. It's not that he is resigned, he goes, that's all."

"You will have to enlarge the hands for me, the hands of Pierre de Wiessant. I'm pleased with my study. One hand almost blaspheming, the other invoking."

"Eustache makes me think of the *God of Amiens*."

"Really? Oh, if I could even remotely approach the art of those great statues. I never get tired of visiting cathedrals . . . But Victor Hugo, no! I refuse to clothe him. I will not give in. What do you think of that, Mademoiselle Claudel?"

Camille was going to answer, but he added: "As for you, get dressed quickly or you'll catch cold. This isn't the time for my best technician to get sick." She had risen, a bit abruptly. He'd wounded her, no doubt, but didn't know how.

"You've told me that your brother wanted to take the foreign service examination? It was on 15 January, wasn't it?" he said, to make up for his tactlessness, and Camille had nodded her head. She didn't see how this related to their discussion.

"I am going to recommend him to the minister. He is a friend. It's probably useless, but you never know. Are you happy?" Camille was happy, certainly. For her brother . . . But what did that have to do with her? Besides, Paul didn't need any recommendation.

She'd gone to get dressed. At that moment she almost hated this smug man whom she probably should have thanked. If she could have done it, she would have made the ceiling fall on his head. Boom! The master, crushed! A pancake, a bag of plaster, of dust. And she? What was to become of her, tossed between Paul and Rodin? The way things were going, she could disappear altogether, they wouldn't even notice. A phantom between two men . . . Muse, model, sister, servant to two great geniuses! Monsieur Rodin had grabbed one arm, Paul the other, and they were sapping her strength a little more each day.

Tête d'Or. Paul Claudel. The book was there, waiting. Camille hurried. She was cold. She would open it only after dinner. She loved to dream over the title first. She often looked at books but did not buy them. "Tête d'Or" – that was beautiful. It sounded like a sculpture. To make a sculpture in gold, a head in gold. To chisel the gold directly. Pour the gold directly, mold it, make it surge from the crucible the way the alchemists did. She would not do Rodin in gold, certainly not. No, it would be a woman, a splendid woman, a warrior who would gradually be transformed into a saint. A Christ – wait a minute, another name with nothing feminine about it.

Earth. That's it, she would make a gigantic Earth-Woman about to sleep with a Sun-Man. She saw the feet of the goddess, sunk deep in the clay, crouching, nearly touching the ground, knees parted. Something fantastic, terrifying, and up above the luminous head, resplendent, transfigured. And the hands, palms extended, offering, giving, without violence, ready to welcome anything. She would be naked, the man lying under her, emerging from belly and earth at the same time.

Oops! The carrot had fallen. Camille bent down. Oh, no, two potatoes! An avalanche! For the moment she was sculpting vegetables. Monsieur Rodin must be enjoying a good soup with his Rose, "so obedient," as he said.

Camille bit into a carrot – if she began to eat a little here, a little there, there wouldn't be a soup. She quickly tired of cooking. But she was so cold this evening, she had to eat something warm. Chop the leeks, cut the potatoes into rounds, click, clack! click, clack! Camille amused herself, making sketches. It was gloomy and isolated at Clos Payen. Come quickly, spring. When spring came, Rodin always stayed late. Happily, Eugénie would dine with her tomorrow and stay over as well. Thanks to her father's intervention, Camille had obtained her mother's permission to have Eugénie come and keep her company once or twice a week. What a celebration each time! What happiness!

Tête d'Or. She gave in. She began to read, waiting for the soup to cook. In the glimmer of the burning candle she turned the pages and devoured the images. What a jolt! Like the wind at Villeneuve . . . She almost forgot that it was her brother's work. Here and there she recognized a detail, a memory, but the current carried her away. The rhythm!

The story of the young peasant Simon Agnel, his violence, his outcries. The meeting in the fields, as evening falls, with his former childhood companion, Cèbes. And the young woman Simon brings to the village to bury. She has died, died in his arms – so young.

> We have joined our mouths like a single fruit
> Having our soul for a pit, and she squeezed me in her
> > naive arms!

Camille laughed. She had recognized the Geyn's butte. It was her and it was not her. She remembered the anticipation, the two lost children growing cold, she and Paul squeezed against one another.

My God, the soup was boiling over! She poured the steaming liquid into the old chipped cup and continued. The two young boys have buried this young girl whom they both loved. There they are alone in the night, walking. The pages turned, the candle burned low. The field by moonlight, the pact of love between the two boys. Sensual, provocative. Cèbes kneeling against Simon:

> Something is dripping on my head.

She read. Paul sculpted words even more violently than Rodin sculpted the earth. Where did it come from, that violence, that luxuriance? After all, she knew so little about him. The two peasant boys embrace. Cèbes leaves now, he disappears into the night. Simon alone, Simon vows to do his work. Simon gets down, kisses the earth, and sleeps an ominous sleep.

Quickly, she turned the page: Part Two. The palace, the king, the princess, Cèbes dying. Death bursts out of the four corners of the palace – a ghastly cancer – it reigns everywhere, terrible, hopeless, and the adolescent Cèbes will not last the night. He is awaiting the return of Simon, who has gone to save the country; he will die.

Camille was in darkness. She'd forgotten to change the candle. She rummaged around. There on all fours under the table, where she had stored a box of candles. She had reached the part where the princess, on her father's order, is putting on a disguise. And there it is! She appears like a sun. She must surely be the Golden Head – Tête d'Or! But wait, since Cèbes called Simon the Golden Head, it must be him. The princess offers men grace, her grace.

> I stand along the ways and at the entrance to dances, saying:
> Who wants to exchange handfuls of blackberries for
> handfuls of gold?
> And weigh with its human heart an eternal love?

Camille could see them at dinner. Yes! Paul absorbed in chapter eight of Proverbs, that was four years ago. Already! Christmas Eve . . . Paul transfigured. The parable of wisdom. Camille read. Never mind the references, and even the story. It was the way Paul arranged the words that was truly fascinating . . .

The men reject the princess. Camille was cold. The kitchen was freezing. How long had she stayed there leaning over the little table, reading, rereading? She cut a piece of cheese, a hunk of bread, a bit of chocolate, and went up to bed. She would not be cold reading under the eiderdown. Quickly, she took off her skirt, her underskirt, kept on her wool stockings, and slipped under the covers.

> The beautiful and illustrious lady, who spoke just now, is
> no more.

Her back against the pillows and the peeling wall, she continued to turn the pages. Here was Cassius. What a victory! She would have liked to make a sculpture of the victorious Tête d'Or as he is described by his lieutenant Cassius. What strength! This is what Rodin should use for the horses of Apollo. Her brother was a visionary – she kept the image for herself.

> O joy! Victory whinnying like a horse
> Rolled over the field of battle,
> Kicking with her glittering shoes, turning her
> Rainbow belly heavenward!

What genius. Here he was, Tête d'Or. She saw him – colossal, bloody – as the dawn broke. Camille didn't realize the time; overcome, she witnessed the death of Cèbes as the sun began to rise, as the mead-owlark sang.

Death.
Death is strangling me with her gentle, nervous hands.

Tête d'Or kills the king and he laughs and chases the princess. He wants everything. He is both man and woman with his long hair, his young face, and the perfidious smile of a young girl, but he kills without remorse. He laughs at murder, chases women, and the princess as well. So she is banished, taking her father into exile – her dead father.

Camille was not expecting this madness, this marshaling of word, of sound.

Part Three. Camille stayed there, curled up in her bed, alone with Tête d'Or. Tête d'Or beaten, abandoned, dying on that stone at the edge of the world. Camille was up there, she was on the Chinchy butte, the trees aflame in the sun, that sun expiring as Tête d'Or expires, lying naked, wounded. And the princess, nailed by the hands like a hawk, half raped by a deserter – supreme dialogue! The bells ring out three o'clock. She is going to die, crucified. In a last kiss, she embraces the man who has just recognized her in everyone's eyes as the queen.

It is you, beloved!
This is beyond grief.
Let me die by your hand!
I was born to live. And I am dying for . . .

Camille closed the bitter book; she was still there in the wind of Villeneuve, while the sun was going down. "My little Paul." The prin-cess slept at his side, there. She saw them both, golden tomb figures, stone sleepers, sculpted in his words. She had never read anything like it. That swift writing, flamboyant, jagged, restrained, he too had the gift, the gift of life, he wrote.

But why was he going into the foreign service? That was folly! He was a poet. What would he do in those gloomy offices full of bureau-crats? Hadn't he mentioned the other day that he wanted to go away, to leave the family, to leave everything behind? She thought of Rimbaud. Yes, he wants to join him. Surely. And the princess? Camille didn't know of any girlfriend, any woman. Where had he found her?

Camille smiled. Was she the one who had inspired him? She could see the scene again. Yes! She had come upon a manuscript, "The Sleeper." How long ago was it – yes, it had been two years ago. She had been looking for a pencil. She had been at Paul's.

"But what's this? Can I read it?"

"If you like."

A little poet in love with the beautiful Galaxaure. She had recognized the Chinchy woods, and there the old Night-Dance. "She is beautiful, Galaxaure. She reminds me of Rodin's *Danaïd*. You know . . ."

"You are not the model this time. Believe me." Suddenly he had turned toward her, aggressive. "Keep reading, you will recognize yourself further on."

Strombo, the huge, horrible female monster snoring in the grotto. The drunken woman who almost swallowed the little slip of a poet, the ogress with her big belly, a "swooning whale" on her back, waving her legs in the air. She had thrown the book at his head. He had laughed, delighted at making her angry. And after all, he was right. No one is really the model for a work. She herself welded various elements together which she constantly reworked. Her sculptures told a story, but they lied as well, faithfully. Models were only an artist's pretext. How many times had she perceived that the model was merely the fulcrum for her dream?

That made Monsieur Rodin angry: "The imaginary doesn't exist. Rely on nature. Be savagely truthful!" Camille had smiled. "There's no creation involved. Create – a useless word."

But at the same time he berated those who slavishly reproduced details: "You must address yourself to the soul."

Paul had done that! Her sage of a brother! She had wanted to tell him. He couldn't be a bureaucrat, an ambassador, or whatever. He had to write, to pursue his dream to the end.

They had made a pact, the two of them. The cemetery at night, the howling wolves . . . He had taken the sword of Sieglinde and Siegmund, they had cut their wrists and mingled their blood.

"Paul, don't leave me."

Paul was ten years old, she felt she was losing her blood, she had sat there on the stone, lost in the middle of the heath.

"Paul, Paul . . ."

188

"Bitch, bitch, you've slept with him!" He leaned over, the child of light, she saw his bronzed lips, his young mouth, his ardent eyes, he leaned over, closer, she was burning, he leaned closer still, she felt the kiss. The child withdrew, laughing, his long curls danced. He held out his hands to her, she was the child, she – the giant. Statue of white gold. Paul was at her feet, he was slowly dying.

"You shouldn't read. You shouldn't read." Yet she couldn't stop herself from reading the title: *Une Mort prématurée*. Again she drew near the young man, who was gold like her; he murmured: "Let's go! I've done what I've pleased, and I will die by my own hand."

"Hypocrite! Hypocrite!" She burst out laughing. Suddenly he got up again and ran away.

"Come play with me. Death to you."

Camille was soaked. She had just awakened. The candle had gone out. The dawn grew pale . . . What had happened? Had she been dreaming? Yet she knew. *Une Mort prématurée* did exist. She had forgotten, but she could still see Paul's anger when she had glanced through the pages on the table. She remembered certain lines that had particularly struck her.

Remember! Remember the sign!
Everything is over. Night elides the name.

And Paul's frightful rage, pulling, tearing the pages: "Get out of here, never set foot in my room again. Go away!" Why had he been so brutal?

Day broke. No more sleep. Suddenly her head was spinning. Nausea overtook her. Quickly she hurried out of bed, toward the washbasin. Along with the fear that gripped her was mingled an elusive and mysterious feeling of pleasure. She had broken all the taboos.

A child was already waiting for her.

Letter *from the Asylum*

Today, 3 March, is the anniversary of my removal to Ville-Evard: that makes seven years doing penance in lunatic asylums. After tearing me away from my life's work, they make me spend the years in prison, a punishment that they themselves so richly deserve.

T HERE IS A HAWK nailed by its wings to the trunk of that pine
tree."

"It's a barbaric custom."

"You will take that bird's place very soon."

"You're not really thinking of doing what you say? You will not nail
me to that tree like a bird nailed by its wings." (Paul Claudel, *Tête
d'Or.*)

My little Paul!

Why had he written that . . . more than fifty years ago?

She had loved this terrifying story – the other face of reality.

The princess – "A Camille at Montdevergues, dreadfully old and
pitiful, with her mouth full of rotten stumps . . ."

There are two thousand others like her. Here at Montdevergues.

The Château
of Islette

MONSIEUR Rodin,
"As I have nothing to do, I am writing you again. You cannot
imagine how nice it is at Islette. I ate today in the middle room that
serves as a conservatory, where you can see the garden on two sides.
Madame Courcelles suggested to me (without my saying a word about
it) that if it were agreeable, you might eat there from time to time and
even always. (I think she has a burning desire to do so.) And it's so
pretty there!"

Camille raised her head. Through the open window she saw the little
wooden bridge, the river. She heard the mill wheel rhythmically slap-
ping the water. Not a breath of air today. She had eaten little, but her
right side ached. The child was bearing down, she felt it each evening,
now, wriggling its arms and legs. With her hand she felt for its head,
spoke to it softly. Old Madame Courcelles scrutinized her out of the
corner of her eye. She would have liked to have Victoire or old Hélène
with her, but that was out of the question. She had succeeded in hiding
her pregnancy. No one even suspected it. She saw so few people, and at

the studio her smock concealed everything. The studio! Yes, Rodin had hardly been reassured. He was afraid of Rose, afraid of a scandal, afraid of making a decision, but he had let her have this child. She'd asked nothing more.

Camille caught her breath. She just felt a good kick. She was doing so poorly today! The child had grown so rapidly.

Camille went back to her letter, the end of her tongue pointing against her upper lip. She was applying herself. Her pen was always drying out, her t's traveled across the page. He kept telling her, "Don't make your bars so long and hard; it looks like scratchings."

". . . and it's so pretty there. I've walked in the park, there is new-mown hay, corn, wild oats, you can walk everywhere, it's charming. If you are good and keep your promise, we will be in paradise."

Camille was waiting for him. Why had he gone back to Paris? To say that he wanted this child would be an exaggeration. One day – when was it? – at almost the same time of year, two years ago, they had been walking together, she had joined him part of the way home, they had just made love. He was on vacation with Rose, he'd returned to Paris for a friend's funeral; she was still in Paris, waiting to join her family at Villeneuve. She had said to him softly, "I would like to have your child." He had not responded, smiling absently, as if he'd been struck by a fit of modesty fueled by fear. She had joked, taken his arm. He hadn't answered her at all. She had just lightly spoken the very words that engaged all her being – her heart, her soul, her life, her art – and he seemed not to have understood.

Camille had a headache. The mill wheel slapped against the water. It was really very hot, too hot. The pen was dry again. As long as he came before the end of the week . . . He felt guilty toward Rose, so he often returned to the country to reassure her. Then, worried, he quickly came back to Azay-le-Rideau, where once more he agonized over Rose. Camille was stifling in this room. She went to the window, no air, nothing, nothing – slap, slap, slap in her head. Yet she loved this old château he had rented for her in Touraine. She took up the pen, dipped it in the inkwell, where was she?

". . . we will be in paradise. You will have whatever room you want to work in. The old lady will be at your feet, I think."

The infernal noise of the wheel again . . . She got up, soaked a handkerchief in the basin, sat down again, and put the linen square on her forehead before taking up her writing.

"She told me I should go bathing in the river, where her daughter and the maid go quite safely. With your permission, I will do so since it is a great pleasure."

She was really having difficulty breathing today. She felt the child, who must be pressing on her lungs. Her heart sometimes skipped a beat. She had to finish this letter, he had to come.

". . . pleasure, and that would spare me going to the hot baths at Azay. Please be so good as to buy me a little two-piece bathing costume, blouse and pants, in dark blue with white bands (size medium), in serge, at the Louvre or at Bon Marché or in Tours!"

No one would see her bathing. She could bathe in the river. She was six months pregnant, and she was used to the cold water. But why wasn't he there? She had a backache, a headache. Slap, slap! Slap, slap, slap! The sound hammered and hammered in her skull, her heart, her kidneys, everywhere . . . what was he doing there with Rose? Had he forgotten that *his* child was taking shape? You didn't abandon a sculpture that way . . .

"Monsieur Rodin, I beg of you, hurry."

"I sleep in the nude to convince myself you are here."

Yet he was happy when he came to their château. She teased him, she called him her Bluebeard, and he called her "my princess." That made her laugh. If only he knew. Paul, where was Paul? If he were there, at least . . . That old Madame Courcelles frightened her. She was like the fairy Carabosse.

The elegant Renaissance château of Islette . . . She was comfortable there, even if she wondered whether he was hiding her away, whether he was doing it to conceal her pregnancy. So what? For a month she'd been living quite happily like a recluse, she had sculpted, made drawings, the weather had been lovely, and the child had thrived – that child who would resemble them both – a shared moment of eternity forever enlarged, multiplied.

When she had told him she was pregnant, he had seemed defeated, punished: "It was the other time, you know, such madness, such madness. I didn't know what I was doing. You were weeping. I knew nothing. And there, I was sure of it."

She had said nothing. How could he have any regrets? She hadn't wanted to hear more. She was the one who took all the risks! She, who withheld nothing – ever – giving herself entirely because she loved. Soon, she knew, the society of cowards would point a finger at her: an unwed mother. She already claimed it, that mark of "shame," but loud and clear!

Slap, slap! Black butterflies before her eyes. She missed him, she called to him. A torrid heat. She had kept on only her skirt and her camisole, yet she felt the sweat running down between her shoulder blades. The flowers she had gathered gave off a strong odor. She took up the pen once more.

"I sleep in the nude to convince myself you are there . . . in the nude . . . but when I wake, it's not the same."

Now it came, the storm rumbled. Good, it would cool things off a little. Her half-eaten bread and jam were there, near the white paper.

"I love you. Camille."

Her heart full, she added: "Above all, don't deceive me anymore."

She was going to fold the letter. Slap, slap, slap! . . .
"Madame Courcelles!" she had cried out, she had fallen; her body was caught in the wheel. "Madame Courcelles!" She was shouting now – her whole belly was tearing apart. She shouted louder, she was lying on the ground, shredded, twisted, her entire body shaken.

"No, no . . ." She wanted to stop them, she wanted to prevent them, then she fled, ran breathlessly, she fell, rolled down the rocks, the hard stone, there, they were upon her, she felt their hands, she shouted, she was gagged, tied down, flogged, hands swarmed over her belly.

"Don't kill me! I love him! No, I don't want to!" She opened, she opened her eyes, groaning. "Madame Courcelles, don't let them!"

The old lady was there, leaning over her. "Don't move, you're in good hands, it's nothing."

She turned her head. She saw the little blond girl, the little châtelaine with her sad, terrified eyes. "Get out of here, go on, scat! Go quickly and fetch the doctor."

Then Camille felt her aching head – slap, slap, slap! – the wheel turned, her head beat the rhythm. The neck broke, the head came unscrewed, fell into the water. The knives slashed the rest of her body; they had penetrated, opened her belly, emptied her out.

Rodin had been informed. Monsieur Rodin was there, standing by the bed. For three days it had rained without letup. The château seemed drowned in mist. No noise, only the water falling all around. Camille was lying in her white sheets. The emaciated face, the two dark circles, she said nothing, she had closed her eyes, she did not utter a word, her long hands flat on the bed, her hair undone, she rested, fragile. She knew. She had not asked but she had understood. They changed her, they washed her. She rested there, as though in her shroud. She had no more to say. She had lost – she had lost it! She had wanted only one thing, for them to leave her alone. The hemorrhage hadn't stopped, she felt it, as if her life were ebbing away drop by drop, slowly, softly – like sleep. She asked only to sleep. She had no more pain. She had become one with nothingness, launched on the dark river. The man there, standing beside her, was a stranger. What good did it do to hear the reasons, her fight with Rose? The worktable on her stomach? Heredity? Her mother's similar difficulties? Fatigue? What good did it do to "know"! The game was over. Death was always dealt to one player in a card party. She didn't feel like playing anyway.

Rodin was there at the foot of the bed. He hadn't even dared to take her hand. He looked at Camille. Camille, who was leaving him. Camille, who was letting him go – his Camille – his *Kiss*. He said nothing, for he carried death inside him. Maria was lying there and refused to allow him to think of that child, whose image he constantly repulsed. For months and months he'd been struggling with that sculpture. 1882: Ugolin, at once male and female. Today he had learned "Pain."

He'd closed his eyes. Why had he gone? Rose was well. He was doing a bust of her so that she would forget, so that she would stop harassing him. All that time Camille was alone, Camille fell, clinging to a little scrap of letter. They'd found the crumpled paper in her rigid hand – a letter to him. Monsieur Rodin carried death inside him. The gates of hell had shut upon him. The two swinging doors forever closed behind him. He was in hell. The drama was over. Gates of love and death. The death knell tolled. No, it was the little bell at the château.

For three days he was condemned, he was judged. He stood near her, his muse, she who had breathed life into him; for three days he heard her raucous laughter, her prodigious will to live. "But I love life!"

"Let her live. My God, I have believed in you. Spare her. Let her be well." Monsieur Rodin kneeled. If she were going to leave him, he would go mad with pain, mad like his father.

Her fingers had moved, she wanted to speak. Eyes opened. Slowly, gravely, she lifted her hand. Her frail fingers stroked the forehead, slid over the eyes of the weeping man.

The Little Châtelaine

To those who love me and whom I love — to those who feel rather than those who think — to dreamers, and to those who have trust in dreams as the only reality.

EDGAR ALLAN POE
Dedication from *Eureka*

W HITE FROST. The day like a blank page.
She had been thinking all day. Walked a long time. Hours and hours. It had been this way for some weeks. Today she had made her decision. It had taken more than a whole year – another year had once again slipped through her fingers. She had done nothing: it was time to gather up the threads, to rework her life stitch by stitch. Since death had not claimed her, she'd had to force life to enter her anew. She had raised up her head. Little by little her strength had returned. She was twenty-seven years old. The month of January was almost over. She could feel spring coming, in her legs, in her body. Even if outside a great white silence covered the village. It had taken a long time before she could get up and savor her days again.

Rodin came often to Azay-le-Rideau. He was working very little, with difficulty. The couple was seen neither at salons nor exhibitions. Camille's parents thought her departure was some new whim. Mademoiselle had withdrawn to the country in order to work better. Not once had her mother written to her. Camille only corresponded with her brother. One day she would tell him what happened. Perhaps, she didn't know. When she had felt stronger, she had made the journey to Paris. Her father had remarked that she looked unwell. "The country air doesn't seem to be doing you any good. You must stay shut in, sculpting. You might as well be in Paris . . ."

It was easy to see that her father was saddened. In Paris no one mentioned her name. He had surely hoped for fame, at least for her sake, but she seemed to be forgotten, and she herself had stopped struggling. He found her attitude rather cowardly. "You must fight, Cam. Attack, don't let them walk all over you!"

She would have liked to tell him what had happened to her, far from Parisian society. The important thing had been to restore herself, to reassemble the scattered fragments. She seemed more hurried. But today, the time had come. No, she was not going to become a Rose! She had made her decision. Thanks to the little châtelaine.

When she was ill, the little blond girl had come every day. At first, Madame Courcelles had tried to keep her away. She had been afraid that this child would only reopen the wound; in the beginning, when Camille saw her, the tears would flow. She saw the little girl waving to her at a distance, as though through rain. Then little by little she had grown accustomed to her presence, to the flowers she brought her. One day, she had brought wild strawberries. And then in the autumn they went on long walks together, the little hand guiding the still unsteady, larger one.

In the beginning, Jeanne, as she was called, spoke little. Someone must have told her not to tire the young woman. But from day to day she'd grown bolder, asking Camille innumerable questions, demanding answers. And then one day, hopping from one leg to the other, she had looked at her. Camille was resting, stretched out in a wicker lounge chair, still weak. Camille had opened her eyes, and the little girl had held out a pencil and paper: "Teach me, you know how. Teach me." Camille had recoiled, but the little hand held out, Jeanne's manner, her eyes wide open in quest of the magic drawing, her dream, had all broken down Camille's resistance. Camille had settled down and begun the drawing. This had lasted the entire afternoon. The little girl went constantly to look for paper. "Do more, Camille!"

"But I can't see anything now." The sun had set before the little girl was willing to give up. Camille felt exhausted. Jeanne had carried off all the drawings like a great treasure.

The next day the same thing happened again, but this time Camille managed to pace herself, demanding a rest at snack time.

Day after day, the little girl was learning, even trying to draw an animal or a flower herself. Rodin had found the two of them one day leaning over the table, the brown-haired young woman and the little blond girl. Their two heads were together over the drawings, the pencils . . .

"But what's this?" He had grown pale. The little girl had held out a magnificent, highly detailed drawing: a startled rabbit.

It was the rabbit she often brought with her, who hopped over the drawings or nibbled at them, to Camille's enormous rage. She called him Matuvu.

"Auguste never could have done such a drawing. And how I would have liked, I would so much have liked . . . to teach him . . . Beauty."

Camille had looked up. He was upset. What an idiot! To come and talk to her about his son, Rose's son, a good-for-nothing who spent all his money on drinking and loitering, when she had just . . .

He had muttered, "Forgive me, Camille." He had left, she had seen him through the window, leaning on the little bridge, his eyes lost in the distance.

A little hand had pulled at her skirt: "Hey, do you think Monsieur Rodin will take my drawing!"

"Of course, dear," Camille had said, stroking her cheek.

Then the time had come when she had been able to return to Paris. Paris! Her birthday, her twenty-sixth. She had forced herself, she was there at the family table, she'd felt like crying. Happily, Nini, Eugénie, was there. She hadn't said anything to her, but Eugénie had understood. Camille had not been well. The snow, the great white January frost. Her color came back. Like that evening just a year ago. Thanks to long walks and him, the young man. With him she began to recover the desire, the wish to sculpt. She had already seen him at Mallarmé's. Mutual friends – Monsieur and Madame Codet – had introduced them.

She could see the café as if it were yesterday. Everything was swept clean, like a first blank page. There were painters, journalists, joyful bohemians. Claude Debussy had introduced her to everyone. Some people had smirked. "She's well known, your friend."

"She's a sculptor."

They were young, they were nearly the same age. They'd known each other only a short time and they were already talking together, discovering the same passions. Hokusai, especially, had immediately brought them together. He, a bohemian musician, and she, still weak, leaning her head toward him. And Camille had rediscovered laughter; she had escaped for the first time in years from the silence of the studio, from Rodin's anguish, from Monsieur Rodin's commissions, from Rose, from patriarchy. She had discovered that she was young, that she was twenty-six years old. Claude was twenty-eight. She contemplated his brown bangs that poorly veiled the two protrusions on his forehead, his nocturnal eyes. She admired his long, agile, nervous hands.

She had finally escaped from the old château, from her reclusive life. Claude was there, like a half-brother. And she had wanted to live, to rush off on her two feet, limping as she went, as if to fly away . . .

"What are you saying, Claude?" She was laughing, a bit out of breath. He had nothing but debts, had left Rome before his *Prix de Rome* ran out, he was enthusiastic, vibrant, impassioned, no second thoughts.

Camille looked at the amber face, the disheveled hair, the enormous pupils, he was like a hunter on the watch, he was describing a melody to her – there were cellos on the lower end: mmmmmmm . . . Then he miaowed with his mouth closed, clicked his tongue, danced, laughing his wild laugh.

Camille felt light, she wanted to get up, too. They left together. He accompanied her.

A white day, a smooth patina – a page, an endpaper . . .

They saw each other again many times. They were always together. Did she know Turner? But how could she? He was astonished by her level of culture, the variety of her knowledge. Thanks to her English friends she had seen reproductions of Turner's work. Rodin had spoken to her about him but didn't think much of him. Despite his great friendship for Claude Monet, Rodin was not following the same path. He had his own way, in his view, and nothing drew him to those artists who were called the "Impressionists." In any case, painting and sculpture were two completely different arts. Rodin went infrequently to Mallarmé's, rarely visited other artists: he sculpted. He was past fifty, stubbornly holding his ground, for he knew he already had one foot on the other side. At moments he despaired: if only he hadn't waited until he was thirty-seven to begin.

With Claude Debussy, Camille discovered her youth once more. Turner wasn't their only mutual passion; there was also Edgar Allan Poe. Sometimes, when Debussy had drunk a little and was excited, he would ask her for news of her old Klingsor. Then Camille would close her eyes a moment, keep silent, and make no response. For a few seconds he thought she was dead. He had brought Weber to rue Royale, where the elite of the artistic world met. One evening she had seen Marcel Proust there. She remembered it, Claude had seemed ill at ease. As she was surprised, Claude had admitted to being a clumsy oaf. He and Monsieur Proust had nothing to say to each other!

She preferred Reynold's, an American-Irish bar. It was the haunt of Toulouse-Lautrec, stable boys, jockeys, trainers, and there was music: the Englishwoman, her son, and the banjo. And there were other women who led unconventional lives. Other women who struggled on alone. That woman with the tired eyes, who accompanied her mulatto son on the banjo, what adventures had she had? Camille would have liked to speak to her, but she didn't dare. The other woman had looked at her rather haughtily. To that woman who performed every evening, Camille and her young man must have represented happiness and material comfort. She was only there to amuse them. So Camille had stopped going to Reynold's. She was not at home there either, amidst the shouting and laughter of the streetwalkers, the courtesans, the kept women flaunting their generous bosoms. On the other hand, the fashionable women, the society women of Weber's world, looked down on her disdainfully.

What she loved was to walk with Claude, to go to exhibitions, to admire a Hokusai together, and to listen to him play. They sometimes spent the evening with Claude's friends, Monsieur and Madame Codet, who always welcomed her warmly. She would sit down quietly, and then, while he played, she would draw.

Camille gained some distance on Rodin's technique, the strict explanations, proportions, models. With Debussy she realized that she was not alone in her preoccupation with the mysterious, the unspoken. Mist instead of muscle, in a way the right of transgression . . .

In the work of Hiroshige, Hokusai's contemporary, rain could become a silvery mist, a white rain that disappeared before touching the ground, or simple parallel lines.

They stood for hours looking at Hokusai's engraving. The enormous wave, engraved by the artist, unfurled before them in an astonishing perspective. "Drops of rain in the shape of animals' claws." The heavy head on the thin stem . . . Camille had grown thinner from day to day. She had the sensual pallor of the great Japanese engravings. His friend Codet had told Debussy that she was the only sculptor to shape marble directly. How did she do it? What terrible power did this "Unknown Woman" conceal? She seemed to pass through life and leave behind her a compelling, contaminating trail. The sweetness of living without life, the dream entwined with nothingness, and the smile . . . A smile that touched your soul!

One evening they had drunk a little. The air was close. A moonlit night. They were laughing. The street was icy. They slid, skated. He was walking her home. She had forgotten that she was marking the time as he sang her a song. She would have liked to waltz; she had never had such a mad notion. He had taken her in his arms, enfolding her on the white road, and they had turned round and round. Her foot had slipped, the one that limped, so he had gripped her more firmly, holding her tight. She had leaned her head on his shoulder. She was there in his arms, impalpable; the chignon had slipped, the long hair had fallen on her shoulders, he looked at her, the snow powdered her with pale gold; she turned around and around, her eyes distant. She looked like Ligeia, Morella, the heroines of Edgar Allan Poe, she seemed to carry death within her, the coming of death, the phantom of this night; he held her tight – dreading that she would disappear – a light vapor – and he would be left with nothing. He had stopped moving for a moment, the couple suspended an instant on the verge of the impossible, he had whispered near her pale, trembling lips: "You are strangely beautiful when I hold you like this. You are so beautiful, you look as though you are about to die."

He leaned toward her a little more. Her eyes widened in fear, in madness, he said to himself, in madness . . . She was seeing something far behind him, she could make out something or someone . . . "Nevermore! Nevermore!"

Now she had offended him. She had run off, limping, distraught. She had melted like the snow, into the snow, like an apparition. For him, "the dream of that dream."

A day like that one, with hoarfrost everywhere. She had been there, like today, in front of the mirrors. She had spent the night curled up, her teeth chattering. In the morning, she had left to go back to Azay-le-Rideau. It had been just one year ago. She no longer knew whether she had lived the scene or only dreamed it. One thing was certain: that night she had left the man abruptly.

No more music. The empty, sad château. Today she was leaving Monsieur Rodin. A life remained to be written.

Almost twenty-eight years old. No salon, no sculpture. It was time. Neubourg Folly and its mirrors, the château of Islette – she was leaving all that behind. She was there alone, as before, in the middle of the room, but this time she would not leave at dawn for Azay-le-Rideau. She saw herself there, reflected in the mirrors. She held her bundle in her hand, her dark cloak weighing rather heavily on her shoulders. It was time to leave. The main room . . . The voice stopped her for a moment: "Beauty changes quickly. True youth, in which the body, full of new sap, realigns itself in its sleek arrogance and seems at once to fear and to beckon love, that moment lasts only a few months. Not to speak of the deformations of maternity, the fatigue of desire and the fever of passion, which quickly slacken the tissues and relax the lines. The young girl becomes a woman: that is another kind of beauty, still admirable but less pure . . ."

His voice. That was before. But she was no longer listening. He had been speaking. She had listened to him receptively, and thought his words were beautiful. But only today had she really heard them – their meaning was ridiculous! He was talking nonsense. Less pure! And what about suffering? And patient love? And "The Beautiful Helmet-Maker's Wife"? And what about humanity in all its tenderness?

"You're wrong, Monsieur Rodin!" She straightened up and made a face in the mirror. She put on the top hat. Well, he had forgotten it there, so she imitated him, she made faces, once more mischievously malicious.

Camille had taught the little châtelaine, with her funny little face, to knead the clay, to work the earth. And then one day it was clear, she had made up her mind. She and Rodin had been working on his *Balzac*. The summer before, the summer of '91, he had gotten a commission for *Balzac*, a colossal statue. Then he had looked for models in Touraine, she had read him whole pages, talking things over with him, as usual. She was as passionately involved as if it were her own sculpture, as if it were a commission she had been given, and suddenly she had noticed the little girl behind her. Furious at being left out, jealous of Monsieur Rodin, she had imitated him, struck poses, touched her finger to her brow, pursed her lips.

Camille had all she could do not to laugh. "Vanity of vanities!" She had seen herself behind him. But what was she waiting for? She was no longer sculpting, no longer creating. How was she any different from Rose?

"I am going back to Paris."

She had made a clean break, interrupting his momentum. She had taken the little girl in her arms: "You will come too, from time to time, won't you, my little woman, that's the only place for sculpting, isn't it, Monsieur Rodin?"

"I have shown her where to find gold, but the gold she finds is her own . . ."

She took off the top hat: "Good-bye, Monsieur Rodin!"

It was scarcely one year ago, on a white day like this, that she had left the other man, broken. "Good-bye, Monsieur Debussy!"

She was condemned to be the eternal fugitive. She picked up her bundle. She would return to take her other things – later. She had rented a studio. New address: Camille Claudel, 113, boulevard d'Italie. Monsieur Rodin had been informed, but he hadn't believed she would do it. She carried her *Çacountala* with her. It was heavy.

Three years of silence. She had closed another door.

Letter *from the Asylum*

I would so much like to be at home and close my door. I don't know if I will be able to realize this dream, to be at home!

113, Boulevard d'Italie

O true sons of the earth! O oaf with big feet! O truly
born for the plough, dragging each foot in the furrow!
O fate of an Immortal attached to this gross idiot!
It is not with the lathe and chisel that you make a
living man, but with a woman.

PAUL CLAUDEL, *La Muse qui est la grâce*

CAMILLE WALKED straight ahead, at random. She was discovering Paris. She was discovering the city anew. She felt that she
was free, looking at the street scene, at the spectacle of daily life with
her big, wide-open eyes. At last she could breathe. The month of June
was bursting with promises, with buds, with children's laughter.

Camille walked rapidly, sometimes stopping abruptly to make a
quick sketch: of that woman going to her appointment, of those two
young people, of that hesitant man. She was on her way. A woman.
She was born in a village of three hundred households, her work was
sculpting, she was walking in the street. A woman. It was indeed the
street that inspired her. A passerby, a family on the bench, workmen
busy at their work inspired her with a vision of future projects.

With her head full of images, of visions, she went back to 113,
boulevard d'Italie. She'd been in her studio for several months. She was
going back to *her* studio to begin modeling. She had to make up for lost
time. She sculpted, she modeled, she searched.

Yet another year lost, but next year she was determined to exhibit some new sculptures. She was no longer working for Rodin, she had time. Hadn't she already lost too many hours waiting, waiting for him?

He hadn't believed her, figured she was just talking nonsense. And then it had happened. He had returned to Clos Payen. No one was there. Death in the soul, he had stopped renting the old place. The placard swung again from the wrought-iron gate . . . Camille had passed by . . . Her studio was a few doors away.

"Well, Mam'zelle Claudel, you've done enough, a good stretch. Look at your boots. You are going to wear out your legs!" Camille laughed. The concierge was her only confidante. Otherwise, she had no visitors, she wanted to work as quickly as possible. But happily there was Pipelette: she never stopped! From her Camille knew everything that happened in the neighborhood.

Of course, Camille wondered whether she wasn't the butt of gossip herself. But she was in too much need of company to risk the smallest remark to her concierge. And then idle gossip amused her. On the other hand, her brother Paul, who came on occasion, couldn't bear the aggressions of this Cerberus. That was what he called her: Cerberus.

"Say! Your Cerberus tossed her bucket at my legs the moment I came in."

"She was washing!"

"I just had time to jump aside, or I would have been soaked."

Pipelette grumbled: "If it isn't a shame, a young fellow like that, always laced up in his shoes, I'd polish them up, I would!" And Camille laughed, with her laugh that had grown even more raucous.

Silence. Solitude. Camille was battling. She would triumph at the next Salons. This very year she had reworked the bust of the master and cast it in bronze. She had seen Rodin again. He did not understand. She had left him and she had paid him a certain homage. He was overwhelmed. "To sculpt Rodin, Camille has done a Rodin." Word of mouth carried the comment to her, and Camille counterattacked: "Precisely! How express the man without his own paw print!"

She braved public opinion, everyone believed they had broken off. She was living alone, no longer worked in his studios, and yet there she was with the master, more beautiful than ever. She had matured. Her eyes still more savage, but everyone could see that she had acquired a certain self-assurance, an inner peace. She was determined, and it was he who stayed beside her, silently, somewhat retiring, almost disappearing. She had placed her cards next to the bust. Everyone could read:

Mademoiselle Camille Claudel, Statuary
113, boulevard d'Italie

After the Salon, she was named a member of the National Society of Fine Arts. For work done alone she had received good notices. They had praised the use "of reddish or green tones in her bronze, which enhanced the face of the great sculptor." They cited Leonardo da Vinci. Raoul Sertat, in *La Gazette des beaux-arts,* was enthusiastic. Rodin had not exhibited. But thanks to her, his name was on everyone's lips.

She was a member, but "everyone knew why . . . He was behind her." This kind of remark provoked even Rodin's anger: "Everyone acts as though they think Mademoiselle Claudel is still just my protégé, when she is a misunderstood artist." Or they compared them to each other, as if hoping they would tear each other apart.

"Listen, M'sieur Rodin, he came by. He'll come back soon, he said." Pipelette had appeared . . . Camille stopped her gesture. She had been in the midst of raising her arms. She was afraid to tire them; when she came home, she put on her clogs, her feet naked.

Rodin had come. Sometimes he seemed to hesitate, as if he were worried. Yet he had helped her. She would have preferred to go out alone, but she hadn't any advance money, and the commissions had not materialized. Her sister Louise had married, and for the moment her parents couldn't lend her anything. "Let her shift for herself!" She hadn't sold anything. She should have cast *Çacountala* in bronze, but it was too expensive. Yet to sell something you had to place examples of your work, copies. He had already offered to help her so that she could exhibit the bust of Auguste Rodin. She would reimburse him. "It doesn't matter," he had said. But she stuck to it, set on the idea. He had shrugged his shoulders. When the second half of the rent on the studio fell due, she found she was penniless. Despite all her savings, she couldn't manage it.

Rodin had commissions. His *Balzac* was going to be magnificent. His friend Émile Zola had struggled to help him get the commission.

The monument to the painter Claude Gellée, *The Lorrain*, was going to be inaugurated at Nancy. As for Rodin, he had been named chevalier of the Legion of Honor.

"What day is it?"

"The ninth of June. If that isn't bad luck!"

For some unknown reason, according to the concierge it was bad luck! Camille smiled. The inauguration of *The Lorrain* had taken place the day before yesterday. Camille had not yet heard any news. No doubt he had come by to tell her.

"Oh, Mam'zelle Claudel, Monsieur Rodin, he was green with rage. He won't cool down!"

"At me?"

"No, the newspapers. Down in Nancy. The inauguration . . ."

Camille was worried. It must have gone badly. It was bound to happen. Camille could see the study for the horses. A disaster! Nothing was right. He should have renounced the commission. She had difficulty imagining the sculptor of *The Gates of Hell* creating a monument to someone known as "the painter of light." He had wanted this commission. She could still see him in a studio on rue des Plantes, dressed in his black suit, polished shoes, top hat. And she had laughed to see him dressed like this, pompous and proper – *m'as-tu-vu*. Wait, Matuvu! She absolutely had to have some news of Jeanne. It had been three weeks . . . Well, she would see her again next summer at Azay-le-Rideau. She had held her sides laughing, and he was furious. "I've just come from the minister. I am going to do the monument at Nancy."

No, she would never get herself up like that for a commission. How could he have done it? Where was his smock, his simplicity, his artisan's hands, his worker's toil in this hodgepodge of pedantry? And as for her, she would have had to put on a hat, a violet, to see the minister. It had all become ridiculous. He was on the verge of being ridiculous as well.

"Look, there he is, your man."

The concierge didn't miss a thing. She wanted to know. Were they together, those two? She had listened at the door, spied on them – in vain. No, impossible! He was dressed up again, as he'd been that day. Camille spied him in the courtyard, which she called the Den of Thieves. Rodin lifted his pant legs, stepping through the debris. She did no better with her hem always in her hand . . . She tried to stifle a laugh: poof! his hat landed in the pool with the little boats. The children shouted joyfully – her little friends, the three plagues, as she called them tenderly, whooped and hollered. He would have to change!

Madame Busybody rushed out. A fine, well-dressed gentleman. Since this morning, Monsieur Rodin had risen in her estimation; she hated those penniless artists who never tipped her. Camille saw her retrieve the hat, chase the kids away, and talk to him. He looked worn out, crushed by events, quite bereft. Camille wanted to run to him. He seemed bewildered, lost in the middle of this courtyard.

Then she quickly opened the door, called him, went to meet him. He saw her, with her hem in her hand in the sunlight, one, one-two, one, one-two, her course slightly broken, her foot exposed just a little, her secret charm, and he clasped her, held her against him, murmuring simply, "I'm tired, so tired."

"Come . . . you'll feel better inside."

He let himself fall into the old wicker rocking chair, her old, worn armchair – the only thing she had brought from Clos Payen. A little later they had bought another armchair for him, "for evenings at Clos Payen."

A glass of cold lemonade. Where had she found it? She lived with so little and suddenly she had everything to give: calm, silence, quenched thirst, peace.

Her cool hand on his forehead. He felt it, that long hand he knew so well.

Then he spoke, telling her everything: the endless journey to Nancy, the Pépinière gardens, the president of the republic, Sadi Carnot, who was there to unveil the statue, the crowd, Léon Bourgeois, the minister of fine arts and public instruction . . . And the military music, the speeches, the statue unveiled, and suddenly the shouts of indignation, the crowd roaring, protesting, sneering, pointing fingers. He took refuge inside, but even there he could hear the remarks.

"Imagine, two little horses like fat spaniels, lost in a shower of putty . . . a bad job by a sculptor in too much of a hurry . . . "

"Listen, Monsieur Rodin, it doesn't make any difference. You've always been criticized. Remember *The Gates of Hell*, the *Victor Hugo*, and even the *Man Walking*, your first sculpture. It has never stopped. So let them shout." She found the words, she gave him renewed strength.

Once again she patiently inspired him with life, desire, faith in his work.

"Remember what you used to tell me. Patience. Patience! Take your time. Listen, you know what the great Katsushika Hokusai used to say, you know, the old fool for drawing. I often repeat his words to myself: 'Nothing I produced before the age of sixty was worth counting. It was at the age of seventy-three that I almost understood the true structure of nature. Trees, grass, animals, fish, insects. Consequently, by the age of eighty I will have made even more progress . . .'"

He looked at her. She had closed her eyes. She was there, squatting on her heels, she looked like an old Japanese monk in prayer, transfigured. He listened, full of respect and admiration.

"'At the age of ninety I will penetrate the mystery of things, at one hundred I will have truly reached a level of marvels, and when I am one hundred and ten, every part of my drawings, whether points or lines, will be fully alive.'"

She still murmured: "Katsushika Hokusai, born of unknown parents on the twenty-third day of the ninth month of 1760, at Edo."

Silence of a summer afternoon. She was quiet, kneeling, meditative, the sun-drenched courtyard behind her. They were there in the gloom, tranquil. The man and the woman, side by side, their two shadows sketching all the harmony of the world on the wall opposite them.

"Ay!" Camille cried and, laughing, fell on her bottom. "A cramp! I want to play the old Oriental and I get pins and needles!"

She hopped up and down, he rubbed her legs and helped her stand up. She was leaning on the package he'd brought. "And now, first, what's this thing trussed up like a sausage?"

He apologized, shyly: "It's me. I'm not very good at making gifts. I wanted to give it to you. I bought it at Nancy."

She hurried to open it. No one ever gave her gifts. Neither her father nor her mother . . . "You must have used all the string in Nancy!" she exclaimed, struggling with the knots. She stopped: she was holding a parasol, a magnificent red parasol, lacy, flamboyant!

He looked at her. Her cheeks were flaming. She was there in her old smock, one foot in a clog, the other bare, and she was contemplating the parasol. "It's too fine for me." Never had she seen such a beautiful parasol.

And suddenly the person who sculpted, who discussed materials all day long, who made tools herself, was overwhelmed. She was a woman after all, a woman entitled to a gift of something useless, superfluous. That was just what she needed – a frivolous thing, the gift par excellence, the gratuitous act. Slowly, with care, she opened the parasol, worried at any sound that hinted even slightly of a defect, a poorly folded spoke, as if her own life were at stake. Now she'd opened it completely, a huge sun above her head, a great thundering flower. She walked up and down, the woman, she was a woman carrying a parasol. She, the tomboy – a man had offered her this gift of love. She whose face was tanned by her long walks, and who was mockingly called the Moor.

"Camille! Camille! Come!"

He explained. She needed to continue working alone. She would keep her studio, he would help her, but he wanted to live with her. For months he had lived in hell, he couldn't do anything. She no longer needed him, he knew. Soon she would have commissions. The Paris newspapers spoke of a state commission, she had received the "silver medal in black and white." Furthermore, he had scolded *Le Courrier de l'Aisne*, which had ignored her. He had written to the editor-in-chief, and then Lhermitte had just told him that he was going to ask her to do his bust. She would make the bust of the great painter. He had not even thought of Rodin. No, she didn't need him to sculpt, but for him she was the woman he couldn't give up, his companion, his life, his wife.

Camille sat up at the last word: he wanted to marry her! So they might live together, love each other in the eyes of the world, her parents, her brother – and he also acknowledged her as a sculptor, as his equal.

"Do you want to, tell me, do you really?" He was going to rent an apartment at 11, avenue de la Bourdonnais. He had seen something quite good. It was time to settle his affairs . . .

Yes, she wanted to, really. She would keep her own studio, but life was going to be a celebration. No more long, gloomy evenings ending in desperate conversations with Madame Pipelette in order to avoid admitting to herself that she was alone; no more nightmares, just the other night, no, don't think about it – the horrible old woman – no more!

He was there as a fiancé. She stifled a laugh, the words were on her lips, "That's why you dressed up in your good suit! To ask for my hand . . ."

Someone knocked at the door. Oh, what did she want now? "I've cleaned your hat! And then there's this . . ." Camille was horrified, she had immediately recognized the piece of paper – it was a bill for the rent. What a shrew! The concierge was taking her revenge. She must have been listening at the window. Monsieur Rodin offered her parasols, an apartment! Well, let him continue paying the rent, and if he thinks of little gifts, so much the better.

Rodin hadn't understood any of this gibberish. Camille would have to be resourceful to find the money. Rose must do better than she did . . . Oh! to escape all this, the nights, the insomnia. Not to have to talk out loud to be sure she wasn't losing her mind.

The emaciated old woman had appeared the other night in the shadow, hideous. It was her child – her lost child, a little girl – but she already had the mask of an old woman.

"Until tomorrow, Monsieur Rodin." She had held out her hand. Frank, direct, she had said all there was to say in this clear, decisive reply. Her no was a terrible, violent, devastating no. And when she said yes, when she acquiesced, it was dazzling, full of light and trust. She gave everything.

Monsieur Rodin left. He did not walk, he flew. He hadn't seen the pool in the courtyard, but it didn't matter, he splashed royally.

"Oh, you saw it, Mam'zelle Claudel. What bad luck. Those kids. He gave them money. This generation!"

"Oh, that's too much! Come on, it's not so bad, they've all gotten something!"

The concierge thought she'd certainly heard everything today.

Since returning from the inauguration, Monsieur Rodin hadn't taken time to change his clothes.

Letter *from the Asylum*

. . . *to refuse me asylum at Villeneuve. I would not make trouble the way you think. I would be only too happy to live an ordinary life and do anything whatever. I would not dare to move, I've suffered so much. You tell me that you'd have to hire someone to help me? How could that be? I've never had a maid in my life.*

Clotho's Waltz

*Oh whither shall I fly? Will she not be here anon?
. . . Have I not heard her footstep on the stair? . . .
Madman! I tell you that she now stands with-
out the door!*

EDGAR ALLAN POE
The Fall of the House of Usher

T HERE SHE IS!" She wrung her hands thankfully. Her saddened eyes looked at the crowd pressing around her. There was
something haughty or distant about this young woman almost twenty-
nine years old. Twenty-eight and a half, to be precise. Was it the slight
slackness of her mouth, the forehead that sometimes seemed furrowed
by a mild migraine? Her eyes were as huge as always, but those who
knew her sometimes caught a fearful glitter in them, or some strange
fixation. But who could compare the woman of yesterday to the woman
of today?

A man was there, still, silent. Young, draped in a large suit, an
oversized hat in his hand, he looked alternately from the artist who was
thanking him to the two sculptures that had provoked such contro-
versy.

The Waltz. Clotho.

Certain people recoiled in horror at the one entitled *Clotho*. The
little old woman in it took no notice of them. She flouted them, with
her scarred belly. One of her breasts seemed lost in a long string of pus,

while the muscular legs jutted out murderously – she killed – and she was laughing with her dreadful rictus. She advanced with ghastly steps, caught in an unwinding shroud.

Claude Debussy could not tear himself away from it. His brown eyes were fixed on this bleached phantom. Why had she created this sinister figure? She had named it *Clotho* – one of the three Fates, the one who presides over birth.

People grimaced, uncomprehending. They thought it ugly, obscene, almost vulgar. Women turned away from it, burying their noses in their perfumed handkerchiefs.

Then he looked at her again. Camille was there, leaning toward him, seemingly pleasant, but there was something spectral about her. All in black, almost masculine, her complexion wan, violet circles under her eyes, pale, too pale in the dark clothes. Lady Madeline in the story by Edgar Allan Poe! He had always thought that Camille belonged to the race of those cursed poets.

She came toward him. She saw him. She stood in front of him, as tall as he. She seemed happy to see him again, but deep in her eyes was the gleam of a hunted animal. He lightly rested his hand on her arm, as if he wanted to reassure her of his physical presence. He smiled at her. "A dream. I thought I was dreaming . . . Where were you all this time? You've done such good work!"

She smiled. "No comment, Monsieur Debussy."

He smiled in response, remembering. She did not like music very much. Rather, she hated concerts, the noisy people, the scraping feet, the discordant voices. With him she had acquired a taste for sonatas in solitude, in utter quiet. She would listen for a long time without saying anything. She didn't know enough about it. So instead of babbling superficial banalities, she would stand up when he had closed the piano and say to him, simply: "No comment, Monsieur Debussy." And he knew that for her, the artist of silence, this was a kind of homage.

He turned to her, indicating the two sculptures, and came back toward her. "No comment, Mademoiselle Claudel."

There she was, snatched up by a group of pedants who wanted to whisk her off; she gently repulsed them and came back to him for a moment, indicating the entwined, turning couple: "*The Waltz* – when I have the means I will make it in a more durable material. It is for you, I am giving it to you."

She had already gone. So he left the Salon, he didn't want to hear anymore, he carried with him the promise she had just made. *The Waltz*, *The Waltz*, which had lifted him for the space of a moment far above his unrelenting black melancholy. He trusted her, he knew that she would keep her promise. One day he would receive *The Waltz* – the couple fluttering in the wind of Death itself.

Camille watched him leave. With him, perhaps, everything might have been different. Perhaps! But she was jostled: "What! Those two vile rags! And again they're signed by Mademoiselle Claudel." She turned sharply, she identified the speaker: that fat, red-faced misogynist, Bouchot!

The two sculptures provoked questions and exclamations. In the distance, she remembered the voice of Debussy telling the story of the sad and despised clown who dreamed of flying away, the poem by Banville that he had recited to her one day.

> Finally, from his lowly platform
> The clown jumped so high, so high,
> That he cracked the tent top
> With the sound of horn and drum
> And, his heart flooded with love,
> He went to roll among the stars.

Their steps in the snow. One last time. A few small discordant notes.

"But why that horrible *Clotho?*"

"Come on, let's go have a drink."

Mirbeau took her by the arm, she could hardly stand up by now. She appreciated Octave Mirbeau. Of all the critics, he was the most courageous. Without equivocating, he dared to say what he thought. When Paul had sent him *Tête d'Or*, he had spoken of genius without fear of seeming ridiculous. He had been one of Rodin's first defenders. Forty-five years old, his hair parted on the side, a small mustache, elegant, affable, he too had heard Henri Bouchot's scornful remark. He comforted her. "Come. I have brought you my article."

They sat down in a little room, she began to read. Mirbeau looked at her. Her face was tense, watchful. Gradually she relaxed, gaining confidence.

The Salon of 1893, by Octave Mirabeau

"Mademoiselle Claudel is Rodin's student and Monsieur Paul Claudel's sister. Everyone is as familiar with Rodin as they are ignorant of Paul Claudel. Paul Claudel has written two books, two dramatic works, *Tête d'Or* and *La Ville,* which are – I beg the critics not to smile – works of genius, a genius still muddled at times, still obscure, but full of striking illuminations. I have said obscure and muddled, and that is, I think, to shore up my self-esteem, for if I do not always understand Monsieur Paul Claudel, if at times the rays of this vivid light are veiled to my eyes, it does not follow that the author must be blamed for something that may be only the weakness of my perception. But were his extraordinary work a thousand times more muddled, more generally obscure, we would still excuse it in such a young man, who hasn't the time to stop for signposts, in whom ideas are fermenting and rushing headlong like torrents, and whose brain is in a state of permanent creation; but I have written of genius, and that is the only quality one can attach to his name.

"Instructed by such a master, living in intellectual intimacy with such a brother, it is hardly surprising that Mademoiselle Camille Claudel, who is indeed part of his family, brings us works whose originality and power of execution surpass anything we can expect from a woman. Last year she exhibited the bust of Rodin: a marvel of powerful interpretation, of free animation, of great style. This year she is showing two strange, passionate sculptures, so original, so moving in their decorative arrangement, so deeply poetic and so masculine in thought that one is taken aback by such beauty in art coming from a woman. I like to repeat this surprise to myself.

"In *The Waltz* and *Clotho,* as these works are entitled . . . Mademoiselle Claudel has boldly tackled what may be the most difficult thing to render in statuary: a dance movement. Infinite art is required to prevent such a piece from becoming crude or fixed in stone; Mademoiselle Claudel has mastered this art. . . . "

She avidly read his description of the two statues. He had understood, he had seen.

" . . . intertwined. But where are they going, lost in the intoxication of their souls and their united bodies? Is it to love or death? The bodies are young, they throb with life, but the drapery that surrounds them, that follows them, that turns with them whips them like a shroud. I do not know where they are going, whether it is to love or death, but what I do know is that this group exudes a poignant sadness, so poignant that it can come only from death, or perhaps from a love even sadder than death.

"Who knows? Something of her soul, something of her heart has miraculously inspired it. . . .

"Mademoiselle Claudel, one of the most interesting artists of our time. Auguste Rodin can be proud of his student; and the author of *Tête d'Or*, of his sister. Mademoiselle Claudel is indeed of the race of Rodin and the family of Claudel."

She thanked him, but he felt something forced. She had tears in her eyes. Had he offended her?

"You know, it isn't out of friendship. Geffroy agrees with me, and so does Lucien Bourdeau. Just yesterday we were talking about it."

How could she explain to him that she'd had enough of being Rodin's student and Claudel's sister? They had her in a vise . . . Besides, neither of them was there. She was a sculptor, that's all. Camille Claudel, sculptor. Sculptor. A woman. Period.

"But where is he? I haven't seen him."

"In the country." She had answered like that, stupidly. If she were to lose the only friend who defended her, that would be a fine thing! But they all irritated her with their questions. They should have asked Rose where he was, what he was doing. It never stopped: "And what is Monsieur Rodin preparing for us?" "Surely you know his plans." "No, no. They are almost separated."

Octave Mirbeau noted her exasperation. They had come back toward the crowd, the questions proliferated. He understood that she was fighting against something. Auguste Rodin was not there. There must have been a reason. No one came. He suddenly discovered that she was alone. Terribly alone. Her brother was not there. He had never seen her mother. Her brother was away, he had heard that he was in the United States, and Auguste had not set foot in the Salon today. She held herself straight, self-sufficient – good stock! – but the sweat ran down her ivory forehead, her eyes grew wider, and she was about to fall. Why were they all after her?

Mirbeau remembered the remark Jules Renard had made to him at the beginning of the year; they had been talking together about Paul Claudel, and suddenly Jules Renard had tossed out: "Paul Claudel, yes! But his sister Camille – unbearable!" The others had laughed in the café: "Ah, yes, Rodin's muse! He, too, has lost his mind, poor man. He doesn't even sculpt anymore!"

Octave Mirbeau could still hear their vulgar remarks. And what about him? He hadn't even protested, content to add furtively: "But surely he's working, sculpture takes time. He must have something in the works. Probably the *Balzac.*" Today, in front of Camille, his cowardice made him ashamed.

"Come." He led her into the gardens, made her sit down.

She was there, depressed, mute, weary. An old woman abandoned on a bench. The cost was too high, too high. Mirbeau remembered Rodin in exactly the same position. When he had returned from Nancy. Prostrate, paralyzed. Two great beasts mortally wounded.

She murmured, "Thanks. I feel better. You can leave me. Thanks."

He did not want to impose on her, he reentered the exhibition hall. Someone came toward him. "She wasn't feeling well. The heat, no doubt. She may want to sculpt but she's a woman! Let's not forget that. And a very beautiful one as well, if I dared . . ."

Camille raised her head. She was packing her suitcase, her things for Islette. Preparing herself. This year she was going alone. She was making the journey for the last time. One more door she was about to close. A place she was losing. A last safe harbor they were taking from her. No more princess, no more little girl, all the multicolored balloons burst one by one.

Azay-le-Rideau. Islette . . . the trunks they'd packed together, the old wagon, the train. They would move in more comfortably later . . .

Little Jeanne had grown, she was kneading the clay better and better, she helped them now. Auguste Rodin was searching for his Balzac. They scoured the country around Touraine, scanning the countryside. Rodin was looking for an "ethnic type." Camille was reading him whole passages, he snatched up everything he could find, devouring it, claiming it. A medallion by David d'Angers, a portrait by Louis Boulanger, sketches, caricatures; a former tailor of Balzac's was still alive, they hurried to catch the train. In that village north of Paris, the bewildered man had taken an order for trousers, vests, jackets "to Balzac's measurements." Convinced that Balzac was dead, he did not understand; Camille had tried to explain more calmly. He obviously thought they were mad.

She had not yet told her mother about their plans. Nor her father. She would resolve the question after the summer. She, his wife!

And then two weeks, three weeks had passed. Several times Rodin had gone off to Paris. "You understand, I cannot leave Rose. She is ill." He would quickly return.

And then she, too, had needed to go to Paris to take care of things at her studio. Her work was not progressing. But no news from Rodin. He had been back in Paris for at least a week. With Rose. Not a word for her; a letter from the little girl, a drawing and a few lines: "Monsieur Rodin left this morning. I'm bored. When are you coming back? Matuvu is fine and sends love."

Camille remained alone in her apartment, stunned. She looked at the date. Why had he done this? She'd felt like vomiting, regurgitating her soul. She was shaken violently by nausea. A week ago he had left Azay, without waiting for her return.

She had spent the whole night walking, seeking an explanation. For a week he'd been there, in Paris. With Rose. A few steps away.

8 June 1893.

Today she was leaving for Islette for the last time, alone. She left him with his Rose. Now he wouldn't need to lie.

She would have no child. Camille had certainly seen his anxiety. He was careful now, he was afraid, not for her but for himself. She saw him again at Azay. She was happy, dared not believe in it, she said nothing, but he badgered her with questions. He doubled his precautions. And there she'd been in Paris, ridiculously useless, rotten fruit. "Those who serve men and those who serve nothing at all." Her health had not returned. The dips in the river must have given her a last illusion, a few weeks of respite that made her subsequent suffering all the greater.

She had stayed quietly stretched out part of the night, hoping that would calm her. She had dealt with it all alone. The next day he had left her a message; a child had brought it: "Will come this afternoon to the studio. I am back. Your Auguste." That was one year ago. Already . . .

She had not been able to drag herself to the studio. He had come, anxious. She had thrown her drawings at his head, the three drawings she'd done that afternoon. A series of drawings, one more frightful than the next. At first he had questioned her: Why was she sitting there on the ground, leaning against the bed? When she told him she was ill, explained what was wrong, she had seen the relief on his face – she would never forget that. So she had thrown her jealousy, her anger, the drawings at his head: "Get out, get out this minute. Leave me alone!" She had thrown him out, and the drawings had sailed after him, like the three dots marking a broken thought . . .

He had killed her child, he had killed childhood in her.

She was not sad. She had just triumphed at the Salon. *The Waltz*. *Clotho*. He had congratulated her. She would soon be thirty years old. She was going to become a very great sculptor. The rest hardly mattered. Life, everything she'd been denied. She would be a cursed artist. She was there, burning with fever. She had unburdened herself of *Clotho*, she had given birth to her anguish, now the way was clear.

Clotho. In one night she had put it down on paper, rooted it out of herself. Then to Monsieur Rodin's studio. He had suggested the materials. He'd received a block of stone that presented an interesting possibility. They had reestablished a relationship around their work; he helped her, she helped him. He no longer slept there, he was living with Rose again. Camille was constantly ill, she found excuses, she lived reclusively, at a distance. Her work was the only thing that mattered. She kept away from him, like a wild animal. Not even one hour of intimacy with her – she did not want that with him, she was out of reach. Distant, she worked.

Monsieur Rodin's studio, to see the block of stone! She had the key to rue de l'Université. He had told her to come when she liked. No one was there anymore. He had told her where to find it. Suddenly she saw herself – once, twice: two nearly finished sculptures . . . she knew she had been the model.

One in particular held her eyes. Then she began to cry: the plaster drapery imprisoned her, the two hands emerging like a supreme kiss. She was there, incredibly fragile, as if she had slipped into death and at the same time called out to someone: "Don't leave me." She thought of Cèbes, Cèbes dying as the lark sang. She was lying down, sculpted with such love. The other sculpture beside it was beautiful, but the first one gripped her, caught her so aptly. She would never be capable of such a prodigious homage to him. It had the quality of forgiveness, it was grace itself, eternity in a kiss.

He had written something in pencil. On the first sculpture: *The Convalescent;* Camille approached the second and read: *The Adieu* – his hand had trembled writing the words.

Silent tears ran down her face. For the first time in months she wept before the sculptor's work. Now she knew he had understood that day, had grasped it all in a glance. What good was it to fight against sculpture? Why insist on living with him? They told each other everything in stone itself, that was their true realm, their nuptial bed, the long desire between them that was constantly prolonged, reborn, and an absence that was as strong as possession. She would never have a husband, a house, children of her own. Just a stone, the stone of the permanent impossibility of their being happy together.

She had once more closed the door to the big studio. She spent that night at 113, boulevard d'Italie. In the glimmer of the candles she had chiseled out *Clotho.* Alerted by the uproar, Pipelette had decided she must surely have a madwoman on her hands. A madwoman, that Camille Claudel! She made a fire. She was sculpting. She's a witch. All night she was moving around, behind the windows, I saw her . . .

That night Camille had plumbed the depths of her private hell. *Clotho* emerged from the labyrinth of madness.

Be not ashamed, and tell him that you love me!

To see the face she will make, for such is cruel love!

It seems saccharine and soft, but it is barbaric and impudent, and it has a will of its own that is not ours and must be obeyed absolutely.

PAUL CLAUDEL, *L'Échange*

Drawing 1

A man is sleeping, still weary. An aged child crouches on the flaccid breasts of a shrewish woman – the familiar topknot of Rose Beuret, the man's sparse beard. Monsieur Rodin encloses the woman with his arms, frightened at the idea of losing her.

Title: *The Awakening. Beuret's Gentle Remonstrance.*

Drawing 2

A man and woman stuck together by their bottoms. Naked. She almost on all fours. Rose's chignon is falling over her face. The fingers are hooked, pressing into the ground. The back almost shaggy.

Monsieur Rodin is gripping the trunk of a tree with his two hands.

Title: *Glued Together – Cohabitation.*

Ah, so true! What a hold!

Drawing 3

Rose. An old woman – naked – brandishes a broom. The nose and the chignon give the face a hideous, menacing look. On the left-hand side of the paper, a man and a young woman entwined, chained to a rock. Irons on their legs. Irons on their hands. The chains bind them to each other and to the rock. Yet the young woman is still clinging. To keep him with her.

In spite of the black metal fastenings. The lovers are similarly naked.

Title: *The Cellular System.*

Camille had written the titles herself. I have seen the drawings. Ravaged by jealousy, they shout their despair.

The Vanished God

*How could the fire have caught? All the servants had
left, and only I remained. And as I was in the garden, I
suddenly saw red in the salon . . .*

*And I, too, was burning! And you, you too will
burn in hell, where the rich go who are like a candle
without a wick.*

PAUL CLAUDEL, *L'Échange*

SHE WOULDN'T LEAVE before Thursday, as it happened. He
had come by, left a note, probably to tell her good-bye. She had
to answer him. She couldn't leave him this way. He was anxious. She
was ill again. She hadn't seen him since the exhibition. He had heard
that she was not well, he wanted to know how she was; hearing from
her would reassure him.

So many things left to fold, to do here on this Thursday. She had
to write to him. She searched around the room, she no longer knew
where she'd put the writing paper, the ink. For some time now, objects
seemed to elude her hands, her eyes. Except when she was sculpting,
everything seemed hazy to her, distant. She no longer knew very well
where to sit, how to stand. Should she keep this apartment or abandon
it? Rodin helped her, as always, but what good were these two locations
that left her scattered, fatigued? She loved her Den of Thieves best.
She felt at home there.

"8 June 1893

"I was away when you came, for my father arrived yesterday. I had been home to dinner and slept there. As for my health, I am not doing better because I cannot stay in bed: there's always some reason to get up and walk around. It is unlikely I will leave before Thursday."

Her father, how proud he'd been when he'd read the articles by Octave Mirbeau! He had despaired for a moment. Now he felt confident again. Paul, too, must have read Mirbeau's article by now. Camille was waiting impatiently for a letter. Who could she ask to forward her mail? What was Rodin going to do? Stay in Paris, leave with Rose? So many things to resolve, alone again. Alone making decisions, alone . . .

The sun struck the white page. Her eyes hurt. She leaned back in the chair, turning her face toward the shady part of the room. What was that in the corner? The parasol, the beautiful red parasol! A few days after giving her this gift, he had invited her to an evening party; he wanted to introduce her to . . . Camille touched her forehead: she had trouble remembering all those names. She had jumped with joy. He would come for her tomorrow, at the same time. What? He wasn't staying! He had stood before her, embarrassed. Rose was not well. But tomorrow he would stay, he would take her out, he would introduce her to a group of interesting people. The red parasol had stood there since. A woman and four days of happiness. That was what she'd had in this apartment. That was just a year ago.

She had a headache, a red hot crown of iron – the pen fell, she picked it up.

She was there on her knees – begging and naked. He said nothing. He simply shook his head. Behind the door, guests, friends, fashionable women. They were jeering at her. She was naked, she had nothing to wear. If he walked out the door, she would die. She begged him. She held out her hands. She begged him. He retreated toward the door. She went toward him, mounting a campaign on her knees. She did not put her hands on the ground. Her open palms were extended toward him. He was there, he did not help her, he was against the door, she called, she called to him. He could do everything. He was the god, they all tore themselves away from her. Her knees hurt. But she went on, she had the feeling he was moving farther and farther away. She would never reach him. Yet he had been there a moment before, against her, he had held her tight, she had pressed her head against him, against his legs, and suddenly nothing, her empty hands . . . The door creaked on its hinges. They were all there, they had invaded the room, some in suits, others in evening dresses, she was there in the middle, they circled around her, she was there on her knees, on her worktable, humiliated. She couldn't see him anymore. They commented on her buttocks, her breasts: "No, the arm is too strong, look at the thigh, the badly turned leg, the twisted foot. Have you ever seen anything like it?"

He had gone back to Rose. Rose drew him, she put her arms around him, enveloping him, as though she were crouching on his back, her bat's wings spread, she dragged him off, they flew away . . .

Camille had fallen. Violently. She had slipped from the chair. Her head was resting on the paper. The sun beat down brutally. Everything was burning. Far away she heard Victoire's voice: "Don't be afraid, Mademoiselle Camille, you just need a little calm, shade. After childbirth it's always like that." The wailing of the child . . . To escape, fly away. She opened the parasol. She flew.

The room had turned violet, flooded with the light of a crazed moon. A woman was coming toward her, her skull shaved, Camille saw the woman lean toward her, gently caressing her long hair. She left again. What was she doing? Camille had raised herself up a little on her elbows, she heard the noise of metal, of steel, the old woman had grabbed her technician's scissors and was coming toward Camille. She looked at her hair: "No, I don't want you to, no!"

The old woman was there. No, she wasn't old. She was twelve years old. Jeanne looked at her, luminous, her two fists on her hips: "Come on, get up! What are you doing there? Come on, you're a big girl now!" She held out her little hand, Camille gripped it, hoisting herself up, the hand was so light. Camille felt supported, she was standing now.

But what had happened to her? She looked at herself in the mirror, a little pale – the sun was about to set. The room was peaceful, a miaowing next to the door, Camille went to open it. A tiny cat was there. Camille took it, patted it. "You don't know, do you, you haven't seen anything? How long have you been there, behind the door, spying on me then?"

The parasol. What was it doing under the table? Camille told herself she had been working too hard these past weeks. The letter. The suitcases. One thing after another. The cat miaowed . . .

"Okay, let's try again." Camille poured some milk for her new friend, a full bowl of it, sat down and took up her pen. First she had to finish her note to him. Let's see . . .

" . . . It is unlikely I will leave before Thursday. Indeed, Mademoiselle Vaissier came to see me and told me all sorts of tales they tell about me at Islette. It seems I went out at night through the window of my tower, hanging from a red parasol, which I used to set the forest on fire!!"

There was a knocking at the door. Monsieur Rodin was there. He absolutely had to see her again before the summer . . . He would have liked to go with her . . . Perhaps he would even join her? He sat down timidly in his old armchair . . . He had just been named president of the Society of Fine Arts. She was the first to know. He would succeed Dalou. He would be able to help her . . .

She was not listening. He looked at his feet. Drowsily.

She did not say a word. Sitting on the edge of the table, she swung her legs. She considered him. The little cat played between Auguste's big feet.

She had work to do.

8 June 1893.

Letter *from the Asylum*

I have put off writing to you because it is so cold I can hardly sit up. I cannot write with everyone else in the common room, where a miserable little fire is spluttering and they make a hellish racket. I am forced to go to my room on the second floor, where it's so glacial that I'm numb: my fingers tremble and cannot hold the pen. I haven't been warm all winter, I am frozen to the bone, cut in two by the cold. I have had a terrible cold. One of my friends, a poor teacher from the Fenelon lycée who came to be stranded here, was found frozen to death in his bed. It's dreadful. Nothing can compare to the cold of Montdevergues. And it lasts the better part of seven months.

The City

Soon you will hear this name: Greed.
When the cities, full of souls, will be put to the torch!
Don't you understand
That the perfect justice for each
Is that he fall in with
All the rest?

PAUL CLAUDEL, *La Ville*, I

PAUL WAS coming home soon. Camille was eager to see him. She wanted to hear the details. She was annoyed with him. He had been there more than a year, now, in the New World, in America.

She was thirty years old. She had contained those years, she had conquered them. The hard way. But now everything was in place. Her body had regained its strength, it was muscular, deft, fit for sculpting. Her powerful shoulders, her long hard legs, all functioned wonderfully on command.

Camille opened the window. She had just dined with the family, and now she stood looking out at Paris. She was thirty years old.

Her father saw the tall silhouette. He admired her. She was something of a success. Her last Salon showing had been highly acclaimed. *The Vanished God, The Little Châtelaine.* She had commissions. She was no longer ill. This afternoon he had watched her walking beside him through the streets of Paris. She strode along boldly, moving her shoulders like a man. She was powerful, and men turned to look at her.

Camille was standing with her hands on the cold railing of the balcony. She breathed in the city, she felt it flowing back to her, felt it in her guts. She was at one with it. Camille was the city itself. She was the streets, the alleyways, and the blood running in its veins, hot and murderous; she was the "prowler," as her brother had written, the prowler invading its streets.

Her brother, her brother's words, his powerful manipulation of images!

Soon he would be here. Probably next month. The poet of *La Ville* (The City). Her insomniac eyes looked at the city. She was the thousand gazes flickering over it. And the mist of hair escaping from her chignon was like the fog clinging to the bare branches. This evening she was thirty years old. Her heart beat to the rhythm of the city, dancing to the tom-tom of the Giant. Paris.

She had Paris in her blood, and she never wanted to leave it again. The slumbering city never stopped for all that, and she could hear the water deep inside it. The meandering water, the river, its damp essence. She was *fully* alive, envied no one, regretted nothing, neither abandonment, humiliation, nor silence. She was not jealous of her sister. She had no husband, no children, no lovers; she had become the woman who takes, the woman who decides, the woman who sculpts with her own hands. She would give herself when she wanted, and to whomever she wanted – just like that, joyous, splendid, free. A woman.

"Shut the window, Camille, it's cold." Her mother. Obviously she'd forgotten. Things were rather worse in that department. Madame Claudel regretted the loss of her connection with Monsieur Rodin. "He was a great artist. He used to come and visit sometimes, with his wife . . ." Her mother was shouting behind her. Camille closed the window. She wasn't twelve years old. How her mother scolded! It didn't bother her anymore.

La Ville. Soon her brother would be there. He had dared to leave on that big ship. Someday she would go with him. It was the one thing she missed, starting off on a journey – standing on the bridge, watching them lift the gangplank, coil the ropes, and the noise of the motors, the quay, and away, away. If only she could be the one who went away.

Someone had told her about it. Auguste's departure. Oh, it wasn't a pretty picture. Roger Marx had told her the sad story. That was a year ago.

Monsieur Rodin had been devastated, weeping as he told Roger that he had no more authority over her. Poor Roger Marx! He had begged her to come back. Roger Marx had vowed to transmit the message. Poor Roger, he was still too young to understand. He admired them both. Why had they separated?

One day Roger had dropped by her studio. He had seemed ill at ease. Camille had questioned him. So he had spilled out the story, pell-mell . . . Morning, the wagon at 23, rue des Grands-Augustins. The neighbors looking on. The furniture and the sculptures heaped together. Monsieur Rodin himself had supervised the move. "He's aged, Camille, if you only knew! He hardly sleeps." Brown spots had appeared on his face. "He never smiles now. I even heard someone say behind his back, while he was climbing into the wagon with Rose, 'Monsieur Rodin – there's a man who's washed up' . . . He is leaving for the country, Camille."

She had interrupted him: "But it's not the end. Listening to you, anyone would think it's like Louis XVI and Marie-Antoinette being led to the guillotine." He looked so despairing. "Listen, Marx, if things go badly, I'll write to him. I promise you."

He had smiled, somewhat reassured: "He loves you. There is only you . . ." She had stopped listening, she was working. Now she was working for herself.

She had brought all her things from Azay, at least what she could pay for. Transport was becoming more and more expensive.

She had written on her own to Maurice Fenaille, a rich benefactor. She could see Monsieur Rodin's indignation: had he ever refused her a commission, stolen a statue? Another misunderstanding. So she had grabbed the letter from him; she had wanted no more of his recommendations. She had left him, she was going to act alone. They both knew it now.

"Dear Sir,

"Please forgive me for taking the liberty to write to you. I have had the honor of making your acquaintance at Monsieur Rodin's, as I am one of his students. I am now working for myself, and I would be most grateful if you would do me the honor of visiting my studio. Ordinarily I receive visitors on Sundays, all day.

"I thank you, Sir, for your generous consideration.

"Yours truly,

"Mademoiselle Camille Claudel
113, boulevard d'Italie."

Rodin had left without a word.

Happily, commissions had come. Monsieur Rodin's letters had to be forwarded. Many were addressed to him. People thought they were still together. She was invited to exhibit in Brussels, Villeneuve had commissioned *The Psalm*. It wasn't the monument on the little square, but after all, she wasn't going to turn up her nose at it. She needed the money. She was living on the advance of her inheritance, which her father had given her when she had moved. As if she had married . . . He had given her a little money besides. Married! But her father wasn't a fool.

She looked at him. He, too, had aged, but he was still the temperamental and tender highlander she had known as a little girl. Good Vosgean stock! The black, piney Bresse! She loved her whimsical father, as ironic as she was and as easily carried away; they sometimes had terrible arguments, hurling the worst insults, pitting themselves against each other, and then they would joke, make up stories, dream, urge each other on.

She looked at him. He had just taken a cigar. She lit it for him. Then he asked her for the papers, he wanted to reread what they'd said about her this year. Camille kept the articles for him. Her mother never had time to look at them. "If you think that's all I have to do. For what you sculpt. It's disgusting!"

Madame Claudel had never budged. She knew that Camille sculpted nudes, that's all. She did not want to know any more.

Camille went to look in the drawer of the sideboard and handed her father the packet of reviews. She did not want to reread them. She needed to go on. All those sculptures were waiting. She still had so much to do . . . before reaching her goal. Only her brother understood. She would show him. And what had he been writing? She glanced at the crystal paperweight on the sideboard, "American blossoms" as such things were called over there. Paul had sent it. She turned the paperweight and the birds flew up. "My dear Paul, I am confiding these discoveries to you alone, don't show them to anyone." What was he doing there in Boston?

Someday she would reimburse him. He had sent her a little money. She had written to him, told him of the freezing winter, the fire in the hearth. One year had already passed. The good reviews, the success of two sculptures, *The Vanished God* and *The Little Châtelaine*.

The Vanished God. Paul had known about the break. Now he was the only one who could understand. He was her brother. And yet they were separated by such a distance. He there, she here. As he was leaving Paris, he had tried to explain: he had faith, he had made confession, and he had written. *La Ville* bore witness to his struggle during the past four years. Christmas Eve 1886. Chapter eight of Proverbs! Wisdom had given her hand to Rimbaud! She had refused to believe in it, to believe that things were like that. So she'd told him in bits and pieces what kind of life she was leading. She would defy God to the end! The struggle with the angel – surely he knew the parable. She had read the Bible, too. They had argued bitterly almost all night long. She had slept at his place that night, at 43, quai Bourbon, exhausted. He hadn't wanted to know about love. At least he had hesitated, stumbling over the words, and she had understood. He was a virgin, this rude boy. He was closed, intact. Now she was the one who hesitated to reveal herself. And yet he seemed to speak of his encounter with God as if it were another kind of love story, a mad love full of fears, flights, and desires . . . She was lame, cursed, Camille the black, the bitch! He had tried to calm her, to understand why she was leaving again in this beginning of the year 1891, why she was always fleeing. From whom or what?

Three years had passed. Soon he would be there. In his letters he hadn't spoken of his faith. She had no faith, no, she never could. She believed only in little Jeanne's eyes, the child's relentless gaze. No reasoning could withstand such scrutiny. A child had saved the world. A woman had understood. She was no longer going to Azay. Never mind! A lightning flash had riven her soul, even to her death. She had an incurable disease: the passion to see things as they were.

What a struggle between brother and sister! But Paul was not God and Camille was not Jacob. She poked fun at him: "My hip is already lame, the ford at the Jabbok river!" She hadn't needed to wrestle with the angel. She had already crossed over to the other side.

He had been impatient, thought her stupid, limited. But she had become doubly violent: "I am not his creature. Or anyone's, do you hear! Anyone's! And if every creature is unique, then He will see. He will be amused. We are going to offer your great Artist work that is unique. I destroy. I will deprive Him of me for all eternity. You can shift for yourself."

Poor Paul! What did he think now? He hadn't seemed happy with this burdensome religion. At any rate, it surely wasn't a simple matter for him. And here she was, leading an ascetic life! She might almost be a nun.

La Ville. He had given it to her before he left. She loved this difficult play with its baroque images.

> The vast blazing of the Night
> Greed . . .

Her father – she had nearly forgotten about him. She had told him to come to the studio the next day. She would show him her next exhibition. Several sculptures, finally. She would not unveil *The Gossips* until next May. Oh, her little companions were well hidden. She had kept them sealed away for some time. No, she would show her work to Jeanne, this work she had shaped directly in the marble. She was both creator and technician. She had done it all, from beginning to end. First, she hadn't wanted anyone else to touch it, and then the workers she had hired had broken two of her other sculptures out of malice. She had been two days late with their pay. So they'd ransacked everything. Madame Pipelette was surely good for something . . . Fortunately, they hadn't touched the block of marble Rodin had given her.

"Whether a single point or a line, it will all come alive." Apparently he had wept when he saw *The Vanished God.* They were left with earth, clay. The span of a life. How many statues were their due?

Letter *from the Asylum*

There is no point hoping for changes in a madhouse. Rules are necessary for all these "nervous, violent, shrieking, menacing creatures . . ." whom their relatives cannot tolerate because they are so disagreeable and dangerous. And how is it that I am forced to tolerate them? Not to mention the worry provoked by such promiscuity. . . . For it is worrisome to be in the midst of all that, I would give a hundred thousand francs, if I had them, to get away.

The Gossips

S o. S H E H A D accompanied him to the station. He had just gone
away again. For three years, perhaps. Or five? For a long time she
had hesitated, questioning herself. She had wanted to go, too. Perhaps
he would have agreed. The two of them had dreamed of it as children.
China! He was leaving for China! Paul was going to China! He had
gone.

She had gone as far as the station – afterward he would take the
boat. Alone. She was alone at the station. No friend, no relative. She
had stood there. He had waved to her brusquely. He didn't like senti-
mentalities, demonstrations of affection. Their mother had never
kissed them.

Paul had gone away to that country she had dreamed of visiting as a
little girl. She had almost left everything behind. Now she walked back
home, her shoulders bent, dragging her feet like a prisoner being led
away. Had it been her last chance?

She was shaking. What was wrong with her today? Her brother had
gone away, well, fine. Curiously, she felt she should have gone too. She

had achieved celebrity. The May Salon had been a great success. She would turn thirty-one at the end of the year. Everyone was talking about *The Gossips, The Painter, The Little Châtelaine* sculpted directly in marble, chiseled by the artist herself. "That hasn't been done since Michelangelo!" She shrugged her shoulders. She had received so many compliments, but the number of silly remarks she'd heard as well, even flattering ones, had made her thoughtful. What was success after all?

Why had she stayed behind? Because she hadn't yet found what she was looking for, because she was a sculptor, and because she wanted to keep searching? Because "the giant" of her childhood always gazed down at her, defied her, ironic, defying the centuries? From the time she was a little girl, she'd had a strange feeling that she would find the answers before she died!

So she wasn't finished – there was an author she wanted to understand, a material she had to study. She had been able to rediscover the method of polishing in use at the time of Bernini: with a mutton bone. She was determined, stubborn. What a fool she was! Like a defect that kept calling attention to itself. She didn't believe in the devil, or the gods, or hell, or seventh heaven; she was a creature of earth.

The May Salon had been a success, but a costly one. Camille was suddenly anxious. How would she spend the summer? There would be few clients in the next months. Good reviews were not enough; she had to eat. She might not even be able to sell her sculptures.

Since she had left Rodin, she had lost contact with the society people, the financiers, the collectors – the whole network. They did not come to her obscure studio. She hardly ever went out. With no dresses, no hats, no "protectors" as they were called, she got few invitations.

She had worked so hard to show these three sculptures at the Salon, one in marble, another in bronze, that all her time had been taken up. Money, too, for tools, plaster, casting, the workers, the caster . . . Fortunately, Léon Lhermitte had paid for his bust in bronze and for the workers. A fine glimpse of the future! In order to prepare for the next exhibition, she would need to exhibit in the meantime, which meant finding money again; and in order to get commissions, she needed enough work to hire technicians, so she could work on a number of sculptures at the same time – and besides she had to pay the cost of transport. Paul had left her a little money, but that hardly solved the problem. Reviews never brought practical solutions. The next day the real problems of sculpture began all over again. It was no longer a question of forging a new art, of modeling, of great thoughts on the future of sculpture. No, it was all much more banal, ordinary, and tragic. How to obtain so many kilos of earth, how to find a block of marble, the cost of this or that caster. You didn't model ideas. And you didn't model directly in clay; you had to have an oven to bake the clay, the casts, the reproductions. She and Rodin had often faced this cruel paradox: they spoke of new forms and servile copies, of ancient and modern, and the next day there they were, faced with questions of money. Only Mirbeau had understood. Perhaps because he himself wrote.

"This young woman has worked with such tenacity, such will, such passion, you have no idea . . . At last she's arrived! Yes, but one has to live! And you can hardly think she makes a living from her art . . . So she is discouraged and demoralized. Such ardent natures, such turbulent souls are plunged as deeply into despair as they are lifted aloft in hope . . . She is thinking of abandoning her art.

"'What are you saying!' bellowed Kariste, crestfallen. 'But that's impossible!'

"Do you have bread to give her, then, can you pay for her models, her casters, her smelting, her marble?

"'Look, the minister of fine arts is an artist himself for a change . . . This art must move him too, since we feel it in our guts! Perhaps someone might speak to him . . . I know that he is accessible and full of good will . . . Not to do everything he can to give such a great artist the peace of mind necessary for her work would be a terrible responsibility, and one he wouldn't want to assume . . . Let's see, my friend, think about it . . . Is it possible?'

"Perhaps, but the minister is not always the master . . . And who knows what goes on in those offices?

"'A collector, then . . . We must find a rich collector . . . '

"But collectors only want works dedicated to them by recognized artists.

"And Kariste tapped the ground with his cane, and to all my objections he cried: 'But she has genius!'"

She would sooner have ended the discussion, licking her chops like old Crapitoche, the cat they'd had as children, who had looked at them like an old, mustached philosopher. She and Paul. She and Paul sitting astride the little garden wall. The future! Travels!

Paul! But what would she have done there in China? Another life, shaking off once and for all the implacable tick-tock of this smug society. He had told her that he was suffocating here – "a pile of spineless bodies . . ." "people swollen with an unhealthy self-importance . . ."

"And what about charity, Paul?"

She sat down on the chair beside the table, the closest one; rather, she let herself fall onto it. Had to get to work now. Right away. The clinging humidity, a June dull with tedium, with bleak laziness. How could anyone want to do anything in this steam bath?

The pile of newspapers beside the red parasol, the bunch of flies glued to the paper; the studio, the half-burned candles, pegged on an iron tip, two dirty glasses, Paul before leaving, the bottle, she, the table, the bare floor. A number of studies mummified in their thick veils. Reddish cloths. Wait, a little piece of cracked earth on the ground, a study beginning to crumble. A whole parched world. She. The table. She and the flies. She leaned over and distractedly pulled out another newspaper. The pile crumbled. A dry sound. The paper crackled. The paper she had folded. The newspapers. To reread them. To shore up her courage, perhaps. To have some pleasure – why not?

"I am seventy-five years old." A grimace at the four old ladies. Four grimacing faces. The mirrors glued in her studio – She –

"'Do you know that we are, in fact, in the presence of something quite unique, a freak of nature, the woman of genius?'

"Of genius, yes, my dear Kariste. But don't say it so loudly . . . There are people who are embarrassed by it, and who would not forgive Mademoiselle C. such an epithet . . .

"'How's that?'

"The catalog is silent and the group is not titled," I answered. "You see, it's a woman who is telling a story to other women, who are listening to her . . . This work is by a young woman, Mademoiselle Claudel."

"'Yes, good Lord! I knew it,' cried Kariste. 'Now I recognize the woman who did *The Waltz*, *Head of a Child*, the bust of Rodin. She is simply a marvelous artist and a great one as well, and this little group is the finest work here.'"

"That's the truth, isn't it, ladies?" The four old women nodded their heads, straightened up, leaning their tired backs on the chairs. Four mirrors.

That dear Mirbeau! He was an unbridled enthusiast. She could see him, with his collar askew, leading his friends toward her little group, *The Gossips*. Camille thought of him. There were people who believed in her, but how could she explain to them that the real difficulties were something quite different from states of the soul. Only Octave Mirbeau had understood the impasse. Mirbeau disguised as Kariste – he was full of inventions!

"After wandering through the exhibition halls, we went down to the garden to smoke. Kariste was full of joyful enthusiasm at this admirable group, at such absolute beauty. Nothing purer or stronger could be found even at Pompeii and Tanagra, when divine artists abounded in the wonder of nature and the cult of life . . . This group enchanted him like a discovery, with its deliciously imaginative composition, its interpretation of truly miraculous nature, of a knowledgeable and supple craft. He never tired of looking at it, of parsing all its beauties."

And Geffroy! Overwhelmed, he would not let her go. "These four women gathered in a corner, one of them telling a story, the others listening to her. You, so young! Those four old women! It is the poetry of old age and gloom. The apparition of intimate truth . . . the poor bodies in proximity, the heads leaning toward each other, the secret being spun out! A marvel of understanding, of human feeling." Everyone had always treated her as heartless, egotistical – it was good to hear. She should send this one to her mother. "But tell me, just between us, who gave you the idea? This secret the four women are spinning out, what is it?" She had smiled engagingly. No one would know. It was a secret. The four little old women! their secret was hers – her enigma.

And Roger Marx: " . . . turned inward, entirely absorbed in attentive listening . . . "

Curiously, certain persons kept their distance. What did she mean by it? And that sudden old age? They felt pilloried, judged.

Indifferent, those four little old women, "the gossips," continued to purvey their gossip, the story weaving itself between them. They were even speaking of genius! Roger Marx stood beside her. They were speaking of genius! There was no more mention of Rodin. No one saw them together anymore, she had no more contact with him. She had emerged as unique in her time. She was creating a new art. Mathias Morhardt had just said to him: "Marx, look, *The Painter* there, our friend Lhermitte, that little figurine she's done. She is starting a new art. And *The Gossips* – those *Gossips!* They are the inexplicable and un-expected effort of genius! That's the long and the short of it!"

Camille had heard them. She had been there in their midst. No one spoke of the master, they no longer even mentioned his name. And yet she sensed him everywhere. In their eyes, in their remarks, their discretion. He had not come; he had not even come. The exhibi-tion had ended and Rodin had not appeared. She had wanted to write to him several times. And then she'd put her pen and paper away.

The *Balzac* was not going well, nor the monument to Victor Hugo. People said he was suffering. Yet his studios were humming with work; commissions continued to arrive, the technicians reproduced his old studies, cut, chiseled. Where was he? What was he doing? It was said that he stayed in Touraine. He had gone in search of his *Balzac*. Alone.

Camille had said nothing. She had been furious when someone came to tell her what was going on. They were about to withdraw the commission for the *Balzac* from Monsieur Rodin. Marquet Le Vasselot had even offered to deliver one of his own in forty-eight hours. Perhaps she ought to . . . She had interrupted brutally: they were sickening, ready to flatter one day and kill the next. They had nothing better to do! A statue took time, necessary time. And whatever the hours in-volved, they would be justified in the centuries to come.

Their old friend Mathias. One day someone had mocked her. She would never produce anything, casting directly on the model went so much more quickly! And this mad idea of shaping the stone herself! Mathias Morhardt had responded sharply – the man had taken them for two yokels! They'd had a good laugh at his confusion!

Mathias, their old friend. He had come at the beginning of the year to ask her if she would accept a commission to do her *Clotho* in marble! She was mad with joy – why would she hesitate? She didn't un-derstand. He stood there twisting his hat in his hands. She insisted: Who had commissioned it? What museum?

She had finally wondered if there was something he wasn't telling her. She had made the messenger sit down: "So, Monsieur Morhardt, let's have it."

Shamefaced, he had told her. Puvis de Chavannes was celebrating his seventieth birthday. He was presiding at a banquet organized by himself, Mathias Morhardt. In fact, it was for Rodin.

"What do you mean, Rodin? Explain yourself!"

Yes, Monsieur Rodin. He would preside at the banquet. For Puvis de Chavannes's seventieth birthday.

"Yes, but what does Rodin have to do with it?"

There was a plot.

"A plot. But you aren't making any sense now!" What was he talking about?

A plot to withdraw the commission for the *Balzac* from Rodin.

"And so?"

All right, on this occasion, Puvis de Chavannes's birthday . . .

"Yes, I understand."

For this banquet a bronze plaque was being made with the profile of Puvis by Rodin. Each guest would receive one. So, in short . . .

"The guests were bought, weren't they?" She finally understood. In this way the artists would show their sympathy for Rodin, and everyone would carry his little engraving along with his full stomach. And what about her? She didn't even have enough money for another casting of the *Clotho*. Buying a plaque was too expensive!

She laughed. No, she was wrong. Mathias Morhardt had simply proposed that on this occasion her *Clotho* in marble should be commissioned from Camille Claudel.

"Rodin's student!" They needed her to commend the merits of the teacher! She accepted, however. "I want to see *Clotho* in marble. So I accept. But I will be the one to cut it. I will be the one to chisel the long threads of webbing around her. No one will touch it. It will take time. But I will make it a little jewel. Myself."

He had said nothing. He had given her carte blanche. He had gotten up, opened the door, and turned around to say, "Yes?"

"No. Nothing."

He had wanted to talk about Auguste. She had wanted to ask, "How is he, really? What's going on?" Nothing. Silence. He stood with his hand on the door, she leaned back with her hands on the table, they looked at each other.

The lunch had been ridiculous. Rodin had read a speech. No one had listened.

She had worked on her *Clotho*. The marble had arrived. She would have it for months. Now she had work to do. Why sit there daydreaming? She wouldn't realize any income from this commission. They had offered her the marble, but as she was doing all the rest herself, they had given her little for additional expenses.

She got up. Quick, to work!

She had been able to make fun of the dinner for Puvis de Chavannes. At the same time, nearly the same day, she had given a dinner, too. A real disaster! Paul had just come back from Boston. He was coming to visit Camille with his friends. His friends!

Early one afternoon, the bell rang. Camille had opened the door. She would never forget it. There was her mother, on her doorstep. She had come to prepare dinner! Camille would not know how, would she? She pushed Camille aside, and then – she would remember her mother's face until the day she died!

The Japanese model was naked. He had looked at her mother, as if in prayer. Impassive. Not a muscle had moved. Madame Claudel had recoiled, Camille behind her. Camille had waited for her to faint. Her mother had turned toward her, to push her toward the entrance. She was red and green at the same time! Suddenly she had pivoted sharply, charged toward the meditating idol, and held out her hand. The other had bowed as if he had been dressed in ceremonial garb. Two minutes later they were behaving like old friends. The extreme civility of the Japanese, who had gotten dressed, had completely conquered her mother's peasant heart.

On the other hand, the lanterns strung from the ceiling beams, the candles pegged on iron spikes, the improvised chandeliers unleashed Louise's anger. And when Camille began to powder herself, she had been subjected to all the provincial Villeneuve remarks her mother could muster. She looked like a clown, a – no, she would not say the word. Camille said nothing, she went on powdering herself.

For some time now she had hidden her features beneath a white mask. That is, when she had to go out in company. She only liked her eyes and her mouth. All the rest had to be white, immobile, dead. She was thirty years old. Thirty years had passed.

The dinner! Her brother was accompanied by a sort of vagrant, an incredible young man, his trousers in tatters, who played the violin. A lover of Debussy. She had jumped when he had pronounced the name. She needed to calm down.

Her mother never stopped commenting on what was being said at the table; at each of their remarks she answered, muttered to herself, gave a sigh: "The Japanese is passable when he's dressed, but that other one! Oh no, with the holes in his pockets. What's his name? Christian de Larapidie? An odd name – Camille? She didn't do anything. Well, sculpture! . . . "

The last guest was the worst. Camille hated him. He had continually made fun of her: "Is it true, Mademoiselle, that at Guernsey, the rocks where Victor Hugo sat are marked by a green cross?" She had not answered this boor, Jules Renard.

Paul had been furious, his nose in his plate. He cracked his knuckles continually with barely contained violence. He found his sister ridiculous powdered like this, like a stale cake. Only Christian de Larapidie seemed to enjoy himself. He drank a lot and grew quite animated. A charmer, with the holes in his pockets and his tattered trousers, he regaled them with all sorts of things, lies, true stories. Who knows? He shared a room with Paul, at the same boardinghouse! But how could they put up with each other? Paul was still a bundle of contradictions! Camille had the feeling she recognized him, this bohemian, rather uncertain young man . . . Louis Laine! My God, she had suddenly thought of Louis Laine! Paul had sent her his two last plays, *L'Échange* and *La Jeune Fille Violaine*. Louis Laine! Yes! She did not like *La Jeune Fille Violaine*. She was horrified by the leper who seduced Violaine. Violaine chased away by her mother, Violaine disgraced, abandoned by everyone, and the murder between the two sisters. So many memories of the village, of the country. Violaine sacrificed. The weight of a sin she hadn't committed. No! This play was too hard and bitter, like the wind at Villeneuve. Ah yes, she had laughed at the old marquis, at the beginning of the play: "The old man with ears full of hair, like an artichoke heart"! She recognized that man, their neighbor. She had once wanted to play with his three children, but it was impossible. What had become of him? "And the marquis?"

"He was put away. Finally! Not a moment too soon!" her mother had answered. "Everyone signed. It had been a long time. They're finally rid of him."

Poor marquis! Put away. In the asylum, and he was so amusing at times. One day he and Camille had played hopscotch. He was a kid at heart! . . . And would Paul, too, enter his little cell? Cloistered, too? No, she wouldn't stand for it. Before leaving for China, he had told her. He couldn't wait much longer. The call, the mysterious voice, exile, "the torment, the severity of love." He had decided to take orders! A monk! He could not escape!

"There is someone inside me who is more myself than I am," he had told her finally; he had sat before her, absorbed, his forehead creased.

What had he seen? What had he heard? Where was he going? To whom? And that light in his eyes . . .

My little Paul!

Letter *from the Asylum*

As for me, I am so devastated by living here that I [illegible] no longer a human creature. I cannot bear the cries of these creatures anymore, it makes me sick at heart. God! How I would like to be at Villeneuve! I haven't done all that I've done just to end my life as a number in a madhouse, I deserve something better.

"Genius, Like a Man Generously Endowed with It"

Just as by cutting away, O Lady, one extracts
From the hard Alpine stone,
A living figure which alone
Grows the more, the more the stone diminishes.

MICHELANGELO

M Y LETTER is too discouraged, don't let Mademoiselle Clau-del see it – I believe that her address is still 113, boulevard d'Italie."

Camille turned the paper over in her hands. The veins in her neck were throbbing. So this was why she'd stayed here instead of going to China with her brother!

The letter was there. He had written it. She recognized the writing. It wasn't a joke. Tragic! This man was throwing up his hands. The artist was vacillating, halted in his trajectory. No, not that!

He was fifty-five years old. No, Monsieur Rodin, you mustn't give comfort to the fools. Not the sculptor of *The Gates of Hell!* No! And with the *Balzac* to finish! Come on, lift up your head. You've got every-thing to live for. Still. Your hands! Your hands idle? Never!

Mirbeau had just brought the letter. He would return tomorrow. If she didn't want to see him again, he would not insist, he would never tell Rodin that he had shown her this letter.

"I don't know if Mademoiselle Claudel will agree to come to your place the same day as myself, it's been two years since we've seen each other and since I've written to her, I am therefore not in a position . . ."

She read and reread. She felt him violently close, too close. Love surged up in her. Sensual, direct, his hands . . . She had wanted his mouth, his eyes, his sex – a great conflagration.

"It is up to Mademoiselle Claudel whether I should come . . ."

Their follies, their projects for sculpture, their discussions . . . How long had it been? He knew sculpture! "God's first thought when He created the world was the model." The two of them together, no one else could understand.

Images jostled each other in her head. She got up, she wanted to escape, to say, No, never again. But they engulfed her, harassed her. "That's enough, bitches! Down, bitches!" She swore at them, tried to control them, they were the Eumenides, the Furies. They were there creeping, hair entwined with snakes, torch in one hand, dagger in the other.

No! Say no to Mirbeau tomorrow! Write him and leave the letter. Flee before he returns. She would leave the letter. She would not see Mirbeau, otherwise she would give in.

"How cruel our life is!"

She had been with him for – no, it wasn't possible – more than ten years – the meeting. *The Gates of Hell.* And his sufferings, his silence, the vanished god. Quickly speak to someone. Don't feel him coming near. Escape. The letter, throw it away, it was not for her, throw it away . . .

" . . . I am sure of his final success, but the poor artist would be sad, sadder still, knowing life, regretting and weeping before she arrives, perhaps too late, a victim of her artist's flight, working honestly, regretting her powers sapped by this struggle and by that belated glory which leaves you nothing but sickness . . .

"Rodin
8, Chemin Scribe, Bellevue."

He was ill. She saw him in bed, a man who was firm, hard, powerful, a child of the people, no, he mustn't be ill. The pen trembled. Escape! Rose will look after him!

> I will always love cherry blossom time,
> From that time my heart has nursed
> An open wound . . .

She was saved. The old musician was there in the courtyard. She would speak to someone. To escape the letter . . .

"It is clear that she has genius, like a man generously endowed with it . . . and in that great garden where empty-eyed creatures went back and forth without even glancing at the work of Mademoiselle Claudel, this word 'genius' echoes like a cry of pain."

She and he. A single, androgynous being. Merged, fused – two great beasts of hell! *The Grip!* – No, what had he called that sculpture? *The Grasp!* "She is the one who overpowers and grasps the man, her prey!" He had explained the double tail to her. She could see the sculpture, and what a scandal it had caused in 1885! Come on, let him lift up his head! She was the male in him. She, the great female, had armed him once again. Camille wrote to Monsieur Rodin.

Tomorrow she would give the letter to Mirbeau.

And I say, then, that youth is the time of illusions, but that is because it imagined things infinitely less beautiful and numerous and desirable than they are.

PAUL CLAUDEL, *Le Soulier de satin*

SAILING FOR CYTHERA: Monsieur Rodin commented on the painting.
She was nineteen years old.
The earth at dawn, still asleep.

24 June 1895.
He had waited so long for her return.
They had taken each other by the hand. Simply.
That night they had not made love.

The hot earth gorged on the sun that retreats at evening.
She was even more beautiful.
"Çacountala, recognized by her husband, was loved again and received by him . . ."

Twilight at Cythera.

Camille Claudel, student of Rodin, has become almost as powerful as the master.

Chronique de l'Indre

I would be very surprised if Mademoiselle Claudel did not take her place one day, suddenly, among the great master sculptors of the century.

ARMAND DAYOZ

Newspaper of the Region of Indre

10 October 1895.
"*A gift to the museum.* – Mademoiselle Camille Claudel, student of Rodin, has offered the museum a fine group in plaster. The work is inspired by the Hindu legend of Çacountala."

17 November.
"Yesterday, on her way to Touraine, Mademoiselle Claudel stopped for a little while at Châteauroux. She was received by several members of the community. . . . Monsieur Buteau thanked Mademoiselle Claudel for the gift she made to the museum of Châteauroux. . . ."

21 November.
"I have resolved not to speak about this bit of fluff which has generously been offered. . . . Not content to place that plaster mastodon

in the middle of the Main Hall of honor . . . they regaled us with academic solemnities that would have taken place in the museum in honor of this plaster obscenity."

December.
    "The city of Châteauroux is currently disturbed by the art of Mademoiselle Camille Claudel. . . . There are protests in the name of flouted convention, of outraged morality. . . ."

"So much the better, after all. It is proof of life!"

"Persons who have not yet contemplated this monolith, this gypsum obelisk, would do well to hurry . . . one foot is already broken. . . ."

"One member of the community has proposed to vote for the acquisition of a curtain to conceal the group from the eyes of the public. . . ."

"Is this the expression of conjugal love after death?"

"The whole thing is covered with a protective coating close to chestnut in color. The patina cost 100 francs! You could get the same result with two sous worth of black sugar and one pail of water. . . . Finally, let us recall the remark pronounced on the work in question by one of those numerous affected types who are born shopkeepers: 'Nonetheless,' he said, 'the work has a certain grandeur.' You're not kidding: It stands three and a half meters tall!"

    The farce of *Çacountala.*
    She had wanted to make a gift to the museum of Châteauroux.

Risotto

What disgusting seriousness
We bring to eating! . . .
What a thing to eat! We are no less voracious than
                                        Master Worm.

PAUL CLAUDEL, *La Ville*, I

O N   S U N D A Y, there would be risotto. She had to send an answer.
It didn't have to be a long one. Just a note. But her shoulders
hurt, her legs were giving her trouble, too. It wasn't warm these days,
and yet she felt bloated, she breathed heavily, like a fat woman. She
had grown dull. Her head especially, her head was already burdened
with memories, with delays, with worries. It was raining outside. Her
eyes bothered her. No, she had not managed to tidy up. These were
the follies of Mars, god of war!

Now she was hot. She threw off her shawl. And then all over again,
from hot to cold . . . She had just sat down, the marble in front of her,
smooth, shining, full, swollen. It was coming along well, but would
it be ready for the Salon? Only a month from now and still so much
to do!

Sunday? It would do her good. Madame Morhardt and the risotto.
She enjoyed eating risotto. All those little grains of rice sliding off the
spoon. That was a dish! It winked at you – full of dimples, a laughing
child. She was thirty-two years old. Well, almost, at the end of the

year. She must not get sick! She had to finish. One month, she had one month left.

Risotto, yes, that would relax her. It was delicious!

"Dear Madame Morhardt . . ."

She felt she had found a haven in their home. They protected her, they welcomed her. From time to time, he would come. She should ask Mathias Morhardt who might hollow the marble for her. *The Gossips* — she was doing them herself, but for the open corner where they sat, she could use a good technician. That would certainly facilitate the work. Provided she could pay! Should she ask him, *him?* But they were all busy. Indeed, at his three studios there was so much to do, so much! The commissions piled up, sculpture from two years ago, three years ago, and the *Victor Hugo* and the *Balzac*, dozens of studies!

Rodin had asked her if she would come to supervise roughing out the stone. She hadn't the time. She would never finish *The Gossips*. If only that was all she had to do, but she had to earn a living. They had said Rodin was finished, but he had never been so busy! Now she was the one who hung back, sagging on her old hooves, breathing heavily, sluggish. Old horse, let's go! Come on, geddy-up! She had referred him to some able workers. He paid well, there was work for them. Jules, Roger, she was fond of them. Everything was coming along nicely. There, at the three studios . . .

But what about her? Should she ask Morhardt? Yes, but what if she should get some inept technician? . . . To hollow out the corner was almost beginners' work. But her *Gossips?* The worker might pierce or decapitate one of them. She had been working so many months on the marble. A costly dream. An act of folly. She had economized, accepted anything that came along. And there was little enough. Monsieur Fenaille, a very wealthy man, had helped her a little out of friendship for Rodin, but would she be ready?

Come on, quickly! Answer Madame Morhardt. Thank her for her brother's articles. And Monsieur Ganderax, their friend. Thanks to him, Paul's articles were going to be published. His parents were satisfied. Even Madame Louise had managed a smile of satisfaction. My Paul, there in Shanghai! The little boy who dreamt of China. His two blue eyes staring at the map, his little finger pointing there, and there,

Shanghai. He was there. Camille was suddenly annoyed at him. This feeling came in unexpected waves. No play had been published since his departure. Only poems, essays . . .

All of a sudden she felt cold. Once more the sun had just hidden its dirty yellow face. Camille wondered what time it was now. With all this day in black and white, she had worked without stopping or looking at the clock. She had stopped only to drink something hot. She must send the letter this evening. Camille wrote quickly: "I will be pleased to dine with you on Sunday evening, not only to feast on risotto . . ."

Don't forget anything: the articles, the thank-yous, the delay, the first-class workers. She had spent weeks redoing their mistakes, watching so they wouldn't damage everything; one morning they hadn't come – they had been offered better pay elsewhere.

Don't forget anything. The marble corner to be hollowed out. They would surely dine outside in the garden. The garden. Mention *The Hamadryad* . . . Monsieur Bing had bought the bust based on the sketch she had just made as he watched! She had decided to employ all her technique. Marble with a golden patina. "The sweetness of what is mingled with the regret for what is not," as Paul said, capturing its essence.

. . . I would do Bing's bust.

She should thank him, too. For the young girl with the water lilies. The young girl she no longer was.

. . . Bing's bust, certainly. I will do again . . . since it finds favor with our master . . .

Dinner outside with Rodin. That was . . . at least six months ago. The whirlwind of these last months, and now she was late! They hadn't lived the same lives. He hadn't had her worries.

Every time she accepted an invitation, an outing, the hours counted double. There was no worker to replace her. They had gone, one after the other, mocking her. One day she had left a technician working alone. She had to see Monsieur Pontremoli. When she returned, the marble was broken. Pipelette had apparently found the young man quite charming; he had told her – "You know, Mam'zelle Camille, the story of the elephant and the ant, it's very funny, you know, it's the story of . . ." and then she had offered him a glass of kirsch. The poor young man was so pale. "Think of it, Mam'zelle Camille, he'd worked the whole day . . . just to eat." Camille had understood. One hour of work, two breakages. Her months of labor reduced to white powder, to pale ashes – wounds in the beautiful sacred, veined flesh, open sores – she saw her blood running out drop by drop. The addition was costly. Too costly.

If she went out this evening, at the hour when sculptors give their eyes and hands a rest and set aside their tools, the hour when contours blend into the shadows that gradually absorb them, she would get up in the morning more hesitant, her eyes still adjusted to twilight, her hands trembling on the tool; she couldn't tolerate too much light. So she had quickly undressed. She had worked, worked without let up.

And still she wasn't ready for the Salon! In one month. All winter she hadn't wasted a single hour. The daylight hours were growing shorter, the seconds weighed heavily between her hands. She hoarded them, greedily, none fell to the ground, she welded them to the marble she had polished and repolished.

Answer Madame Morhardt! Dinner! With him. Yes, it had been a long time since then . . . July 1895.

The big trees, the lovely restaurant, the swan's neck of autumn, the sun on the lake, the delicate dishes, the silky wine, the red-gold kiss, the trees above them, and the cry of the swallows. Lower. Lower until it hovered above their heads, more piercing. The cry. Rodin had said: "They are the creatures being killed."

Camille had not understood. The swallows?

"The nymphs! You hear them? They are crying. They are born with the trees. They watch over them and share their fate. The nymphs . . . the hamadryads."

She had taken his hands: "Tell me . . . the hamadryads?"

"They are joyful when the rain from heaven waters the oak trees, and in mourning when they shed their leaves. It is said that they die at the same moment as the tree they love."

He had spoken. She had leaned toward him over the table, sitting on the edge of her chair, linked to him by their clasped hands. He would never get used to the gleam of her eyes. As if she were sculpting you in a single stroke. He would not have liked to pose for her. Her violent gaze stripped one terribly naked – shaken, blasted, plundered. What did she see? What did she read into things? He closed his eyes.

". . . a messenger between mortals and immortals. They were mediators. Honored as such." He took her hand and leaned over it. He did not kiss her hand. He had stopped himself. "Like you, a hamadryad! An intercessor. For me."

She laughed harshly: "Between heaven and hell, purgatory!" She pulled back, dropping his hands. "A purgatory all to myself!"

He shrugged his shoulders. She said: "I don't like compliments, flattery. I love life, that's all. Neither hell nor the immortals . . . Life, here and now."

He had looked at her, changing in the light of the guttering candle. The swallow had cried out more sharply in its haste to fly away, far away. She was no longer the tense, stubborn young girl. This evening he had seen the gentle, silver sheen of the hair escaping from her chignon. He had never seen this natural rebellion in any other woman. She was never properly groomed. She often made an effort to smooth the strands, he had noticed; before going out she would turn around, and in a single movement the hair would come undone. The little strands curled around her face, will-o'-the-wisps, a crown of thorns following the gaze – by turns vicious or tragic.

Her black dress blended with the night gathering around them – the halo of candlelight on the table – she wrinkled her forehead.

"Why are you smiling, Monsieur Rodin?"

"I was thinking of Daphne transformed into a laurel tree. And Procne into a swallow. In each of them we see the woman she is ceasing to be and the tree or bird she is becoming."

She was silent. "The woman she is ceasing to be . . ." What was he trying to say? Even to become a bird. No, not that, not that death of the flesh – of her flesh. Leave me a little time yet! Leave me a desirable being. No, she could not bear that. She would never cease to be a woman. Hold on, Monsieur le Professeur! "And what about Dante?"

Now he was startled.

"A snake glued itself to the body of one of the damned, and transformed itself into a man while the man changed into a reptile. Let's wait for the end of the game, Monsieur Rodin."

He did not laugh. He did not smile. She held out her hand: "Let's make peace."

"Truce."

She had done the bust. Monsieur Bing would exhibit it. At least if she managed to finish a few sculptures. *The Hamadryad!* "Time flies, time flies . . ." She had barely a month left. Now the studio was completely icy. She used to go out in the evenings. A good hot supper. But she had refused too many times. Male friends had abandoned her, even her brother. And the women were too busy; they were not very welcoming. And then, she had heard a few remarks: "She is beautiful in spite of that slight limp, don't you think?" "That foot adds to her charm."

But that was nothing. The armor was solid. The real danger was not from that direction. The few commissions she had obtained were quickly laden with innuendos. She had met Monsieur Fenaille one morning on rue de l'Université. He was interested in her way of polishing marble. If she could do his bust, he would like . . . Suddenly rumors were rife. They had dined together and she wasn't even embarrassed! "Anyway, that's why she got the commission! – you know, the marble!" There was Fritz Thavlow, the Norwegian painter. Bing . . . Friends of Rodin. They admired her work, but tongues would wag.

And then one day the dagger was thrust in to the hilt, as it had been with Sadi Carnot. (She had little interest in politics, but she had seen all the newspapers with their headlines announcing: "President Carnot assassinated," "Sixteen centimeters from point to hilt!" "Attack against the president of the republic." *Le Matin, L'Intransigeant.* One year earlier, 25 June 1894. She remembered it. She had seen Rodin again the evening before.) Someone had said: "Sculpture is just a pretext – a good way to meet men! The courtesan with dirty hands." She had looked at the speaker. For a second she had reeled at the shock – for a second. *"Sculpture is just a pretext."* No one really took her seriously.

All this sniping didn't bother her. Ten years earlier she couldn't have stood it. She had gone out very little, but she was young, people had gathered around her, asked her questions. She had thought they were interested in sculpture. So she had explained a little, thinking that they admired her. Past thirty, she hadn't changed. Now men quickly turned away from her. Even artists, writers, and journalists. As for women, none of them wanted to know how she used her chisel, how she shaped the clay.

Jane's words came back to her: "It's not what you do that interests them. It's you, your big eyes, your insolence. They will talk about the sculpture afterward. Besides..." Her insolence had become ill humor. Her intransigence an old woman's bad character. And if Bourdelle was known as "the sculptor Bourdelle," even though he was a former student of Rodin's, she was still "Camille Claudel, a woman of genius, Rodin's student."

"Sculpture is just a pretext."

And another person had said: "Yes, she's never found a husband." So she had retreated, becoming more solitary and savage than ever. She would be sculpture. There would be neither father nor lover. And when she died, people would say: "There was a woman!" With that admiring tone they used to hail the death of a great man.

To regain their esteem, she decided not to go out anymore. Her sculpture alone would speak for her. Others cut off an ear, she would kill herself by inches, more righteous, more demanding than a Carmelite nun. Even Rodin, whom she met from time to time, had not seen how supremely alive she was, still full of surprises. She was preparing herself. She had observed the world. The world of men. The world of power. The "giant" was waiting for her, patiently.

Meanwhile, she was hungry. Risotto was for Sundays. And everything was closed now! Could she go out at this hour, alone? And where would she eat? A poor woman in a restaurant – and all by herself...

There was Pipelette! "Madame the concierge is out today. Address any inquiries to..."

Tomorrow the
Opening

I don't know how to dress. I am unskilled in woman's arts.

> *I have always lived like a boy. Yet all the same, I'm not so bad. I would have liked you to see me in a beautiful dress. A beautiful red dress . . .*

PAUL CLAUDEL, *Le Pain dur*
Act 3, scene 2

Monsieur Rodin,
"I thank you for your kind invitation to present me to the president of the republic. Unfortunately, since I haven't left my studio for two months, I have no dress suitable for the occasion. I will have my dress only tomorrow for the opening. Anyway, I am desperate to finish my little women in marble, there are two cracks it will take me all day to repair, but I hope they will be ready tomorrow for the opening (if there is still time to enter them). Therefore, please pardon me and do not think I am ungrateful. With all my thanks, *Camille Claudel.*"

On 12 May 1896, Camille Claudel did not attend the Salon. No one, neither she nor a courier, had brought *The Gossips* in marble. They had waited until the last minute.

Where had she been? When friends came to the studio that evening to find her, it was quite empty. In the setting sun, *The Gossips*, magnificent, brilliant, was finished. A dress of scarlet silk was hanging from the beam. It had a number on it. It was a rented gown.

Letter *from the Asylum*

In first class I won't be able to eat anything at all. I don't want to touch all the greasy fat that makes me terribly sick. I've asked for baked potatoes noon and night, and that's what I live on. Is it worth paying twenty francs a day for that? I have to say, you are the ones who are crazy.

Letter *from the Asylum*

I have already told you that those in first class are the most miserable. First of all, their dining room is drafty, they sit at a tiny little table, all squeezed together. All year long they have dysentery, which is not a sign that the food is any good. The basic food is as follows: soup (the liquid from badly cooked vegetables without any meat); an old beef stew in an oily black sauce, sour the year round, an old dish of macaroni swimming in grease, or an old dish of the same sort of rice, in short, just plain grease; for hors d'oeuvres, a tiny slice of raw ham; for dessert some stringy old dates or three tough old figs, or three stale biscuits or an old piece of goat cheese. So much for your twenty francs a day. The wine is vinegar, the coffee is chick-pea water.

"Among the Finest Sculptors . . ."

We can say that she is among the finest sculptors of the day, if not the finest.

MATHIAS MORHARDT

THERE. Almost at the top. The "giant" was not far off. The critics had spoken of genius, she had been made a member of the Society of Fine Arts and even a member of the jury. The featherless bird was going to take its place of honor. Camille compared herself to the old shabby, bristling crow who struts and flutters on his perch. On one foot! And he doesn't see that he has no more feathers, no more crest.

Winter had come. After the brilliant reviews of the last Salon, there were a few lines and the claptrap of Master Renard. And she didn't even have any cheese to drop. Ah well, there she was. With her thirty-three years upon her.

She shouldn't complain. She still had a few green feathers, she was still a pretty bird! Bone structure and a few fine green feathers. Her *Gossips* in jade had been a triumph at the Salon at the Champs-de-Mars. Indeed, she had thought she would never make it to this month of May 1897. And look what they had written:

"What a marvelous thing! That this exquisite work took weeks and weeks of laborious effort, that it took all the patience and passion of the young artist to ensure its realization at this level of truth, we have no doubt. But never mind!"

Well! They'd had it easy. They weren't the ones who had suffered two terrible years.

And she had been so cold. All the time. The winter dragged on and on, creeping into her legs, her stomach, her arms. She would never be done with such cold. So she had made herself a fire, but with kindling, a small fire. Camille laughed all alone. She liked to amuse herself: wood was expensive, it would be better to use it for sculpture.

Camille Claudel! The Salon of 1897! She warmed her hands near the fire. Thanks to Mathias, to Fenaille, to the few who had believed in her, she had finished her admirable *Gossips* in jade. Her success only underscored their contempt. She was so widely discussed, she couldn't have any material problems! If only they had known, if only they could have seen her curled up against cold and hunger. She hadn't even been able to ask her father for money; he didn't have a large fortune, and he had to help Louise. Poor Louise, who had just lost her husband. So young, she, too, was so alone . . .

Monsieur Rodin! He hadn't changed. He had wanted to present her to the president of the republic. That was folly. She searched. Pipelette had no dress for her. Madame Morhardt was not her size. Her sister? Impossible. Other women? How they would have laughed! She always had her parasol, but no hat, no shoes. One night she had made herself a dress – from an old rose-colored curtain. Monsieur Rodin's face fell when he saw it – he, who so loved beauty! Finally she had suggested that she come as she was. In her old black dress. But he had said that everyone would think she meant it as a provocation.

Once she had disregarded their opinion, and she would never forget the lesson she had learned. She had embarrassed them, dishonored them. There had been a large reception at the home of Maurice Fenaille. The illuminated fountain, dinner, coffee, liqueurs. It had all been torture. Rodin had gone off at the beginning of the evening. He was dancing attendance on the beautiful and shallow Madame Fenaille, who looked so charming in an evening dress. Camille had understood that her wretched appearance would only detract from the quality of her sculpture. Finally they would have "pity" on her. Her luxurious art, her polished marbles, the refined cutting and shaping of the stone, the riot of beauty she offered them, the golden patinas that evoked the Renaissance, the expansive opulence – her work was out of character with the woman. Which was credible? That evening, Rodin had taken her home without a word.

He had just bought the Villa des Brillants at Meudon. How was he doing? Clearly, the studios were always busy. But the *Balzac* was not progressing, and *The Burghers of Calais*, inaugurated that year, had been in the works, let's see . . . since 1885. More than ten years! As for *The Gates of Hell*, the less said, the better.

"Artists of all styles and schools, having thought long enough, are now preparing for future battles. In a silence propitious to annual sojourns in the country, it is fitting that we decide whether the year now ending is bringing us the revelation of some precious personality. In perfect sincerity, a single woman emerges from the group . . ."

Thank you, Monsieur de Braine! Camille was crouching by the fire, she raised her head. It would be hard.

"But her name provokes immediate argument."

She knew that. The critic taught her nothing she didn't already know. But she would earn a second chance. Mathias had just shown her his article. "My friend Mathias."

"*The Gossips* had shed the first rays of glory on her name. Yet today she does not dwell on her celebrity."

Certainly not.

She had too much to do, and then there was the *Clotho* in marble. Nearly finished. But she was waiting for 1898 on firm footing. Well, *one* firm foot; the other was her share of the dream, of flight, of the beginning of an ascension.

"Mademoiselle Claudel with her *Gossips* in jade . . ."

Jade! No one had dared to carve directly in jade. Camille smiled.

Grand Guignol

If truth must die, my Balzac will be hacked to pieces by future generations. If truth is imperishable, I predict that my statue will make its way.

AUGUSTE RODIN

NIGHT. A dark corner. Destruction everywhere. Yes, every-thing had come back to her: the men, the two technicians she had hired to help her work. She had very little money, so she had taken on the poorest workers. Stone breakers. What a strange idea! But she had wanted to make progress. She had no referrals. She had heard at the studio on rue de l'Université that as a last resort, when there was too much work, you could recruit such men. Properly supervised, they could lend a helpful hand. She had gotten a helpful hand, all right – she had landed on the ground. She had made one remark, and one of the men had walked toward the door, she thought he was leaving, when the other grabbed her from behind and twisted her arms. Of course, they weren't expensive! She hadn't paid them, but now her pockets were empty. And saying what she often repeated when her statues broke: "I'd rather it were me" – well, this time she'd gotten her wish. She lay like a broken puppet. She had called for help. No one had come. And it had been her fault, living like this, all alone. It was bound to happen. She had lost consciousness twice. Her dress was

269

torn, she was bleeding. She hadn't moved all night. For the first time in her life she had been afraid.

It was Mathias Morhardt who found her. He was supposed to come in the morning, they had made a lunch date. Her teeth were chattering so hard she couldn't speak. Her throat, her throat. She showed him her neck. She wasn't badly injured, but she had lost her voice from fear. Mathias was distraught; he had wanted to call Monsieur Rodin, her mother, the doctor, but she had clutched at him to stop. He had finally calmed down, left the door open, crossed the courtyard, and told Pipelette to go and fetch the doctor. They had soothed her, tended to her needs. Morhardt had brought her home, his wife had nursed her.

"She has just spent a miserable week because of two wretched technicians who persecuted her with extraordinary malice. We have had them arrested by the prefecture of police . . ." Why had Morhardt informed Paul? Now he was worried. She had to answer his letter. She had already been made to testify.

A few days later she had moved back to her studio, more determined than ever.

Rodin had left for the summer in Touraine. Sketch after sketch, the *Balzac* defied him, eluded him. The nude studies, the studies of the body, Balzac in a jacket, Balzac with his hands behind his back, Balzac with hands crossed over his stomach, Balzac as an ordinary man, Balzac with his prominent belly, Balzac in a dressing gown, Balzac in a smoking jacket . . . From day to day Rodin had grown more irascible.

Camille had worked. Rodin had shown her a new study. She had laughed, imagining the head of the commission. Especially Alfred Duquet, advocate for the discontented. This was before the holidays. Already! Poor Alfred Duquet would have to confront a Monsieur Balzac with his heavy cloak half-open, naked. Naked as she could never have imagined, obscenely naked.

Rodin was standing there; no, he didn't think it was at all amusing. He was angry. He thought she took his attempts seriously. Monsieur Duquet had already dubbed this study a "colossal fetus." The quip had struck with full force. He had seen nothing, noticed nothing. He complained. He had to deliver his statue in twenty-four hours. "No, Camille, listen to me. In twenty-four hours!"

He didn't look well. She studied him. He continued: "Jean Aicard

is discouraged. You know, the president of the Society of Letters."
Yes, she knew. This group had been in existence nearly ten years.

"Émile Zola led the way. And now Zola is busy with that Dreyfus
affair. I am abandoned." Dozens of people were concerned about him,
all of fashionable Paris! And he felt abandoned! He ought to write, defend himself.

"No, everything is happening at once! I have the flu. Constant
headaches. I am in a state of exhaustion, you have no idea. And you
never come! I have to leave."

Then the other day someone had reported to her Duquet's nasty
remark: "That man is not well. If he should die, we will have lost our
ten thousand francs." These people were utterly crass. They were the
same men who sent the bailiffs to Balzac's door. And now they were all
in a rage, exercising their vocal chords because a sculptor was trying to
do justice to his model. She raised her head to him. "You remember?
Monsieur Rodin – a statue costs the time that it costs . . ."

He smiled, he wrote. Tomorrow he would ask his secretary to look
over his letter, unless she wanted to help him . . . He timidly apologized: he made mistakes, he didn't know how to construct a graceful
sentence. "After all, spelling mistakes are like mistakes in drawing!"

She had come back to her own place. She was cold and alone.
Alone with all that work! She had to succeed. She did not have any ten
thousand francs. If she were going to die, they wouldn't lose much.
No, it didn't help to envy him. She simply had to carry on, that's all.

She had accepted a commission from Mathias Morhardt. It was
delayed but she could not give up on it. Rodin hadn't the time to concern himself with her; she hadn't wanted to bother him. You were a
woman sculptor if they let you.

Mathias Morhardt's commission . . . Camille didn't dare visit
him anymore. What could she say? She hadn't finished it, and instead
she'd done smaller sculptures to have something to sell. She hadn't
sold anything for months and months. The commission, finish Morhardt's commission. For once she had one. Ten busts in bronze that
would be sold for three hundred francs a piece. Ten busts of Monsieur
Rodin. For which she had to pay the smelter, do the work of chiseling
herself, and engrave the medallion. At times she felt like putting a bul-
let through her head. Would she be paid? She hadn't received any advance. She hadn't dared to ask for one. Morhardt had advised her,

moreover, to demand nothing until the work was finished: "It's the *Mercure de France,* they have no confidence in a woman, you know!" So she'd had to borrow money to begin the work. She would soon be a thousand francs in debt.

She remembered: Léon Maillard! The two engravings she had done for him. He hadn't paid her for them. How could that have happened to her, a friend of the master! The worst thing was that she had already delivered them. She had written to Rodin to ask him to intervene. The engravings were at Léon Maillard's or somewhere else, but not a sou. It had been almost ten years . . .

Rodin was ill. Well done! "I am sure that you have overeaten at your cursed dinners, with the cursed world that I despise, which robs you of your time and your health, and gives you nothing in return." Why wear herself out? Why bother? He was heading for disaster. "I am powerless to save you from the harm I see. How are you going to work on the model for your figure? . . ."

My God! He had so little time left. As soon as the model was done, the studios would gear up and move into action. In a few weeks, he would still manage. The May Salon was approaching. As for her, that was another story . . .

"You reproach me for not writing at sufficient length. But you yourself send me only a few lines that don't give me much pleasure.

"You are right to think that I am not very happy here. I feel I'm so far away from you, and like a complete stranger."

And then that journey to make. How tiring.

"With fond affection, *Camille.*"

Mathias Morhardt had come to see her, to take her out of her solitude. No, she would not go to this dinner. Thank you very much! If Rodin were not there, conversation would turn to the Dreyfus affair. If Rodin were there, they would only talk about the *Balzac.* Between the two . . .

She knew the Dreyfus affair by heart! "Listen to me, Camille," Morhardt had said. "I am president of the League of the Rights of Man. This affair is important, you know! Just because you're a woman doesn't mean you should ignore politics. Well, that's how it is with you women when we neglect you a little!" As for Rodin, perhaps he was concerned about Captain Dreyfus, but he only talked about himself, about his *Balzac,* himself, only himself.

Ten busts of Monsieur Rodin! Ten busts. No! Impossible! Ten busts for Mathias Morhardt! He must have been joking, have pity on me! In her exhaustion she wondered whether the face she was touching here, now, was a reproduction – and a poor one at that. The features hadn't been properly modeled, it wasn't going well.

"Camille, what is it? You were so far away!" Auguste was there, nearby. She could no longer distinguish what was real from her sculpture. Everything was shimmering before her tired eyes.

"What a good fire! It feels fine at your place! What a shame! I would love to have a peaceful corner like this . . . It's just not possible at Meudon! Nor at the studios. Always such a crowd! A real commotion! Visits, interviews, press dates, the committee, friends, but I'm only concerned with one thing, Cam . . . I'm worried about making an artistic mistake . . . Listen. I remember what my old master Barye said to a fellow student – you know, Barye. He often came to the Jardin des Plantes, he was a sculptor of animals. I can see him now . . . We were fourteen, fifteen years old. In his threadbare suit . . . he looked like a poor secondary school tutor . . . I have never known a man so sad, with such power. He constructed his works himself and sold them at bargain prices. And had trouble doing it. A man of genius!" Camille listened to Rodin.

" . . . Yes, I can see him saying to a complaining student: 'As for me, on the contrary, I am grateful to fate; I have been making sculpture for forty years and I am not dead yet.'"

Camille looked at the tired man beside her. She still loved him. Why? Perhaps because of stories like the one he'd just told her.

She got up, poked the fire, wrapped herself in a blanket. She was there on her knees, she had just put back the poker. She rested her two arms on the cloak, as if in prayer.

Rodin contemplated the sculpture she had nearly finished. A bronze, *Woman/Dreaming by the Fire*. But how had she done all that! She must have had help. And yet Morhardt had told him that she worked too hard, she didn't eat enough. He looked at the form draped in the light cloth, kneeling. He would have liked to touch her, to caress her. She looked like a nun.

"You have . . ." Suddenly he could see the document, the document by Louis Boulanger – 1837 – the description of Lamartine. It faded out, her image superimposed: she was Lamartine, no, she was

"Balzac in a dressing gown" – they always found him dressed in a long cashmere robe, tied like a monk's habit, "with a silk cord." He had it! That was it!

"What were you going to say?" Camille stood up, she came toward him.

"You look like a nun . . . You know that Balzac wore a monk's habit as his dressing gown!"

She laughed. "Great men! They can do anything. Of course, he was tremendous, both literally and figuratively. You're making progress on the *Balzac?*"

"I think so. But people are pressing me."

"And that horrid man, that dunce Duquet?"

"I must exhibit at the next Salon or no more money! They annoy me. They don't want to understand."

Not to think about money! He had plenty. Brutally she told him: "You know what I am looking for. The design. The general features. Nothing more. No more details, no more anecdotes. Simplicity. Hokusai – yes, you know my passion for Hokusai. You mentioned religion. Yes, in a way. But let's be clear, not like Paul, no. Never. You remember the sentence . . ."

She leaned forward a little more, pulling the blanket closer around her body; there she was, collected, an Oriental statuette, an ancient Buddha. She told him the story of the "giant," described the fabulous stone of her childhood. A giant like Balzac! "Whether a single point or a line, it will all come alive. When I am a hundred and ten years old, my art – "

He suddenly got up. He embraced her, turned her around, clasped her. She struggled, shaken by raucous laughter. "I'm speaking seriously to you and – "

He devoured her, took her. He had regained all his strength, as if he were sculpting. The blanket slipped off the warm, voluptuous, earthbound body that was never wrong, the flesh he knew so well. He knew how.

In the space of a few moments, Camille forgot that she had work to do.

The date of the Salon was approaching. Camille had to answer Rodin. Through Le Bosse – there was a good technician – he had sent her his last study for the *Balzac.* Quickly, he wanted a response. Le Bosse had to come for it. Camille hurried.

"I think it is very fine and very beautiful, and the best of all your studies of the subject. Especially the highly accentuated effect of the head, which contrasts with the simplicity of the drapery . . . in short, I believe you should expect great success, especially with your experts . . ."

One month more. She no longer knew where she was going, what she was doing. She worked. White eyes, white hands, white face. Her heart beat. Too fast. Too tired. She was hot.

Mathias, his wife, and the doctor were leaning over her. What had happened? It was nothing! Exhaustion and lack of food.

And then there were the envious. Rodin had advised Morhardt not to publish his article on her. Fortunately! It hadn't occurred to her that once again it might provoke "anger and revenge."

One month. One month left. Ask Morhardt where Rodin had bought the block of rose marble, and especially, especially – she begged – be careful with her bust of the young girl. It was fragile, so fragile – burning hours of her life exposed there. He was afraid. Quickly she reworked it. They mustn't touch it! They must protect it!

The exhibition would be held at the Palais des Machines. The administration had almost thrown her cards in her face. Her bust was stuck away in the dust and the sun. It was so fragile. Write to Rodin, let him know.

One night. One night left. He had to do something. But where was he? One more night to work.

The day of the opening of the Salon, in the huge space of the Champ-de-Mars . . .

"Move along, young lady." Camille hesitated a moment. Did she dare to say that she was exhibiting, that she had to get through? She didn't even have a card. Three days ago they had nearly thrown her out. Her white lace collar, her little black dress, it was understandable if they took her for a student. It was just her luck, and no one had been free to come with her! Did she dare to say she was a sculptor?

The Salon had just opened. There was an enthusiastic crowd. The huge hall trembled from top to bottom. Decked out with entries for the exhibition, the Palais des Machines gallery was so vast it seemed endless. Camille would be truly triumphant at the great Exhibition in 1900. She felt it. Then they would see!

"What are you here to see?"

"The *Balzac*, like everyone else. People have been talking about it for ten years."

A group of giddy young people in flowered suits and reddish hats pushed through the multitude, and she followed behind them. There, she was in!

Then she reeled. There it was. No need to go farther. It stood out, five meters tall against the great nave. Five meters! She shouted. He was going to fall on her. The giant! The great ghost gazed at her, his mouth twisted with irony and pity. She was pushed and pulled to him.

"Cast right in his plaster gown," immaculate, lifting his head painfully, "his eyes seeking the sun and already overcome by darkness" – someone had said that, someone nearby had just said that. She no longer knew, she was about to die. That was thirty years ago . . . It was yesterday. And here she was, hiding herself as if she were naked, slipping away. Beside the sculpture stood Rodin, tranquil and serene in the shadow of a large hat. Camille had put her hand to her mouth, trying to stifle another cry. This time she was in agony – between the giant and Monsieur Rodin she had just seen *The Kiss*, the work conceived fifteen years before. *The Kiss!* "Where are you going, Mam'zelle Camille?" – "To Monsieur Rodin's." – "At this hour?"

She retreated, borne back by the crowd. Give it to me! Her two hands groped blindly, but she was swept back to the exit. She was left at the door. She was forever retreating. Away from the artist!

The *Balzac!* Rodin had found him. It was over. Someone exclaimed: "An unspeakable hoax!" She froze.

"If Balzac were to come back, he would repudiate his statue." She didn't move.

"No, I can't criticize it, I don't understand it." She remained paralyzed.

"What sculpture! That Rodin, he shows us all the way!" She held her breath.

"You've seen it, one senses the pitilessly modeled nakedness beneath. He seems to palpitate and shudder with the beating of a heart about to stop." Camille was naked.

"You're dreaming, my friend. Your *Balzac!* A grand *guignol!* That's what you'll find beneath. A miserable grotesque!"

"Ah, my poor woman, are you all right?" A man approached. "Sit down here, I'll go look for someone. It isn't very sensible to go out at your age. There are more than two thousand people here. You wanted to see the *Balzac.* And the entrance fee isn't cheap. Poor woman!" She raised her eyes. It was just as well this man was talking. She could hardly make him out. "Don't move, now. I'm going to look for someone. We'll get you home." He went off.

Then she fled. As she was leaving, she perceived her bust, the fragile bust exposed to the sun and the dust, stuck off there in a corner. The enormous crowd was crushing it, too. Never mind! She was running now. The hot street, the pavement. She fell, pushed herself up. Quickly! Quickly! The passersby turned to look at her. Some jeered. "A madwoman!" "A vagrant!"

Quickly, quickly! Boulevard d'Italie. There was Pipelette, the courtyard, the studio, the closing door, the shadow . . . She fell to her knees. Crawling, she looked for matches to burn the drawings, all the sketches of the grand *guignol.* Bang! Bang!

Why had she told him?

The fabulous stone of her childhood.

She had given him her giant.

Her secret was gone.

Letter *from the Asylum*

Imagination, feeling, the new, the unexpected that emerge from a developed mind are closed to them, with their pasty faces, their thick brains forever shut to the light; they need someone to furnish it for them. They used to say: ". . . we use a dreamer to find us our subject matter."

There should be someone, at least, who would be truly grateful for their living and know how to give some compensation to the poor woman whom they robbed of her genius: but no! a lunatic asylum! not even the right to have a home of my own! Because I'm completely at their mercy! That is exploiting the woman, crushing the artist — they want to make me sweat blood.

The Twentieth
Century Begins

*A woman sits looking at the fire, this is the subject of
one of my poor sister's last sculptures . . . When I
think of her soul, this is how I would see her . . . Sitting and looking at the fire. There is no one. Everyone
is dead, or what amounts to the same thing.*

PAUL CLAUDEL, *La Rose et le rosaire*

SHE WAS THERE by the hearth. All the kindling was used up.
It was raining. She sat in front of the fire. It was out. 19, quai de
Bourbon. Camille Claudel, 19, quai de Bourbon. She had no more
cards left, and hadn't had any for a long time now. No more Pipelette
either. She stared at the empty blackened hearth. The ashes were
damp now.

She had written the letter.

It was raining hard. It rained and rained. A bit bent, her shivering
back wrapped in a cashmere shawl, her tears were dried. But it was all
over.

She had written the letter.

The door was closed now. Paul had been there earlier. She had
been so glad to see him again, her old Chinaman. They hadn't seen
each other for five years. He'd been anxious. But everything was going
well. She had regrouped, gotten back on her feet, as they say. Finally,
hopping on one foot! Last year she had exhibited *Maturity*. A great success. The usual reviews, of course . . .

Her old Paul! He was thirty-three now. China! Shanghai! Hong Kong! He would have to tell her everything – remember, you promised? – but her sister Louise had come looking for Paul. "Mama is waiting." Louise had vaguely nibbled Camille's biscuits.

"We're in a hurry, you know."

Camille had also returned to Azay to claim her things. Old Madame Courcelles had wanted to make her pay rent! "You understand, I have kept your things, your busts, your studies here, as you asked me to do!" Camille had looked at the half-broken busts. She had taken the clay; it might be useful. "And then Monsieur Rodin said you weren't coming back."

She sent the letter now.

Jeanne mimicked all Monsieur Rodin's gestures. Her little Jeanne. She must be nearly fifteen! Plump, her hair frizzed, cheeks rouged, eyes dull, she had barely greeted Mademoiselle Claudel. She had fidgeted, impatient to be off, stiff in a flowered or flounced dress. So dowdy! A boyfriend was waiting for her: "You know, he's taking me . . . We're going fishing!" Jeanne exclaimed.

Going through her things, Camille had rediscovered a soiled, half-torn drawing of Matuvu. She had questioned Madame Courcelles: "Oh, he is dead. We ate him. A bit tough, he was."

Camille had questioned: "But the drawing, the girl? . . ."

"Oh, she hasn't touched it for a long time. It was fine when she was little. Now there are boys . . ."

Then there was Mélanie. Camille had never quite understood how she lived. It didn't matter to her. Mélanie sometimes stopped by for a visit. She smelled a bit of wine, of sweat, but she had a fine laugh. Her response to every concern was simply to shrug her bony shoulders. She would chase away worries by saying, "Come on! geddy-up, darling!"

She brought newpapers she had unearthed heaven knows where. Camille didn't want to know. "Here y'are, m'zelle Flaubel, that'll cheer you up." Ten times Camille had told her: *Clau, Claudel* – or simply Camille. She had laughed, shrugged her shoulders. "M'zelle Flaubel!"

She had come recently, a bit red in the face, her blouse unbuttoned. "Say, he's not your boyfriend, M'sieur Auguste!" Camille hadn't understood. "M'sieur Rodin! . . . Hey, look! . . . there're three bankers lending him money! Funny, huh! Wait, I'm trying to find where I read it!" Camille had held herself very straight.

"There, for the International Exposition! He's having a pavilion built! And in style! Wait, oh, I can't read very good, Louis something! Him, he must think he's the Sun King! . . . That looks like the orangery of a castle. Oo la la! They're going to bring all his work together. Even the Americans are coming. Oh, how exciting! Seems he don't know which way to turn. It's my friends who told me. Fine gentlemen. I told them that you knew him in your time, M'zelle Flaubel. But it didn't impress them. They don't know your name! Seems they come from all over the world to ask his opinion. Worse, they all want him to do their portrait! He's called 'the Sultan of Meudon'!"

She'd looked up a moment from the paper. Her hazel eyes dreamy, she had sighed: "A boyfriend like that, I wouldn't have let him go, not me. One of them – one of my friends, he often sees him, I don't ask their names – told me that he's helped lots of women. I wouldn't have let him go!"

The paper hung there like a last autumn leaf. Camille had wept, silently.

> The wind, the wind, the wind blows high
> The rain comes scattering down the sky
> She is handsome, she is pretty
> She is the girl of the golden city
> La la la . . .

"See you tomorrow M'zelle Flaubel! Maybe . . . " She went off singing her music hall song. She would come to drink something, get warm when Camille made a fire, she would sing her the new songs. She would tell her about life out there.

Evening fell. Tears, tears, tears, hours, running down two tracks that finally stopped, dried up. She had waited too long. So she had taken her pen, ink, and paper – without revisions, without hesitation, without anger, without pain, without a shudder, without bitterness, without envy, without reproach, without regret, without love, she had written the words meant for him.

She had folded the paper, sealed the letter, and sent it off. She had closed the door again and felt nothing. She looked at the night around her.

"The twentieth century is beginning and . . ."

I have found the lost bead!
I have found my lost number . . .
That hoarded tear. That unchangeable diamond . . .

PAUL CLAUDEL, Le Soulier de satin

FROM MONTDEVERGUES, poor Camille sends a rosary to Mama made with a heart-shaped bead called a "Job's tear." (Paul Claudel, *Journal.*)

Camille had kept a single bead in the hollow of her hand. She no longer knew what to do with a rosary. How many dozens exactly. And then you had to add a few little beads . . .

In her palm she warms a tiny sculpture, her heart filched from the world.

Standing near the stove. The freezing snows of Montdevergues. The huddling old ladies, poor trembling moles.

Camille paralyzed in full flight. Her wing folded against her left breast. A new Çacountala. A tragic surrender.

"Everyone is dead or what amounts to the same thing. And that is why I am holding this bead indefinitely between my thumb and index finger, and I cannot go on." (Paul Claudel, *La Rose et le rosaire.*)

Cross Your T's

DEAR SIR,
"I beg you to do your best to prevent Monsieur Rodin from coming to see me on Tuesday. If at the same time you can gently but firmly suggest to Monsieur Rodin that he should cease his visits to me, you would give me the most palpable pleasure. Monsieur Rodin is not unaware that many mean-spirited people have taken it into their heads to say that he was responsible for my sculpture; therefore, why should he do his utmost to give credit to this libel? If Monsieur Rodin really wants to be of help to me, it is quite possible for him to do so without making people think that I owe the success of works over which I have taken such pains solely to his advice and inspiration . . ."

Rodin refused to see visitors. Rose was disturbed by them. A single wave of the hand had sufficed. She had turned them away. Mathias Morhardt had come by. Leaving the studio at Meudon, he had said simply: "I will come back tomorrow. Monsieur Rodin wants to be alone."

Monsieur Rodin had not lit the lamp. He sat there, his two arms dangling. One by one the tears slid down his cheeks. He did not wipe them away.

In his right hand he held a letter. No need for a signature. Besides, she rarely signed her letters. Or her works – "Time effaces all signatures, Monsieur Rodin," she had said, and burst into her hearty laugh. He had recognized the way she crossed her t's: the lines were even longer now, they pierced the paper. He had known right away. His friend Morhardt had given him the letter and he had understood. So he sat there.

For the first time in his life, he was afraid. He, the Sultan of Meudon, sought after by people from all over the world, courted by all the women; he had money, commissions, success. The *Balzac* was finished. His last kiss! Fifteen years of work.

Suddenly he was afraid of all the time he had left to live, without her. He felt brutally empty, useless. *Vanitas vanitatum.* She was there before his eyes, that somber figure he had modeled two years earlier.

The t's trailed across the paper. Here he was, entering his sixtieth year without projects, without sculpture, without her!

She was only thirty-five years old. At that age, he had undertaken *The Age of Bronze*, his first scandal.

Letter *from the Asylum*

It's really too much! . . . And to condemn me to perpetual prison so that I won't complain!

All of that actually comes right from Rodin's diabolical brain. He had only one idea, that with him dead, I would come into my own as an artist and become greater than he. He had to keep me in his clutches after his death, just as he did in his lifetime. He wants me as unhappy with him dead as alive. He has succeeded on all counts, for unhappy I certainly am! . . . I am so weary of this bondage.

Dear master and friend, I have just seen Monsieur
Philippe Berthelot, to whom I have imparted your
wishes concerning the poor and admirable artist . . . I
have insisted that we join together in our efforts . . .
all hope of cure being illusory? . . . What I would like
is for you to agree to reserve a room in the Hôtel Biron
for the work *of Camille Claudel.*

MATHIAS MORHARDT
to Auguste Rodin, 5 June 1914

WITHOUT GIVING her time to decide, he took her head
violently between his hands, like a prayer, like a quest, and
kissed her hard on the lips. "No, no, don't leave again!" His hands
squeezed her hard.

Then she felt a rush of pleasure, she wanted him to regret her, she
wanted to do as he did with his models. She decided to take what she
wanted and then leave, insolently. She had learned a great deal with
him, tenderness but also havoc, sweetness and humiliation, waiting.
She would throw it all at his body that night; she was also a great sculptor of men. The hot body became clay, she was pitiless, indifferent, the
artist lashing the human being and drawing out his last spasm.

She undressed him. He peeled her dress from her body. She held
it, that sensual pulse throbbing between her hands, and swelling. She
had seized it first, like an abduction. He took her breasts. The couple
faced each other like two ancient warriors – she erect, her chest like a
breastplate of white gold, he with his bronze sword glistening in her
hand, the searching blade. The white bed like a sandy beach struck life-

287

less by the sun. He looked straight into her eyes – she was her own murderer. Suddenly she turned brutally, vulgarly, and burst out laughing. She undid her hair, glancing at him as it flowed down her back. His sex was in her flowing hair, she rubbed her neck against him and quickly turned around, caught him by the lips, then let him go. "Monsieur Rodin" – his name sounded like a shot, she was arrogant, he wanted to kill her; he had understood the label, the insult.

Even here she had become his equal. He did not dare to say that here, too, she had outdistanced him. He understood that he would never possess her completely, he had lost. She was forever indomitable; he had been wrong one day – too many days.

Then suddenly he wanted another child with her. Like a woman who tries to keep a departing lover, he cried out his demand, a man playing his last card. He had reached her. Camille stopped, transfixed, her eyes devastated. She looked at him and slowly folded her legs, she was wounded to death – the child, a remembrance that seared her memory.

Perhaps she had been dreaming.

Maturity

*There is a symbol here that all minds concerned with the
great modern problems, feminism, democratic art, and
so forth, can scarcely mistake: the symbol of a poor devil
with an altogether awkward behind, with its two fat,
pathetic cheeks, who is trying to tear himself out of the
muck, and struggles, and twists, and asks for wings!*

PAUL CLAUDEL, *Rodin ou l'homme de génie*
September–October 1905

Frou-frou . . . frou-frou . . .
Petticoats whirling,
Frou-frou . . . frou-frou . . .
Redingotes twirling . . .

"Ah well, see, M'zelle Camille, you're making progress. Soon
you'll come and sing with me. I earn something from it, I do, some
sous, not like you. And then, there're extras."

Mélanie was satisfied. If M'zelle Flaubel had listened to her
sooner, she wouldn't have been there. Not bad, this girl. And beautiful, too. She had sold everything, nothing left in her apartment. Even
her personal things were gone.

"Look, tonight I've brought you some peaches. I'm going to the
country. They're taking me. And then some vegetables. I'm leaving it
all for you. Just need to recuperate from time to time!"

Camille kissed her, she liked her very much, Mélanie.

Since the Salon, since the *Balzac*, Camille had already moved twice.
There had been 63, rue de Turenne, and then 19, quai de Bourbon. She

felt fine there. The high walls, Mélanie, the empty studio. It was true that she'd sold everything. *Frou-frou!* She had to straighten things up a bit. This afternoon. For now there was sculpture. Her great sculpture. Six years ago she had thought everything was over, finished — *the grand guignol!*

She was wearing a scarf to protect her hair. She was singing *Frou-frou!* She was laughing more often. She had started work on her great sculpture.

Camille worked. The distant noises from the street were muffled by the vigorous tapping of her mallet. She was not yet forty years old. She was still beautiful, shapely. Her great sculpture! She had discovered that she had all her life — well, nearly all her life — before her. Hokusai had only just begun at sixty. He had considered his earlier works childish stammerings. Camille struck. The old, slightly torn smock, her clumsy clogs no longer embarrassed her. She had time now.

Paul had left for China again. Go, you Chinaman! More silent and closed than ever. One year. He had only stayed in France a year. One day he'd announced that he was leaving for a certain period of time. Camille had known. He was in Ligugé. He wanted to be a monk.

Camille couldn't read the newspapers anymore. His photograph was everywhere, the name of Rodin. She was finishing his busts . . . Truly nauseating! She had to pay to the end! Mathias Morhardt was waiting for the ten busts. She found Rodin ugly, wrinkled, pretentious.

In her weary head, the friends who supported her were confused with those who had signed in favor of that Captain Dreyfus. She hated them all. She was the one on trial. But no one had come to her defense. It was Monsieur Rodin they continued to pity. He had to be helped. Everyone did his part — the fashionable world!

And Monsieur Rodin had asked that the names Forain and Rochefort, notorious anti-Dreyfusards, be added to the list of subscribers to the statue of Balzac! He had been afraid to get mixed up in these political debates: "He didn't want to get involved in the Dreyfus affair!" You never know!

And Morhardt had so often reproached her — "Take an interest in what's going on. Look at Monsieur Rodin! All his friends are Dreyfusards!" She was laughing now. She imagined all their faces! Grand *guignol!* But at least she wasn't a coward.

Only Clemenceau had been brutal. Since Monsieur Rodin was

afraid to see too many of Zola's friends in his corner, Georges Clemenceau had withdrawn his name from the subscription list: it was written in black and white in *L'Aurore*.

You can't have everything, Monsieur Rodin. You had to compromise a little, didn't you? And he hadn't wanted to pay the price. Come on, then! She had no Legion of Honor, no decorations, no top hat! Ah, it had been a long time since they had laughed together over that scandal.

"You can buy the Legion of Honor. And other decorations too, you know? Just address yourself to Monsieur Daniel Wilson. What? The son-in-law of the president of the republic, yes indeed . . ." Nothing had changed. Even him! Even him! He probably hadn't wanted it and was now grappling with his conscience. He no longer sculpted. Receptions, interviews, women, travels, decorations, official busts, how could he refuse all that? She would have liked to take him by the hand, once more. They would have saved each other . . .

"My dear friends,

"I have the express desire to remain the sole possessor of my work. My interrupted labor, my reflections, everything demands it now. I am concerned above all with my artistic dignity, and beg you to declare that I am withdrawing my *Balzac* monument from the Salon at the Champ-de-Mars; it will be erected nowhere."

Bravo, Monsieur Rodin!

"The artist, like the woman, has his honor to protect," he had said. A fine turn of phrase! But how could he withdraw his work without returning his commission?

She didn't even have anything to eat, she was reduced to selling other people's works. Henri Lerolle, her dear Lerolle, had given her a painting as a token of their friendship for Claude Debussy. She loved this picture, she looked at it often, at different times of the day, in the changing light. But one morning the picture, too, had gone. She had explained it to him. "You will forgive me, won't you, since you know the panic of artists reduced to the last extremity . . ." He had kindly signed the painting so that she might get more money for it. Never had she endured such shame. She was not an animal! No, cut to the quick, sick to death, she had forced herself to look her old friend Lerolle in the eye as she explained her predicament.

It was spring. Toward evening she had set out for Meudon. She wanted to see the *Balzac* at his home, in the flesh. To understand. She had just given away a bit of her heart, a last small crumb – this painting.

She went along the rough ascent toward Meudon, the Villa des Brillants. The shade, the evensong of the birds, stronger, more piercing. There, the slope, the Val Fleury, as they called it in the papers. Dozens of times she had read and reread the description. She couldn't be mistaken. "The Villa des Brillants" on the summit above.

Camille had more and more difficulty breathing. The birds were calling loudly now, and quarreling. Time was suspended, the roads disappeared, everything gradually grew blurred. Her feet on the muddy path. Soon she glimpsed the villa. So she crossed over to it.

She looked like those gypsies who pass through villages. She was youth, she was the unknown woman who passes through your life for a moment – the sudden stroke of fate, of luck. She had no child in her arms. The lengthy stride, the carriage of the head that made her look like some wandering princess – where was her kingdom? Where did she come from? The dogs who saw her stopped barking, frightened. A great she-wolf, Camille walked toward the advancing night. Her eyes glittered, her skirt slapped against her long thighs. Beneath the rising moon, white now, she seemed to leap – she appeared, disappeared. She went on, over great swathes of mown grass. Her hair swung against the nape of her neck. She stopped, withdrawn, the magnificent beast was there, lying in wait, and his savage cat's-eyes pierced the murky dusk.

He was there, two steps away, a bit bowed – a black spot. He was lurching. No, not him! Impossible! Was he suffering? He seemed about to fall! She called softly to him, softly as a birdcall: "Monsieur Rodin!" He hadn't moved.

"Monsieur Rodin!" My God, he was going to collapse. So she burst from the hollow where she had been crouching, she wanted to help him, to hold him up. "Auguste!" The cry burst out.

He had turned around violently, and now they were facing each other. He smiled complacently. The same eyebrows, the same hair, the forehead, the bushy beard, but it was not him. Everything was there and yet nothing was right. This man was a parody, a caricature. She recoiled, dumbstruck. His son! His son, Auguste Beuret. No, not this drunk who held out his hands to grab her, not that licentious gaze. She disappeared.

The lights had just been lit in the Villa des Brillants. Yet it was still day. What a muddle! The noise of dishes, of cooking. Her mother at Villeneuve? The lane of chestnut trees, the regal lane that led to the Louis XIII house, the house of overlapped squares of white stone. The white stone . . . Camille had settled down a little.

He had just come out. She could distinguish his silhouette, the shadow of the man she wanted to love again. He drew near. As he did each evening, he looked at his *Balzac*. The great diagonal! A woman limping!

"Auguste, my sweet, you're going to catch cold." Rose's voice. He turned. Camille had time to catch the gaze, the head, the forehead, the beautiful mouth, the tragic face. Bewitched, her heart suddenly went out to him. Had he seen her? She had been so ready to disappear. Was it because of her that he stood there unmoving, like a man awestruck? Camille threw herself behind the nearest bushes.

There was Rose, overcoat in hand, disheveled, thin . . . "Leave me alone. I'm tired. I must think! . . . I want to think."

Camille had difficulty recognizing him, his complexion was so pale. Embittered, mean. Rose was twenty meters from him. He turned. "Have you taken the dog for a piss, my sweet?"

Rose came toward him, put the overcoat on his shoulders, and led him toward the house. A second – an eternity of horror. Silence fell once more. The final act.

Camille departed slowly, distressed. Thirty-seven years old, almost thirty-eight . . .

She had seen him three years ago. Exactly the same scene! *Maturity* or *The Paths of Life*. She had sculpted what she had just seen. She did not know then, and it had happened! "Man abducted by old age," the hideous figure of compromise, comfort with "her sagging breasts" – Paul had described her sculpture in these terms. He had made her laugh. He had looked at the man, "the pitiful old couple."

"There is a time for discovery, says Ecclesiastes, and a time for exploitation." Paul had turned toward her tenderly: "You were the discovery, little sister!"

Never had she felt so close to him. He had left for Ligugé a month later. He had broken all the vessels, cut all his ties, he had even renounced writing and gone off with just the essentials. Her Paul. He was ready for the monastery at Liguagé.

Always in China. No news of him for months. He had always written her something. But this time, nothing. The people she had seen who had been there were evasive: "Yes, he was well." "Health – oh, no." Camille felt they were all hiding something. She was anxiously awaiting his return. He would soon be thirty-seven years old. She was almost forty. *Frou-frou!* . . .

Three o'clock in the afternoon already – my God, the housework. She set down her tools, recovered the plaster, knotted a scarf over her hair, and caught up the dust rag.

She was a simple woman. She always had been. Between the monastery and success there was everyday life, humble as it was. Her work was to sculpt. So she had taken up her work. That's all. There was no other explanation, no secrets, no dreams, and no nightmares! Nothing explained anything. There were no models, no geniuses; she had done *Maturity* two or three years before Monsieur Rodin had become senile. She had made the little kneeling figure to exorcise her shame. No, all that explained nothing!

She had thought that after the break she would never sculpt again. Everything was over, wasn't it? But no, she would sculpt until her death. She had acquired the necessary tool – great patience.

There was terrible human wretchedness, and there were also practical problems: problems with the casting for Captain Tissier, who had bought *Maturity* – she had used the advance to reimburse Monsieur Fenaille; then there was the smelter Rudier, who worked for Rodin and wanted six hundred thousand francs for the job. Too much! These were her problems.

She exhibited nearly every year. A few new sculptures. But she chiseled them in marble, cast them in bronze, and sold them at laughable prices. By turns she was showered with praise and insults. "A complete figure of feminine genius," "a caricature of Rodin's genius" – dear Romain Rolland, he certainly had a way with words! Camille Mauclair: "For ten years she has exhibited works that have assured her a place as one of the three or four sculptors our epoch can claim." Eggs to pay for, the process-server, Adonis, who visited her more and more often. So what?

She had tried to find time for each thing. The postman on New Year's Day, the increasingly scarce and costly workers, the few loyal friends. Of course there was Mathias Morhardt – but she had difficulty putting up with him, Monsieur Rodin's friend! Eugène Blot, a new publisher, who took care of selling her sculptures or personal objects; Monsieur Fenaille, who tried to commission a little statuette from time to time; Henry Asselin, introduced to her by Eugène Blot . . .

Without admitting it to themselves, everyone was worried. Her febrile temperament, her nervousness, her total lack of fastidiousness, her abrupt gestures, and especially her raucous laughter . . . Her broken, piercing laughter that burst out like a gust of wrenching sobs . . .

"Oo la la! Don't forget that the postman, the sewerman, and the sweeper of quai de Bourbon are coming to greet me on New Year's Day! . . . Yours, always the same."

"The dairywoman shouts she gave me so many eggs that aren't paid for . . . Adonis Pruneaux is coming after me again (this time they won't say that it's Venus running after him!)."

"If you had wanted to protect me, I wouldn't be in this state, certainly not, certainly not!"

"I am still going to be awakened one of these mornings by the amiable Adonis Pruneaux . . . an event I would hardly find seductive, despite the white gloves and top hat this amiable civil servant always dons for the occasion. Excuse these graveyard jokes!"

"The only man running after me at the moment is the process-server." She had mimicked the visit of poor Adonis Pruneaux. He had nothing more to seize. There was only the artist herself. "Take me! The artist is for sale!"

And there were her visits to the Saint-Louis hospital: "A little eleven-year-old cousin is being cared for on my recommendation (he tried to commit suicide by cutting his stomach open with a knife in two places); we still don't know if he will live. Monsieur Pinard supervised the operation by one of his students; it's a dreadful business and evokes lasting feelings of distress."

She had not answered their questions. But every day her eyes glittered more disturbingly. Eugène Blot collected her letters, which now came at an impressive rate. But there were so few of them to help her . . .

She had continued to work. They lowered their heads a little more sadly. Her gaze embarrassed them now – as if she knew. "For," as Asselin said, "it was the delicate expression of a great and absolute openness that was unembarrassed by either forms or nuances."

There was great sculpture. She had worked at it each day. They questioned her. Was this the *Perseus* she had exhibited for the first time at the Salon? But she had put a finger to her lips and had recovered the statue with a cloth before they entered.

Paul was about to return from China for the second time.

Letter *from the Asylum*

I received the hat, it fits, the coat is fine, the stockings are wonderful, and the other things you sent me.

    I send you a kiss,

                                           Camille.

    Give me your news and tell me if you caught the flu.

    I have received your letter, which reassured me, because seeing as they were changing my class, I assumed you were dead, so I didn't sleep at night, I froze.

Such power — love, despair, and hatred expressed with such terrifying sincerity that it overflows the boundaries of the work of art . . . Maturity . . . That spirit in a supreme, initiating blaze was bound to be extinguished.

PAUL CLAUDEL, *L'Oeil écoute*
"Camille Claudel"

ONE MORNING they made the decision for her: she would not have time to grow old. They took away her time, her life, her memory — buried her alive in hell.

She became unalterable — like the asylum itself. Preserved, in a sense. My Paul!

The cloister. To the convent with her!

Was it all worth the trouble?

Rose Beuret, rooted to a stairway at Meudon, struggling to safeguard Monsieur Rodin. They came in increasing numbers: the admiring women, the dancers, the society women. It was Rose's turn. "They won't chase me away! I've taken care of him like a child for fifty-two years! They won't get away with calling me crazy, they'll have to lock me up . . . They've taken the marble statues," she cried to Judith Cladel.

Poor Rose, born in Champagne, like her, like her old mother.

Claude Debussy, dying in torment.

And Paul, where is my brother? You remember, the young girl in white at Château-Thierry. To the convent with her!

"That naked young woman is my sister! My sister Camille. Begging, humiliated, on her knees, this haughty, superb woman, this is how she represented herself. Begging, humiliated, on her knees and naked! Everything is finished. This is what she has left us to look at forever." (Paul Claudel, *L'Oeil écoute*, "Camille Claudel.")

The Red Dress
Pierced

Before the final shadows part: [*She creates a statue of*]
Perseus.
*What is this head of bloody hair he holds aloft if
not the head of madness? Yet why did I not see it, instead, as an image of remorse? That face at the end of
that raised arm, yes, I seem to recognize the distorted
features.*

PAUL CLAUDEL, *L'Oeil écoute*
"Camille Claudel"

IT WAS COLD on that day in November 1905.
"Pardon my graveyard humor."

Once again that morning, she had written to Eugène Blot. She
would be arrested the day after next. Once again Adonis Pruneaux had
arrived at dawn, as the law specified. But he was no longer smiling. He
had his orders. Nothing could move the process-server this time. Not
the momentarily distraught face of the youngish woman he had summoned from her bed – a poor pallet. Not the dance step she had traced
at the announcement of the news, not the leg that had given way, land-
ing her on the ground, not her crazy laugh. He had simply waited for
her signature.

"No comment, Monsieur Pruneaux." Why worry? She no longer
understood anything about "administrative considerations." She had
tried, but everything had gotten even more muddled. Especially in recent weeks. The papers! The references! Those things, too, required
time and money.

There was no more money. The great sculpture grew impatient

there, under its hood. She had redone everything. What she had ex-hibited in 1902 had been only a pale approximation. No, now Camille was on the verge of discovery.

A rainy, gloomy November. "The haggard days of November" – ah, how right her brother was. Especially the darkness everywhere. The endless black rain. Paul!

He had returned one evening. He had reappeared. She was waiting for him. Quai d'Orsay had notified her. He was there, at her studio. They had embraced stiffly. And then she had seen the wounded face, the mad eyes, the trembling body. He was burning; she had under-stood, she knew! And the rage, the kisses, the abandonment. He had been betrayed.

He had told her about the Scarlet Woman. A woman. Camille didn't want to know. What was the point? His entire being was crying out, wasn't that enough? She didn't want the details. Every love story sounds banal to others, vulgarly banal. A mere anecdote. She did not question him, she said nothing. It wasn't indifference. No, on the con-trary, she knew only too well! She respected the mystery of beings.

They had dined together. Finally! She had gone out to buy some-thing to eat. He had given her money. He did not want to see anyone, especially the family. Neither of them had eaten much. Paul was there, prostrate. Remote. She had a sudden desire to put him to bed, to stay beside him all night, to join him in his pain. There was nothing to say.

Paul! Child of November. She could see him munching on an ap-ple. The sad child there, near the laundry at Villeneuve.

He had shut himself up at Villeneuve. She remained in Paris.

The days of November 1905. She seemed to hear the knell, the lit-urgy for the dead, the rusty weathercock, the icy presbytery. They held each other by the hand. They were cold. Sleep. Their great-uncle con-tinued to chant in the shadows.

A fog as damp and heavy as the sea buried the port
                and the streets.
I am the only one left alive under the lamp, and under me
        rushed the waters of that great unheeded multitude
To whom I read the Miserere!
"Have mercy on me, O God, according to thy steadfast
                love . . ."

She was shaking. The day after tomorrow she would be arrested. Yesterday, Asselin had brought her some wood. She had told him: "If you come to lunch, bring something with you or we won't eat!" He had also brought something to warm them. Dear Asselin! There were still a few logs left. She had only two models now: Asselin and Paul.

After all, they were going to seize everything. So what good was it to economize? And besides, she had to finish the great sculpture that was so close to her ultimate vision. *Perseus* was growing.

Camille arranged the logs. She waited for the flames to leap up. She walked back and forth. She looked at her hands, her blue nails.

"The neighborhood of hide-cutters with blue teeth."

La Ville! Paul had foreseen everything! That was it! She had known that city of horror. You remember, Paul, rue Mouffetard, and the tanners of la Bièvre, the neighborhood of hanging, hideous sides of meat – and "the Field of the Poor," the "Boulevard of the Empty Stomach"? You used to walk for hours. The monstrous city.

Gradually the fire warmed her hands. Her fingers flexed. She would be able to work. She undid the linens, unwrapped the figure. Slowly the face emerged, still unformed – premature. A whitened chrysalis. For the second time she was going to meet the monster – her great "giant." "Mustn't laugh at those things."

Villeneuve! The old housekeeper, Victoire. Victoire Brunet. One evening in November . . . She was six years old, maybe seven. The fire in the hearth. The old woman. The old woman was there, cracking nuts. She spoke in a low voice. Victoire, the gamekeeper's daughter, who now worked at the Claudels'. She told stories that made your teeth chatter all night. And the child listened with her enormous eyes, too blue, too deep.

"Once upon a time there was a very unhappy grandfather. He wanted sons. So he prayed to the gods for them. He had only one daughter, Danaë. And he begged! And he pleaded! Poor Acrisius! He hadn't any boys."

Camille mocked him inwardly. He had a daughter, that should have been enough!

"Then the gods said to him: 'Your prayers will be answered. Your daughter Danaë will bring into the world a son named Perseus. But Perseus will kill you one day!'"

The little girl was delighted. Well done!

"So the old king grew frightened. He was terrified and wanted to prevent the oracle from coming true . . ."

Victoire told her story, and little Camille opened her eyes even wider, those eyes ringed with night.

"The king locked his daughter in a bronze room under the earth, far away . . . But Zeus, the mightiest of the gods, penetrated through a crack in the wall and came to Danaë in a shower of gold . . ."

Camille crinkled her sparkling eyes.

"One day, when the old king was passing by, he suddenly heard an infant's cry coming from a distant room. He hurried there, began by killing the nurse who had betrayed him, and decided to cast his daughter and his grandson into the sea."

Camille held her breath.

"He shut them in a wooden chest and cast them far away . . . far away."

Camille could see the arrival of the mother and child. Found by a fisherman, they were brought to the court of Polydectes. She could still hear Victoire pronouncing the foreign names. All day long, and the day after, she had amused herself by repeating them.

"One day Perseus, who had become a handsome young man, wanted to offer Polydectes a lavish gift. So he proposed killing the Gorgons. They were three sisters, three monsters. But only Medusa was mortal. Their necks were protected by dragons' scales, their hands were bronze, their wings gold. But worst of all their gaze was so unsettling, so powerful, that it could turn to stone whatever caught their eye."

Camille thought they were so beautiful. She was there, quite small, and her eyes blinked at the Gorgons' flight.

"Perseus knew that all he had to do to triumph was to kill Medusa. He armed himself with a shield so highly polished that it mirrored the sun. Then he went toward them, but he didn't look at Medusa. And yet he saw her. He raised his head, looked into his lifted shield, and shuddered at the sight he saw reflected there. Around Medusa's head coiled terrible snakes. Then he remembered. She had been a beautiful young girl, but the goddess Athena, jealous of her ravishing hair, had transformed her into this hideous creature. The serpents turned and twisted around her face, but the hero did not lose sight of her in his shield. He advanced."

Victoire lowered her voice: "To be on the safe side, he chose the time when the Gorgon was resting. Asleep, her eyelids were lowered."

Camille was furious. What kind of hero was this who killed young girls in their sleep! Wake up! Wake up! cried little Camille.

Suddenly Camille started. What had happened to her? She had just fallen asleep on her sculpture. She was no longer standing. What a cold night! She was trembling. Yet the fire still flamed. She was shivering, she touched her forehead – it was burning. She couldn't get sick. Oh no! Not before finishing – completing the movement of the snakes, the eyes of Medusa, and above all the winged horse that emerges from the severed neck, the golden horse . . .

She was staggering. She had to sit down. A few minutes near the flames would warm her up, get her in shape. She let herself fall near the fire. The sweeping fire of hell. Her limp hands could no longer control it. Hell was there, calling her. She heard the crack of the whip, and the marshaling of the four irons! The metal gates were closing, the golden snakes coiled and twisted around her face streaked with red earth. She knocked with all the strength of her fists, she knocked on the great gates with her bloody hands. And the echo sounded again and again. One, two, three, four! She left at a gallop. Away, away! Wait – Asselin was trying to catch the reins. She laughed now, the bit in her teeth. She rose up, her wings spread. What were they all doing here? Her father held out his arms. But she had no dress to go dancing in. She smiled at him. Her old, gray-haired father. She whispered in his ear: "I am like *Peau d'Ane* or Cinderella, condemned to tend the ashes of the hearth, with no hope of seeing the Good Fairy or Prince Charming come to change my rags into dresses the color of time."

Then Paul took her by the waist. She saw herself reflected everywhere. A great ballroom. Everyone was looking at her. She was so beautiful, so beautiful. Who was she, this mysterious woman in red? Camille saw herself – she took her dress in her hands, her amazon's dress, flaming and crackling, quivering with all its spreading red silk. And they all fell back. And she danced, she danced a Gypsy dance! But why were they all hiding their eyes? Ah, yes, again Monsieur Rodin. He was furious at a negative article in the press. But what was he doing? He had a big hatchet in his hand. He was coming toward her. She was afraid. She grabbed a pick. But he cut off the head of his *Saint John the Baptist Preaching*. He laughed derisively. Camille had stopped dancing, she was there, ready to defend herself. It was odd how weak she felt, weak . . . Her head was spinning, her mind was giving way . . .

"Is nature finished? Are they putting the finishing touches on the trees? . . . I will not complete anything again . . ."

That was 14 November 1905. The following morning, Asselin, who came to pose, found Camille terrified. She let him in only with great difficulty.

"She was gloomy, defeated, trembling with fear, and armed with a broomstick bristling with nails."

She told him: "Last night, two men tried to force open my shutters. I recognized them, they were two of Rodin's Italian models. He has ordered them to kill me. I am an embarrassment to him, he wants to destroy me." And she fainted.

She'd had time to glimpse Monsieur Asselin's incredulous face.

He did not believe her either. Her old friend.

Horror has forever bent her in a defensive posture! Ah, we have sought in vain to take her hand and embrace her! Too much of this sort has been done to her! One should not lead her on! You people who are not inclined to muster your powers to fend off a bad conscience, don't you see some resemblance? And as for myself, am I quite sure I haven't sometimes seen that panic-stricken face in the mirror?

PAUL CLAUDEL
Seigneur, apprenez-nous à prier

S HE IS KNOCKING with her two fists.
She is left with hell – the two gates of fire.

"I would like you to see that Mademoiselle Claudel receives some relief until she leaves this Gehenna . . . I thought of you because, like me, you are an admirer of hers." (Rodin to Morhardt, 28 May 1914.)

On the threshold of this terrifying door, Camille stands strong. The mask is encrusted on her face. She admires the white snakes that crown her head.

"'Apollo! Apollo! God of the gate! My Apollo of death! Apolesus! You have damned me! Why have I kept these ornaments of mockery, the scepter and the prophetic bandages around my neck? Go and be cursed! That's my gratitude to you!

"'Gift of death, in my place try to make another as sumptuous!'

"It has been so long since I have thought of these terrifying lines referring to the image of my poor sister Camille . . ."

She is still able to kill. The beautiful, tall young woman with the magnificent dark blue eyes takes the chisel. She is determined now. The sculpture of Perseus shatters beneath her furious blows.

"In the last lines of the tragedy, we see a face turn toward us fixed with the same horror, the face of the Gorgon that my sister, at the end of her conscious life, also saw reflected in the shield of Perseus." (Paul Claudel, *Conversation sur Jean Racine.*)

Everything is ready. The gods can now intervene. A woman goes forth without memory, without a future. The doors open.

A woman transfigured in a final blaze. There will be no more sculptures.

Who would have dared give her the commission for *The Gates of Hell?* This is what she had waited for from the age of twelve.

The Pictorial Magazine

Why did I want to make such puppets by the lot?
What was the use if they have brought me to this end?
Like one who crossed the sea, then drowned in spit?
My art so praised, and once honored,
Did defend me once; but now has brought me to this
pass:
A poor old man, I serve others and to their power bend
So that I am undone, if I do not die first.

MICHELANGELO, 1546

I WAS SURE that my sister's works would please you. The poor girl
is ill, and I doubt she can live long . . .

"With all her genius, her life has been full of such disappointment
and disgust that its prolongation is not to be desired.
Paul Claudel. 15 November."

Camille had raised her head: "From the fourth to the sixteenth of December?" She heaved herself up now. "I want to be there."

Eugène Blot had just promised her a major retrospective exhibit of
all her works. There would be thirteen of them. Camille looked at the
mock-up of the poster he held out to her. Her hand still trembled, she
was so pale, so emaciated in the big bed.

Major Retrospective, Camille Claudel
Gallery Eugène Blot
5, Boulevard de la Madelaine
From 4 to 16 December 1905

She rested her head on the pillow. She smiled like a little girl promised a wonderful, coveted gift. But inside, something was missing, something had given way.

They dressed her, they supported her now. They were there, the few friends and her brother. She looked at the clothes Mélanie had found. Eugène Blot had been looking for an outfit for her to wear to the grand exhibition. Madame Morhardt had been consulted. But Camille thought of the beautiful dress in her dreams, a dress the color of fire. She would never have it now. Just a parasol! Which wouldn't do her any good.

In a soft voice she asked that *he* be barred from entering the exhibition. Oh no, that would be too easy! He should have come sooner. Not now. No more now. Never again.

A beautiful red parasol – today.

She pushed away the helping hands. She looked at herself. She was dressed in dark blue. She said to Asselin: "Do you remember my last letter? . . . 'I am like *Peau d'Âne* or Cinderella, condemned to tend the ashes in the hearth, with no hope of seeing the Good Fairy or Prince Charming come to change my rags into dresses the color of time . . .' Thank you. See, the princes have come. Soon I shall find them again."

Then she leaned toward Paul and whispered in his ear: "I would have liked you to see me in a beautiful dress just once! A beautiful red dress!"

She took the powder and whitened her face and neck, which had aged very little. Still too much powder. The dress had to be brushed. She laughed weakly: "It isn't very good. I've never known how to dress." She had always lived like a boy. Always surrounded by men.

"What is it you say, Paul? Oh, yes!" She has no womanly arts. "But I do, Paul! Sculpture!" She had raised her voice menacingly, as if rocks were rolling pell-mell to the bottom of a gorge. Paul shrugged his shoulders. She wouldn't stop talking. They had just sat down. Asselin leaned over to put on her boots. "A sick woman, she is a sick woman." She didn't want that. She would plague them. She swung her legs under her poor friend Asselin's nose. "The right or the left? The respectable one or the crazy one? The nice one or the naughty one?" Asselin dropped the right boot and picked up the left one, and changed them again. He dared not stop the ankles swinging under his nose. "Monsieur Asselin can't do it, no he can't, can't, can't . . ."

Her father! Apparently he was going to come too. He would make the trip to be at this retrospective. She would be glad to see him again. Such a long trip at his age. Seventy-nine years old. She was anxious. "Are you sure Papa can stand the traveling? I would so like to see him." Paul reassured her.

"Hold still, Mademoiselle Flaubel, I'll never manage to do your hair." Poor Mélanie! As resistant to pronouncing Claudel as the hair was to the brush. Her hair slipped, escaped, twisting around the fingers of the inattentive young woman. Mélanie was discouraged. "I've never seen anything like it! And your face. Put on a bit of color!"

Camille took the pot of rouge Mélanie held out. She dipped her finger, sucked it, rolled her eyes, dipped it again and daubed Asselin's nose as he continued trying to put on the boots. He looked at her without getting angry. No one reacted. Eugène Blot told himself they were going to be late to the opening. Never mind! They had organized this major exhibition for her. She had so little time left to live. Poor young woman! Paul was irritated. It was cold. He remembered the other woman who had left him in China, the other woman he hadn't heard from. She, too, made brutal gestures, had sudden fits of feverish laughter. Unbearable! Their presence! Their absence! "Camiiiiiille!" – not without turning your heart upside down with the flick of their handkerchief.

What was going on? Camille got up. Was that why? A few seconds of thoughtlessness, of teasing, the beautiful dress, the boots, the hair, the rouge on Asselin's nose . . . They let her do whatever she liked. They put up with anything. And Blot hadn't even tried to hurry them along the way he usually did. They would be late, and he just sat there saying nothing. So that was why? Paul? And if I made a mess of everything now, would you leave me? Without anger. Without laughter. She understood.

She was going to die. They all thought so. There had to be an exhibition. From 4 to 16 December 1905. Quickly, before she . . .

She said nothing. She took her handkerchief. They had bought her an embroidered handkerchief. Too. She pressed it against her heart briefly. Louise's embroidery on the bed at Wassy? "From now on I'll be sensible, calm. You can lace them up, Monsieur Asselin. I'll stay still." She leaned her back against the table. She said nothing more. The little starling . . . it was all over.

Gloves. Cape. Hood. They enveloped her. Already. The horses were stamping. She said nothing. Far away now . . .

I remember everything, winter, feast days.
The families, the times of joy, the times of mourning . . .

The horses moving in step. The princess dying. In step. In step. Paul was sitting across from her. She shut herself off from life for a few moments. The king's daughter's final lament.

. . . times, countries.
And my dresses were in the coffer of cypress wood.

A melody played in her head. To the horses' step. She let herself be led away. The coachman reined in his beasts. They would go gently. She thought of a funeral cortege; a hearse passed by unnoticed. "She was an artist, and quite gifted . . ."

"Paul . . . you will read me what you've just written at Villeneuve. I would like . . . Tell me how . . ."
She had difficulty speaking. The sobs. The exhaustion. The horses' fetters.
"The title! You know. I love the names you give . . . Tête d'Or, Avare, Lechy Elbernon, Lechy, Lucky, Lucky . . ."
"*Partage de Midi* . . . I've reworked the end of the fragment . . . You know, *Une Mort prématurée* . . ." He stopped, embarrassed. She knew. He was twenty years old. He hadn't wanted her to see. He had torn the paper . . .

By what long, painful, underground paths
By what long, painful paths,
Still distant, incessantly weighing
Each other down, do we go
To lead our souls in travail?

They stopped suddenly. The carriage shook.

Major Exhibition, Camille Claudel.

311

Camille looked at the sign over the entrance. They had dropped *"Retrospective."* She had liked this word that pointed backward. They hadn't dared. To go back in time. Forward. Backward. What did they call that invention? She had read in the papers. "The Pictorial Magazine," no, that wasn't it. The cinema . . . ah, yes, a long word: cinematography. Everything was moving. She had been captivated by this article.

"Excuse me, I was forgetting . . . Not used to it." Camille smiled. The cape. The hood lightly sprinkled with snow. Yes, it was snowing. The gloves. Someone took her things. She was cold.

Cinematography. They had found a way of fixing movement. Her endless discussions with Rodin late into the night at Clos Payen . . .

"*Marshal Ney* by Rude. There you'll find the whole secret of gestures interpreted by art. Look closely. The different parts of the statue are represented by successive moments. Thus you have the illusion of seeing the movement completed."

"And photography?"

"Photographs of men walking? They never look like they are moving forward. They appear fixed on one leg or jumping at hopscotch . . ."

"And the three acts of *Sailing for Cythera?* You remember . . ."

No, she didn't remember anything.

"Cami-i-ille. All your friends are here." "The Pictorial Magazine." Magnificent. Eugène Blot led her in. The mad dance began: "Monsieur Roger Marx. What a pleasure." "Yes – one of your friends. Bonjour Monsieur." "And . . . oh, no . . . You! You needn't have troubled." "What? Ah yes, I've heard of you, sir . . . Yes, I see. Your friend. She likes sculpture. Yes." "Oh! no, what? Yes, a woman artist. Difficult? No. When one is in love, you know . . ." "Ah, Monsieur Mirbeau. I want to talk with you quietly and – what? Oh! Sir . . ." Who can that be? "No, from so far away? You shouldn't have made such a trip."

Her father? Where was her father? She looked for his eyes. Paul. Where was Paul? He would know.

"I'm honored, Countess."

"She is a poetess . . ." Eugène Blot was delighted. He had never had so many people at his gallery. Surely he would sell something. What a good idea this had been!

"A woman artist. No. I am not alone. You write. That is difficult, too, isn't it? What's that? Ah yes. Mathias Morhardt. Yes, I accept. He is coming all alone? " "Oh, Monsieur Fenaille, how can I thank you for all that . . . "

Madame Fenaille in a silk dress – supple, sinuous . . .

"Camille, don't stare at people so. It's rude."

"Mama, that dress!"

"We don't point either."

"It's ugly, don't you think? How can she walk? She looks like a Japanese woman, doesn't she?" Madame de Frumerie pursed her lips. She looked like an old date left out on the sideboard since last summer. "It seems it's from that new couturier – Poiret? What a name!"

Camille was not listening; Camille did not answer. Madame Fenaille wore a red dress, so beautiful. It was unbelievably beautiful. Madame Fenaille had a dress. Red.

"You're getting tired. Drink something."

The circus! Look after the artist! There's still the final turn.

"Oh, no. You shouldn't have. Really. You already know them all. You know, I've done nothing new."

She had not yet seen her sculptures. Just caught a glimpse of them. Between two suits. Three dresses. A hat.

Thirteen sculptures. Ah, a little corner for *The Beseecher*. No. She didn't see anything anymore. And they? If this went on, she would imitate them and buy the catalog – "Thirteen Sculptures."

"Dear Camille Mauclair. I thank you for your article." "Oh, Gabrielle, Gabrielle Reval. Camille Mauclair. Yes, of course you know each other. I'm confused. I was saying to . . . "

She went from one to the other. Ah! *Maturity*. She on her knees – again.

"Oh, Monsieur Morice." Because he was tall and thin, he always reminded her of her father.

Her father? He would not come now. What could have happened to him? Dear Charles Morice with his vehemence, his sudden insights, his denials. Everyone who was anyone was there.

She tried to catch Octave Mirbeau's eye. She would have liked to sit down a little, to chat a moment. With him. She loved his vision of things. Sometimes he was hard – he didn't give anything away. She glimpsed him there, with the Countess de Noailles; a smile curled his mustache. For a second his eyes turned toward her. She read the message. "Don't compare yourself to her. Be careful. The Countess has money. You don't."

Two women artists! But one was high and one was low – someone had just stepped on her foot. And limping as well – poor, lame. She was really having trouble with this leg. With him she had never thought about it. No, mustn't think of him. Morhardt, she hadn't seen him yet. Francis Jammes waved his arms above a hat – but what a hat! "What pins, what feathers, what lace!" Monsieur Jammes was desperately attempting a coded dance around this still life. Camille did not understand. Then he tried the supreme tactic: to turn the fat lady by facing her. The technique of revolving doors. She was swept along, pushed. The mastodon clung fast.

"Ah, Monsieur Jammes, what joy! What . . . ?" Camille smiled at him. He was leaning affably toward the still life – "feathers, fruit . . ." She loved the attention he brought to people. The way he listened, his constant attention . . . Those who knew how to listen . . . whatever happens.

"I am delighted to see these delicious motifs of the inner dream that animates your sister's genius."

Dear Francis! Dear Paul! They had tried to defend her against him. Rodin had just attacked again. Don't think about him. Paul had been sharp in his article: ". . . carnival of rumps . . . vulgar figures, as if they were pulling beets with their teeth." Paul had hit hard. He wrote well. The images. Many people had passed around the article, laughing: "Monsieur Rodin, his rump pointed toward the lofty stars!"

They were laughing. She was sick at heart. She hadn't wanted to affirm herself against him, against the master. But why was he making war on the great sculpture of *Perseus*? Why had he kept her marble *Clotho* while she and Morhardt were surprised that the museum of Luxembourg had not yet received it? Why? A kind of appeal? To her. Hatred was all they had left. Implacable. He was celebrated, adored, surrounded by women. She was dying. Who could have said which of them was better off? She no longer knew. Dear Francis! He had understood their stubbornness. "The blows of the defeated do no harm." Monsieur Rodin was flourishing. She was in her death throes.

"Dear Francis! You were all feathered behind that lady. A real musketeer."

"Camille, your father is here. Without that lady, he would not have – "

She left him, bucked the crowd. She was in a hurry. The old man – seventy-nine years old – had come. Her father.

Seated near the door with his starry, sea-blue eyes, Louis-Prosper smoked his cigar. He was waiting for her, dreaming. He was there at Villeneuve, at dawn – the adolescent girl stamping, crippled, her mane of hair. He pressed her against him. Francis left them together. The old man withdrew a little, moved out of the way, his wide forehead, the hands, ten transparent fingers describing swirls of fierce pride.

The tall silhouette that backed little by little toward the white opening. The words left unsaid. He took his hat, his cane. The coat. More bent now. He had not wanted her to accompany him. Modest. Papa! come back. Once. They had not even embraced. The blanketing snow. The door held open. Papa! The scenes! The conflicts! Their two vessels launched in the same storm. No, not again. A dark carriage was waiting. The funereal horses. The steam from their nostrils. He lit a new cigar. The old male. The two heads raised against each other. The creaking of wood. Papa. He climbed in. He was leaving the square. The horses backing up. The whip. The snow thicker now. She did not tell him that she loved him. A wave of the hand. A sign? No, flicking ashes from the cigar. The hand resting there. Gray, silver, spotted, white. Luminous drops of snow. Black.

"You're going to catch cold!" Francis was there. What was she doing outside? On the sidewalk.

"Come."

Francis's arm. Claude Debussy. The waltz in the snow. She kept confusing them. Last summer, Paul had introduced her to the young poet he had traveled with in the Pyrenees. And then Francis had converted. Paul and Francis. Two men thirty-seven years old, mature but rootless. Both the same time, because of a woman. God, that summer in Orthez!

"It's no good."

Francis's hand. She had forgotten them.

"The pictorial magazine." She couldn't bear them any longer. She hadn't wanted to see them. Earlier she was waiting for her father. Was it the cold night, the champagne she'd drunk – she'd drunk too much – ten glasses? two glasses? She no longer knew; someone had handed her a glass, she had taken it. Her cheeks were violet. Mélanie would have been pleased. She'd said she would stop in to see Mademoiselle Flaubel's stones. Francis's fingers. Her life running in reverse. Go back, Camille – "Pow! Pow!" *Guignol.* The great overheated hall, their tenfold arms. Japanese dolls. The throbbing shadows. The dance had begun.

Shame. Rebuffs. Compromise.

She had put up with them long enough. Agnes de Frumerie, "sculptress," with her five statuettes of gossiping wives. She was strutting about there.

Henry Cochin! Bishop *Cochon* – pig! It was easy. She knew. A champagne toast. "I salute the talent of Mademoiselle Claudel." "To yours, Cochin." "Monsieur Rodin is absent and I've found him only in numerous imitators."

What was she complaining about? She was first among the master's harem! The favorite! And Henry Marcel: "*Perseus,* her rickety hero. A shrewish vulgarity."

Look, speechifying cockatoo! Camille stared at him. "Old moulting savage, if you could only see yourself – an old broomstick. Good for sweeping filth. Go on, continue . . ."

"I'd told you." Whirling of the great fury, "Henry Marcel, you are hereby crowned." *Vanitas vanitatum.*

"And you, dear Romain Rolland. What is ugliness? A woman on her knees, begging someone not to leave her? My petrified heart, humiliated for all eternity? Naked. I was naked, Monsieur Rolland. On my knees and naked. You didn't like *Maturity,* that is your privilege. But spare us the facile excuses. A little dignity, please, when you write reviews. 'A taste that is all too clearly a caricature of Rodin's genius.' A direct hit, Monsieur Rolland. Right on target."

She went toward him. She raised her clear eyes toward him. She told him. Right on target.

Eugène Blot was already leading her away. "No scenes." It was true. It was his exhibition. His evening. He was going to sell something. Isn't that so, Monsieur Blot? I'm here gratis. You've already paid me everything, and double as well, haven't you?

Monsieur Blot was afraid. She was there, her cheeks a vivid red, her eyes metallic, their hue slightly altered. Fortunately, Jammes supported her. Paul would return.

She hadn't seen them just now. The fur-lined hell of jeering beasts rolling their shoulders, coiling their necks, rubbing ankles. The shell of the fashionable world! Eaten! Moth-eaten! Gnawed away!

Monsieur Blot detained her. It was late. Camille cried: "I invite you all to my place. To the studio! To finish the evening. I have champagne." She turned toward the gallery owner. "Before I left I asked Mélanie to buy something to drink. You advanced me some money, remember! For my exhibition. We must celebrate. I expect you."

Gloves, cape, hood! Francis supported her. She didn't want his help. She was fine. Eugène Blot accompanied her to the carriage. The storm was growing worse. "Tell Paul to join us. He has taken our father home."

Papa!

She breathed.

The two men were cold. The horses waited in torment. The coachman wrapped in his muffler no longer seemed human. She reread aloud the text of the poster – "Major Exhibition Camille Claudel. From 4 to 16 December 1905."

Eugène Blot was satisfied. It had been a good idea. "You're happy?" Camille looked at her feet, white with frost.

"Too late, Monsieur Blot."

Letter *from the Asylum*

*I don't belong in the midst of all this, you must get me out of this place;
after fourteen years, today, of such a life, I cry out for freedom.*

If your legs are still whole!
You shall have me cheaply.
Is it really for sale?
It is for sale, why not?

PAUL CLAUDEL, *Le Soulier de satin*

I WOULD HAVE DONE better to buy myself some beautiful hats and dresses to set off my natural assets. This miserable art is more suited to old men and poor suckers than to a woman relatively well endowed by nature." (Camille Claudel.)

There are no more decorations here – no more busts to finish – no more great men – no more dinners.

> I am going to my earthly homeland
> With those of my race,
> My brothers, in a dark night . . .
> Those who summon you are mad. (Paul Claudel, *Le Pain dur.*)

The great circus is over. They wouldn't even sell her a Legion of Honor. Even if she had the money!
There are no decorations here. Only numbers.

"Something
Eternally Childish . . ."

*Camille wore the most extravagant dresses, and espe-
cially hairdos laced with ribbons and multicolored
feathers. For this inspired artist had something excessive,
eternally childish about her.*

HENRY ASSELIN

THE TWO ROOMS at quai de Bourbon were filled with smoke
from all her guests. Monsieur Asselin tried to catch a glimpse
of her through the haze. He was huddled in a corner of the divan, a
sort of crumbling old structure – the overturned mattress bursting at
the seams. Monsieur Asselin trembled, his heart was breaking. He
would stay until the end. He could do nothing for her. He was there,
that's all.

That spring night leaped to the unleashed rhythms of champagne.
Asselin, hunched up on the disemboweled bed, looked at the old marble beside him. Just the other day she had put her hand on the block
and murmured tenderly: "Poor old marble! It is like me, Monsieur
Asselin. Clunk!"

She had explained. There were "proud" marbles and "clunk" marbles. When they were struck with a tool, the first gave a clear sound, the
others simply said, "Clunk!" They would soon split. She had shrugged
her still-lovely shoulders. "They are rotten inside, you know!"

At the foot of the bed she had piled old stones. Collected here and there. Monsieur Asselin looked at the pile. The scene came back to him.

On a night like this, he had stayed with the revelers until dawn. Confused, dressed once again in her old sculptor's smock, she had said to him: "Monsieur Asselin . . . You will stick with it to the end, won't you? Follow me, then."

She had led him to the fortifications. She put her head down, next to the earth, next to the broken stones. She had wept. An old woman in a cemetery. A dead child? He had thought so. In the midst of the rubble, in the spring breeze, a dirty dawn, she, hollow-eyed, he, silent beside her – terror-stricken by this old woman's face.

She had walked, hopping quickly from one leg to the other, faster and faster. He'd had trouble keeping up with her. Not a word. Just that long pause at the fortifications of Paris. Then the return. No explanation. A few guests had dozed off on the ground, on the rags. She hadn't even looked at them. "Until tomorrow, Monsieur Asselin. Your bust must still be finished."

It had begun . . . the evening of the Blot Exhibition. People – friends, poets, journalists, society women – had come to her studio. Asselin had been there, as he was this evening. A party that would never end. The champagne flowed – "a classy spread." He asked how she had done it. Blot had lent her the money. Mélanie was serving. Then they hadn't seen Mélanie. Just two fat, leather-sheathed legs kicking in the air. Some of the society women had been offended. It was time to leave. "Already! You never know who's here . . ." They felt ill at ease, they patted their pockets. Others held more tightly to their bags.

"Look. Their hands full of rings! And that neck dripping pearls . . ." She had emerged from the fog of cigar smoke. Asselin would never forget what he had seen that evening.

In one hand she held an unsteady tray piled with the blue dress, the cape, the gloves, even the boots he had laced up a few hours before. With the other she was leaning on a man – no, a human wreck of a vagrant, bearded, staggering, covered with scabs. And she, queen of the Volscians whom Virgil had described so well. But instead of a band of gold, instead of the tiger skin thrown over her back, instead of the lance consecrated to Diana, she held a bearded animal who stared at them and laughed derisively, babbling incomprehensibly.

Silence. Everyone moved away. Gravely she walked toward Eugène Blot, kneeled before him, solemnly handed him the folded clothes, even the handkerchief she had tried to clean. Asselin had wanted to scream – they all had. Paul. Paul's face! Asselin would never forget that either. He had backed up flat against the wall. The poet seemed turned to stone. Only Francis Jammes had approached her, helped her up, stroked her cheek, attentive to that soul being torn apart without the slightest expression or grimace.

That night, they had sounded the *hallali*, the death knell.

It was 4 December 1905.

When she had ceremoniously returned the clothing to her agent, Asselin and Mirbeau had understood. The convent or hell. She had to go quickly. She had lit the fire. She was tearing her heart out bit by bit.

They had all come back, the gluttons, the buffoons.

"Monsieur Mirbeau, you're not eating? And Asselin. The two faithful – my thieves!" Sobs mingled with laughter. She rested her head on the writer's shoulder. His arms trembled as they supported the fragile neck. Who really thought about her? Perhaps the vagrants she had gathered together that very day, a few hours before the celebration, found here and there during her dreamlike walks through the city.

"You remember, Mirbeau, the dinner? . . . I never told you. Our dinner. I didn't yield to you. Poor Mirbeau! See, you have escaped time. But you were my art critic. I do not sleep with that race." Those laughing blue eyes met his own.

"A pity. I might have . . ." She was gone.

"Perhaps . . ."

She was there, lightly touched his lips. "I respect you. It's even more difficult . . ."

A breath – had she embarrassed him? What had she wanted to say?

He had been the first to attach the word *genius* to his subject. There had been the Salon of 12 May 1895. Suddenly he had found himself in the presence of something unique, a rebel against nature: the woman of genius – *The Gossips*. He had wanted to meet her. Once or twice he had glimpsed her with the master. Then he had invited her alone. Besides, people were saying they had separated. The dinner!

"A rebel against nature!" he had written. And she had come, a fabulous bag lady! Her devastated eyes, offering their misery to the fashionable world, "squandering" the little money "they had taken such pains to get her!" – Oh yes, dear Monsieur Blot, she understood. She did not want charity. That was too easy. Three studios! The Alma Pavilion! Authentic commissions! Offer her that. But not charity. Have some respect for her.

Mirbeau stood with his back against the wall, quite still. No one knew. At that very moment he understood why he had written that article more than ten years before.

Banished by society. Anarchic. They would soon arrest her – why not? For months he had been waiting for it to happen without knowing precisely what it was he dreaded.

Camille Claudel: a genius. He had dared. "The equal of Rodin." Mirbeau passed his hand before his seer's eyes. "Monsieur Rodin is more shocking, but Camille is more revolutionary. She puts society on trial and – "

"Excuse me, Mirbeau, I'm worried . . . Camille just ran off into the night alone, and the storm is raging."

"We can't do much more, my dear Asselin. We must let her follow her own path, free. If we love her . . . Henry, do you know what a genius is? A divinity that in ancient times presided over every life. We are the ones who need her, Henry."

Mirbeau looked at the studies, the models wrapped in damp linen, the bust of Asselin. Tomorrow, everything would disappear. Every spring, the studio was suddenly empty. Did she sell anything? No one knew.

The Passion

Neither painting nor sculpture will now soothe
The soul turned at last toward the divine love
That opens its arms to us upon the cross.

MICHELANGELO

S o HER LAST NIGHT began.
She was forty years old, 1905, 1906 . . . I am forty-two, forty-three. I am forty-five. She scurries away. The heavens shed their tears. Her weaving gallop. Mad? The streets. Turns and returns. Undone. 27 November. Camille at four o'clock in the morning fled from her own home. 1909, 1910, 1911. No one knows where she is. I run, I panic. The blind city of her memory. For how long, the city engulfs my steps. Where is she going? Stop. The gray cornerstone, there, sit down. My leg. It's bleeding now. Out of breath. I spring forward. Chest. Suffering. She cannot go on. A heart attack. My heart. Monsieur Rodin! The sidewalk. The murky pavement. She sits down. She calls out to him. Storms! Night of fire. Reproof!

And didn't I love him, after all,
Didn't I have something to complain of, too?

324

The stream widens. She looks at the water seething around the soaked stocking. *The Little Fairy of the Waters.* 1890. "Do you remember, Monsieur Rodin?" She slaps at the dirty water.

She sees the trousers, the legs. He trembles. He is cold, too. Why are they both there beneath the abject rain? The other evening, no, last year . . . The lighted window of the Hôtel Biron. She escapes. She wants to see him again. He lives in Paris now, on rue de Varenne. The high entrance way. Get through. Scale the fortress. The torches. Behind the frozen night. She, cowering. The phonograph, the yelping music. He is there, his back to the window. Camille could touch him, if the glass weren't there. He is drawing, but his hand trembles. 1910? He is not old. Camille goes to take his hand, to warm it as she's done before . . . At the other end of the room, an old woman, powdered, peroxide hair, waving her two thin arms – clinking noisy bracelets.

"Look at her! Madame is a real little bacchante!"

It's a nightmare. Camille watches, horrified; Roger Marx – Charles Morice. But what are they doing there? Camille restrains herself. She is about to scream.

Monsieur Rodin puts on a record. Camille hears. Grinding of teeth. Boom! Boom! A candle now. She undresses. She dances. The master cried: "The extraordinary mistress conquers like a flame." And the other, who croaks from her bottom: "I am the reincarnation of your sister Maria."

"Mademoiselle Claudel has put all that is sacred in the act of love into that magnificent work, *Çacountala.* Charles, you wrote that – and look, listen to what they've done with me."

Camille has fallen. With the weight of her heavy heart. She can still see Charles Morice getting up. Charles, who looks like her father. Charles leaves the room and Rodin dances with rage. "Get out – all of you! The duchess and I don't need you."

Camille slips to the ground. Her head makes a slight, crystalline sound on the glass. Ping! Monsieur Rodin hurries over. He leans his flabby face over the mirror. He is ill. The night is empty for all eternity. Hell itself has the taste of ashes. Since she is no longer there.

"Get rid of those people who only want your money. Watch out. The jealous are prowling the gardens, waiting to murder you." Rodin is pulled back. The door opens. The guests go away, one by one. Silently.

One last time, the voice crackles: "Useless to disturb him, since I am there. I take care of everything. Monsieur Rodin is myself! Me, the Duchess of Choiseul."

"Go, Dora, attack!"

The old man lifts the woman up. Though blind, he has seen the body lying in the gutter. Someone was suffering, groaning. Quite near. Camille caresses the animal, warms herself a moment near the body of the beast. "Thank you, sir. It's better now. I must have fainted."

Nightmare! Shame! All that was the truth. They had all foreseen it. Monsieur Rodin had a muse, outrageous, obscene, an old duchess who stayed with him at the Hôtel Biron – la Choiseul, as she was called! Monsieur Rodin? Impossible!

"He doesn't work anymore." Camille smiled. Let them try another lie! The shoulder torn before dawn – her ashen face. It was all true. Why hadn't the Duchess's dog, Dora, killed her? Why?

"Greater love hath no man than to lay down his life for his friend."

The city is mute. A labyrinth of tears.

> She who remains waits
> For someone to open the door and push her.
> No one has come.

Camille is lost. She would like to go home. One by one she counts and recounts the paving stones. The hard stones . . . she has left her stocking. She falls. Her hands slip on the rough ground. Pale and limp. Jesus falls for the first time.

> And I went out all alone
> Through wild and arid places, bearing
> A full vase with me, through the salt desert,
> And it was broken
> And the sea of tears spread out in me.

The sky grows purple. Slap! Slap! Slap! The château at Islette. The dung cart. They are in the past!

> O mothers, who have seen the first and only child die . . . !
> Farewell . . . farewell, O flesh of my flesh!

Camille is standing up, moving neither forward nor backward. I am watching. Waiting. There is no more rain, there is no more wind – only a woman pierced to the heart. She remembers that she must die.

Time has stopped. Blood. Tears. Spittle. The woman comes toward her. She is finished working. She squeezes the poor flowers tightly to her. She sold almost nothing this evening. Against her heart the roses shed their petals at every note. She has begun to sing.

And weep, weep . . .

I hear her approaching.

> Henceforth doomed to sobs
> By this new crime of the waves
> That so overwhelms her
> Between the thunder and the Ocean
> She calls out in the Void
> And weeps . . .

Face to face. The singer half opens her coat. One flower is left. The dry blouse. Delicately she wipes Camille's face. The muddy fabric, dirty now, that gave birth to a single flower. The old singer goes off. Camille, the flower between her fingers. Still a few drops . . . She lunges forward.

Let us look at her once more. The sixth station.

> Laugh at me because I am drunk and I don't walk straight!
> I am lost and I don't know where I am.

She falls for the second time, "My little Colin-Maillard. Paul! The little hands playing with Victoire. Pat-a-cake, pat-a-cake . . . "

On all fours, braced against a wall, a she-wolf, bristling. Camille hoarse, bloody lips, retreating before the gathering light. She sniffs the still-distant dawn. Panicked, she yields, beats a retreat. She becomes dangerous. They are leaving her so little space. Hide yourself in the entrance way. Camille, come.

> Who is pulling my hat from behind?
> I'd like some drink. Two little girls in blue . . .

She goes wild again. No more lion-tamer, Monsieur Rodin! The sky revolves, shot through with blood.

"*I've caught him red-handed now. The wretched scoundrel makes use of all my sculptures in different ways, he gives them to his pals, the chic artists, and in exchange they get him decorations, ovations . . . That's how he has profited from my alleged vocation!*"

In the city, a woman is speaking. She is alone. She is walking. She is trying to make her way home. She is explaining to everyone. Passersby cross her path, indifferent. She is dirty.

"*They had me taken away expressly to provide them with ideas, given the poverty of their imagination. I am like a cabbage devoured by caterpillars; every time I sprout a new leaf, they eat it . . .*"

The purity of the face: it slips through the dawn, intact, almost transparent, in the coming day.

And his idea is only to go to sleep somewhere . . .
Put a paving stone on my back.

"*You can be sure that by letting him go unpunished, it only encourages others.*"
Ninth station. Spring 1913.

Turned toward us one last time, those eyes full of
blood and tears.
What can we do? No way to keep him with us
longer . . .
And we see the crowd, crying out and judging him,
who washes his hands.

PAUL CLAUDEL, *Le Chemin de croix*

D EAR DOCTOR,
"Yesterday we saw the director of the asylum at Ville-Evrard.
The certificate is quite sufficient. . . . If it were possible, we would like
to try and proceed with the internment even today.
"I remain respectfully yours, Doctor, . . ."

"I saw that poem *La Vague* in her studio on quai de Bourbon, under the
shifting shade of the tall poplars the lonely woman in her coarse-
grained white smock. Patiently from morning to night . . . She is going to struggle . . ."

A cock crows. At Montdevergues, Camille is still not asleep. Villeneuve is awakened by the copper rays of the sun.

"I have no way of knowing the exact date. Is it so important? The artist
is the contemporary of his entire life, he has a presentiment of events

he doesn't remember." (Paul Claudel, *L'Oeil écoute*, "Camille Claudel.")

It was the end of the year 1897.
Camille was thirty-three years old.

Someone
Will Betray Me

What? There is your Jesus! He makes us laugh.
He is full of violence and obscenities.
He provokes the psychiatrists and the police.

PAUL CLAUDEL, *Le Chemin de croix*

BEHIND THE DOOR, there is a body collapsed on the dark old cloak.

> I am fallen again, and this time, it is
> The end . . . Jesus falls a third time,
> But at the top of Calvary.

The studio. They have all gone. She glimpses the sculptures in their dirty cocoons. She hears the old rodent working patiently at the ghastly decay. Embryos – and death leaves us.

Six o'clock, perhaps. The sparrows pilfer the spring with little chirps. She is going to kill. This is the season for love, life is burgeoning, malicious. The time for departures to Touraine . . . Azay-le-Rideau . . . promises . . .

The first noises – "the poison of the concierge who seizes everything in her path." She hastens to close the shutters. Quickly! Camille hurries, fastens the shutters. Everything closed up. So no one will come in again. Ever again.

One evening, a paper was slipped under the door. She had to pay. And then they condemned her. She thrashed about, running to find a sou, a thousand francs. She promised sculptures. Her work became currency, vain promises, too late . . .

She escaped in laughter, celebration. Never mind where, if only they don't find her! Her dress was torn, she couldn't go anywhere now. Her body exhausted, she stopped running. And so she left herself with no way out.

Her sole recourse was to destroy her last sculptures, the cracked marble and the pile of stones next to the bursting mattress.

"Your bust has lived the life of roses." There, she had warned him.

She smashes Monsieur Asselin, her last friend, to pieces. She crushes the plaster, determined. Her strength is doubled. It is perhaps seven o'clock. The neighbors hear, but turn a deaf ear. It will soon be over. They have informed the family, the police, you never know.

Tomorrow the garbage collector will come to fetch the debris. He will bury it somewhere in the fortifications, as he does every spring. Those are his orders. She pays him for that.

She is all that's left.

Father Died Suddenly
at Three O'Clock in the Morning

It is 3 March 1913. A telegram slipped under the door. The letter she doesn't read. Seven days, seven days left. That's enough.

> "Verily, verily I say to you,
> One of you will betray me."
> "Will it be me, Lord?"

The night is not yet over. She does not move. Not a gesture, not a sound. She knows. She waits for the dawn. She waits for them. Who will come? How many will there be?

She hasn't gone out for a week. No more food either. No useless gestures. Naked. To be truly ready, she has stripped herself down.

> They have taken everything, there is nowhere to hide.
> There is no more defense, he is naked as a worm.
> He is delivered to all men, and revealed.

The entire studio sways toward her. When they enter, she will be snatched up into the void, thrown forever off balance.

The night is clear. The dawn comes slowly. A gentle morning. Drop by drop. In the studio there is only one figure left. Unique.

She is terrified. That is why she doesn't move. Only her lips are pulsating. Weakly.

She is dying slowly on her feet. She will not defend herself. She awaits the clay – the little vein at the base of her neck throbs too quickly. The knife will slice the pain.

"My soul is sick unto death."

He, too, has abandoned her. Even he! The fourteen stations are well fastened to the wall. She cut them out of a recent newspaper. He is there, silent on his cross. Color prints!

And Paul! He had written *La Jeune Fille Violaine* – "Scandal must be avoided" – "Unspeakable, reprobate" – the leper, Paul! The leper. Not a quiver on her face. Poor Violaine!

Her eyes – even a bit larger. There on the ground, at her feet, insidiously, furtively, a great pale tear, and they advance, and they creep. The shutters grow light. She knows, she is waiting.

No noise, as if the whole world had disappeared. She will go out. There will be nothing left, no more Paris, no more towns, no more country – a wasteland stretching to infinity, a cloaca turned to stone!

She pulls herself up on the edge of the cliff, the first to reach the Geyn. She has gotten there first. She must turn around. Someone is going to push her.

Hush!

Oh you, have pity. She calls for help. They are not going to abandon her. She is going to die. It's been so long since they've forgotten her there. So long.

They have thrust their way in, boots and helmets. The door forced.

The mob has seized her by the throat, like a stag.

She is struck, thrown to the ground. She does not say a word. A naked woman, it's intolerable.

333

She allows herself to be led away. Without a word. Her wings clipped. Her camisole is threadbare.

Outside, the ambulance is waiting. 10 March 1913. The two horses whinny under the whip. Barred windows, jolting as they go.

Letter *from the Asylum*

It has been fourteen years ago today since I had the disagreeable surprise of seeing two policemen enter my studio armed with all sorts of weapons, in helmets and boots, utterly threatening. A sad surprise for an artist. That's what I got as recompense! Such things happen only to me.

Letter *from the Asylum*

I don't want to stay in first class at any price, and when you receive this letter I beg you to have me put back in third class, where I was before.

You lack one thing; go, sell what you have, and give to the poor, and you will have a treasure in heaven; and come, follow me.

The Gospel according to Saint Mark

S HE IS POOR among the poor.
Camille does not even want to be in first class.
She will stay in third class.
At the bottom. My Paul, will the last truly be first?

"The order is to live.
"Mine is to die.
"Ignobly, between two workers disgruntled at being awakened so early." (Paul Claudel, *Le Pain dur*, 1913.)

Interdiction

Often, for amusement, sailors
Capture albatross, vast birds of the sea . . .

M ARCH 1913.
"Camille put in Ville-Evrard on the morning of the tenth. I was quite wretched all that week.

"The madwomen of Ville-Evrard. The senile old woman. The one who constantly chatters in English in a soft voice, like a poor sick starling. The ones who shout without saying anything.

"Sad in the hall with my head in my hands. The awful sadness of these souls . . . " (Paul Claudel, *Journal.*)

"17 March 1913.
"You would not recognize me, for you've seen me so young and so dazzling in M – 's salon . . . I await your visit with impatience. I am not reassured. I do not know what will happen to me. I believe it will end badly!! It all seems dubious to me! If you were in my place, you would see . . . Remember the Marquis, your ex-neighbor, he just now died after being shut up for thirty years. It's dreadful."

Those are not things that would happen to me.

Somewhere in Paris, Auguste Rodin is the victim of a stroke.

"Rose Beuret accompanied me: 'At times he does not recognize me. He says to me: Where is my wife? I answer: I am here, aren't I your wife? – Yes, but my wife who is in Paris, does she have enough money? . . .

"'He remains sitting in his room, sitting in front of the open window. I speak to him gently . . .

"'You are fine here, under the protection of your great Christ.

"'Ah, he once said with an expression of humility, that was a man who worked!'

"Judith Cladel."

On 17 March 1913, the director of the lunatic asylum at Ville-Evrard wrote: "You can visit Mademoiselle Claudel on your next visit to Paris, barring complications in her mental state, which are hardly likely: the general state of her health is quite good."

The formal order not to allow visits to Mademoiselle Claudel and not to give her any news was received only a few days later.

> . . . *Exiled on the ground amid the jeering pack,*
> *His giant wings will not let him walk.*

CHARLES BAUDELAIRE, "L'Albatros"

I Agree to Meet You

Don Camille. "And what is this precious thing that you offer me? A place with me where there is absolutely nothing else! Nada! zilch!"

PAUL CLAUDEL, *Le Soulier de satin*

M<small>R. AMBASSADOR,</small>
"The grave is set with a cross bearing the numbers: 1943 – no. 392. Mademoiselle Claudel possessed no other personal effects at the moment of her decease, and no papers of value, not even mementos, have been found in the administrative file. I remain respectfully yours, Mr. Ambassador, . . . "

"Mr. Mayor,
"The Paul Claudel family has found among the poet's papers the letter, a copy of which you will find enclosed. The members of the family of Paul Claudel wish to give Camille Claudel, the older sister of Paul Claudel, a sepulchre more worthy of the great artist that she was."

The Bureau of Cemeteries responds:

"Sir,
"In response to your letter in which you express the desire to transfer the mortal remains of Madame Camille Claudel, interred on 21

October 1943 at the cemetery of Montfavet, in the section reserved for the hospital of Montdevergues, I regret to inform you that the ground in question was requisitioned for the needs of the military.

"The grave has disappeared."

Jean-Louis Barrault

The theater is man's active reflection on himself, on madness, on chance, accident, the charter of the world.

NOVALIS

A YOUNG MAN, his rucksack on his back, is walking on the narrow road leading to Brangues. Six kilometers to meet the old poet who has agreed to see him. Paul Claudel is nearly seventy-five years old. For twenty years, the play that represents "his life's summation," *Le Soulier de satin,* has been waiting to be performed.

The young man dares. Nearly five hours of on-stage performance at the Comédie-Française.

1943. One month before the premiere, a seventy-nine-year-old woman dies at the hospital of Montdevergues. She is called Camille, like her brother "Camille the Moor," who will appear each evening from his hell of fire in the first act of *Le Soulier de satin.*

"Deliverance to captive souls."
(Final line of *Le Soulier de satin;* Claudel adds:
"The instruments of the orchestra fall silent
-one by one.")

342

"The sequestered woman has left! She has left the cell. And the person emerging, radiant in the rising sun, is no longer a madwoman, a terrified old crone . . . she is that sublime figure posed before him by the Eternal to encourage Himself to create the world!" (Paul Claudel, *Seigneur, apprenez-nous à prier.*)

Is that where my story begins . . .

A little girl, scarcely six years old, enters a garden in Normandy bathed by the late afternoon sun. The young man is there. Beside him, a woman "with an angelic smile" whom he calls Madeleine. Her eyes never leave him. He has a Company. She is an actress.

He directs the plays of Paul Claudel. The fifties.

Is that where it all began . . .

At the age of twelve she is taken to the theater for the first time. Once more she is in the sunny garden. She recognizes them. Jean-Louis Barrault has had the courage to mount the very first production of *Tête d'Or*. The sixties.

The poet has just died. She will not meet him.

Is that where it all begins to unfold . . .

I lost my heart there, under the flaming trees: that hall where Tête d'Or and the Princess had just concluded their love scene. I didn't want to leave them ever again.

1557. An old man is dying. He is eighty-two years old. The soul of the old master is still capable of loving. She is called l'Anguissola. She is not yet thirty years old: an artist, a "colleague," his first and last student. Michelangelo sends her one of his drawings, "so that she might paint it in oils after finishing it with her own hand."

She attaches herself to Bunarroti, better known under the name of Michelangelo. A few years later, she goes blind . . . retires with her children. Venerated until her death sixty years later, she agrees to receive a visit from Van Dyck, who does her portrait. She is nearly a hundred years old.

Is that where this story begins . . .

343

The Company was created. Mine.

Late one afternoon, I entered a sculptor's studio. Coppers, bronzes, in a corner a bust chiseled in stone. All that captivated me.

Huge doors were waiting to be shipped to another continent. Made of some unfamiliar material, they seemed to be endlessly transforming, shimmering with the reflected light from the sun and shifting clouds. Changing from the earth tones of burnt sienna to frozen blue, from the most varied grays to colors as dazzling as a white-hot blade.

Sculpture was becoming a theater ready to welcome the dreams of poets.

She.

She was emerging everywhere. This began with the text of *L'Oeil écoute* . . .

Little by little she began to appear in this or that dialogue, without betraying either her mystery or the dreams of the poet. My Paul!

Nine months before this book was written, the play *Une Femme, Camille Claudel* was given its first production. They were all there, the people who had worked with me. Jeanne Fayard – a whole summer bent over notes, texts, letters, she and I trying to gather all the scattered information, following clues. Camille, whom I pursued over many years, whom I had begun to love. The people whose paths I had the good fortune to cross: Jacques Cassar, who was also devoting himself to this great figure, sealed up for so many days and nights! We were able to meet many times before the brutal death that tore him from his patient and colossal labor. Still others appeared each evening, bringing information, a presence, a relationship. I still remember with emotion François de Massary's attendance at the production. Gradually connections were made – details here and there. The Rodin museum allowed us to see the sculptures, to photograph them. She had so loved "Monsieur Rodin"! A professor from London arrived one evening, providing a new link in the chain.

For a long time, the direct descendants of the poet whom we loved so much gave us their support despite the difficulties.

Following in her father's footsteps, Renée Nantet decided to resurrect this woman of genius. Henri had seen her in the asylum; he had accompanied his father. He spoke to me of her hands, always moving. In the void.

Was it on that day that everything fell apart for her . . . Camille.

12 November 1840. Birth of Auguste Rodin.
8 December 1864. Birth of Camille Claudel.
The little girl is twelve years old, kneading the clay of Villeneuve.
"Have you taken lessons with Monsieur Rodin?"
Was it on that day that everything began to play itself out . . .

Last evening the young man returned.

For several weeks Jean-Louis Barrault took us in. On 28 April 1982, the last performance of *Une Femme, Camille Claudel* took place at the Rond-Point theater.

I was in the midst of finishing the book.

For the last time, we would bring down the photos of her sculptures, still dispersed and hidden away in the museums of the world.

Nathalie Alexandre, Micheline Attal, Sylvie de Meurville, Pascaline Pointillart take their bows. The guests hurry to the "Festin de la Sagesse." Camille Claudel bursts out laughing, her noisy laugh, with her deep blue eyes . . . We would like to stay with her. She is going back into the drawer . . . Then the young man comes forward. He takes her by the arms. He is still holding her there.

The performances will be held over. We'll let the two of them talk. She was waiting for him so long. You remember? October 1943! Did the old poet speak to you about her one evening . . .

> I separate from you, sister
> Once of a name
> By me named impious!
> Let us go!
> I have done what I wanted to do, and I shall die by my
> own hand.

He was twenty years old. Is this where everything begins to unravel . . .

28 April 1982.

A story begins . . .

Perhaps a child is already pulling this woman by the skirt. "Camille, come on! Come toward the light . . ."

Others will search, others will write . . .

29 April 1982.

Camille

PHOTOGRAPHS BY DAVID WAKELY
(EXCEPT AS NOTED)

The sand and "gnomes" on the Devil's Gift.

ABOVE: *The "giant" at Villeneuve.*
TOP RIGHT: *Portrait of Louis-Prosper Claudel (artist unknown), 1905 (Private collection).*
BOTTOM RIGHT: *The Claudel home at Villeneuve.*

Le Jeune Romain *(Young Roman; or, My Brother at 16)*,
1884, bronze (Private collection).

La Vieille Hélène (*Old Hélène*), *1882, plaster*
(Private collection).

ABOVE: L'Homme penché *(Man Crouching)*, *1886,*
bronze (Private collection).
RIGHT: Les Causeuses *(The Gossips), 1886, bronze*
(Private collection).

ABOVE: Le Dieu envolé (*The Vanished God*), *1894,*
bronze (Private collection).
RIGHT: La Petite Châtelaine (*The Little Châtelaine*),
1895, marble (Private collection).

Buste de Paul Claudel à 37 ans *(Paul Claudel at 37)*,
1905, bronze (Musée Rodin).

Buste de Rodin (*Bust of Rodin*), *1892, bronze*
(*Musée Rodin*).

Les Causeuses (*The Gossips*), 1897, jade
(*Musée Rodin*).

Çacountala, 1895, marble (Musée Rodin).

Camille Claudel at the asylum at Montdevergues, around 1935.

Appendix 1

Article by Mathias Morhardt

Published in Mercure de France *in March* 1898
(*Extract*)

...AND ACCORDING TO the ideas of Mademoiselle Camille Claudel, which I would like to follow more exactly, the most essential task of art is to capture movement.[1] But this is also the most difficult thing to explain. Certainly it has been quite neglected by all the great sculptors since the Renaissance. Rather, their efforts aim always at capturing the fragment, the beautiful hand, well posed, well analyzed, well studied in its contrasts of light and shadow; the beautiful, powerfully shaped animal standing, immobile, against the chiaroscuro of the background; the nude, patiently and often minutely observed in the tranquillity of the requisite pose. But who among them is concerned with movement? Who endeavors to follow the modifications of the hu-

---

1. I observe here that on this point Rodin's opinion differs from Mademoiselle Camille Claudel's. For him, the modeling is almost everything when it comes to sculpture. He attributes only secondary importance to movement.

man form in the process of energetic action? Who has evoked – as the Japanese, the Chinese, the Greeks have done with such wisdom and genius since the dawn of time – the idea of pure movement in its equivalent form? For if a leg at rest and a leg walking are two different things, isn't the leg walking all the more vivid and real! Certainly, movement deforms. To use a comparison that is made by Mademoiselle Camille Claudel herself, there is an essential difference between the rapidly turning wheel and the stationary wheel: the stationary wheel is round and its spokes are equidistant from each other; the rapidly turning wheel is no longer round and has no spokes at all. Movement has, in a sense, devoured the anatomy, the very skeleton of the wheel. And a similar thing happens with the human body when it elongates or retracts, changing proportions and destroying its equilibrium. Hence, to consider the anatomy of a body walking as if it were in repose is a gross error of observation. Movement, in effect, embodies a state of becoming. The artist cannot hesitate between what has been and what will be. He must choose. In what has been he must preserve only what is necessary to explain what will be. The Greeks, who were not ashamed to modify their proportions, knew how to submit to this imperious demand. The Chinese and the Japanese have been astonishingly deft at the art of indicating the mobility of beings and things. Furthermore, all peoples who are gifted with eyes to see and have looked at life have exclusively occupied themselves with interpreting it in its living form, which is the form of its transience. Bas-reliefs and the most rudimentary carvings of primitive peoples exhibit this same concern with truth, and attest that only our modern civilization has disdained the highest, the purest possible expression of art, namely its dramatic expression. While the savages of America and the nameless tribes of central Africa are adept at indelibly evoking the trot of a zebra or an antelope, we confirm that our most expert artists are incapable of understanding even a horse's gait. This, and this alone – Mademoiselle Camille Claudel is convinced – can explain our decadence. And this, above all, is the source of the mysterious impulse that, in her view, clearly separates the art of the Rembrandts and Velásquezes from the art of the Phidiases and the Hokusais.

Even the respectful, scrupulous observation of nature does not, then, suffice to create masterpieces. There must be a particular passion.

There must be a special gift that allows one to derive from the very observation of life the thing that constitutes the basic element of any masterpiece, and is in a way the testimony of truth: a sense of Beauty. The Greeks, like all other artistic peoples, had this gift. The statuettes of Tanagra, the dazzling "snapshots" that have forever restored to us the ordinary events of their daily life, demonstrate that they knew how to observe, and that their observation was neither banal nor silly. For this is not a matter of mere copying. Indeed, it is essential that the copyist have the eyes of a poet. It is essential that he know how to read the meaning of the spectacle before him. When Monsieur Edouard Pailleron looks at contemporary society, he writes, very sincerely I believe, *Le Monde où l'on s'ennuie* or *La Souris*. Shakespeare, who works with the same examples, the same men, the same passions, and who deals with the same catastrophic events, writes *Coriolanus* or *The Tempest*, *Hamlet* or *Falstaff*, *Othello* or *Macbeth*. Mademoiselle Camille Claudel is closer to Shakespeare than to Monsieur Edouard Pailleron. Nature as she sees it and explains it through her work has an immediate quality of grandeur, a true sovereignty. The little groups that date from the period when she watched through her window the daily dramas played out in the 'Den of Thieves' – the children seated in a half circle around the blind musician; the two little singers, hats in hand and hands on their backs, looking up at the closed windows; and so many others – have the sacred quality of eternal works. *The Painter*, which she executed in 1894 at Guernsey after the sketches she did of Monsieur Y . . . painting landscapes, is of this order.[2]

This little bronze, which represents the artist standing with the paintbrush in his right hand, his thumb hooked through the palette in his left hand, solidly planted on his two legs and mixing his colors carefully before applying brush to canvas, surely conceals no mystery. Mademoiselle Camille Claudel took notes, she copied profiles, and soon after she reconstructed her character according to these notes and profiles. Thus she modeled her figurine of *The Painter* without wondering whether she was creating a new art.

---

2. *The Painter*, a little statuette in bronze that belongs to Monsieur P . . . was exhibited at the Salon at the Champ-de-Mars of 1897. Plaster copies survive, belonging to various collectors and to M. Bing.

The appearance of *The Painter* merits consideration as one of the important landmarks of her career. It is the first work in which she showed her power to evoke life directly. And her mastery has been evident from this time: *The Painter*, with his head bent slightly toward his shoulder, is a work of frankness and power. Its tone of imperious sincerity instantly commands the viewer's attentive respect. New or old, it derives from a magnificent and living art.

But as soon as she set out on this path, Mademoiselle Camille Claudel gave us even clearer proof of her genius. Just as the painter observed in Guernsey had given her the idea for the small figurine we have just discussed, so four women facing each other in the narrow compartment of a railroad car, who seemed to be sharing some precious secret, must have suggested to her that prodigious masterpiece, *The Gossips*.

An intimate corner, unexplained, indeterminate. Two plaster benches, arbitrarily placed at right angles, convey decaying walls. In the corner, a woman announces by the warning, cautionary gesture of her right hand raised to her mouth that she is about to speak. And around her and in front of her, the three busybodies, frustrated by curiosity, lean toward the already half-open mouth and the revelatory gesture, their faces greedy for knowledge, impatient to know and to hear. All the heads converge toward a single focal point: the face, the very lips, of the woman about to speak. The back, the shoulders, the neck of each of the women obey the same movement. They are bent to a single will. A single force subjects them. A single shudder, a single anxiety inhabits them and shows them ranged similarly on the two benches, identical as sisters.

Yet each is quite distinct. The one seated opposite the woman who is about to speak is almost completely crouched over. Her torso is supported by her two arms, which are leaning, crossed, on her knees. And, as if to get a better view of the direct emergence of the precious secret and also to ensure a kind of complicity in curiosity and in the joy of hearing, she seeks the head of her most immediate neighbor and mingles her hair with her own. Her feet are raised on their toes, both to elevate her knees a little, on which she is leaning her torso, and so that her eyes should be at the desired level. The other woman, in order to lean further forward, has put her right hand on the bench. She is leaning heavily. Yet she eases the strain a little by placing her left foot as far away as possible, so as to establish, by a gracious and natural movement, a sort of counterweight. The third busybody, next to the woman harboring the priceless secret, is seated nearly on the diagonal. She is leaning with her left arm on the bench and with her right arm on her knee. More fortunate than her two neighbors, she can bring her face quite close to the Gossip. She looks into her face, into her eyes, with all the force of her will, with all her anxiety not to lose a thing, not to miss a bit of this marvelous secret. And in the effort she makes, her neck is swollen, her lips half open, her back bends, her whole being bears witness to her extraordinary passion.

I believe I am not mistaken in saying that there is almost no modern work that has the breadth of *The Gossips.* At least I cannot think of any in which the drama is developed with such swiftness, such simplicity, such lucidity. Moreover, it is not specifically related to anything familiar. It has the providential clarity of creations that do not derive from something known and do not confirm us in familiar habits, whose mysterious filiation is unexplained and yet suddenly, according to the inexplicable and unforeseen will of genius, *are.* And indeed, these *Gossips* quite definitively "are." They "are," not only by virtue of the dramatic character of their expression. They "are" because a kind of miraculous logic governs each of their parts in relation to the purpose of the whole. Here, every detail participates in the beauty of the work and contributes to it. Let the eyes proceed to reading line by line, becoming intoxicated with the splendor of the words, the glorious caprice of the statements and their harmonious combinations; or let them run, conversely, from the drama that moves them toward the elements that compose it: the work constitutes its own defense, and no examination, however minute, can triumph over the secret of its perfection.

The poem is magnificently written. For it is indeed a poem, these four women seated in a circle around a dominating idea, around an inspiring and informing passion. It is a poem in which the extended necks, the raised heads, the supple and luminous torsos constitute the splendid strophes. It is a full-blooded, throbbing poem, full of shoulders lifted by inner emotion, and heaving chests attesting finally to the prodigious richness of life. But it is also just a fragment of nature, revealed to Mademoiselle Camille Claudel by a random incident, a chance movement observed in passing. No magic, no effort, no research explains it. It is endowed with a supreme grace that belongs only to itself. It is alive. It is permanently alive. The modeling and invention have a triumphant energy. The very fidelity of the artist and her respect for the human form are manifest in it with a strange grandeur and freedom. Truly, the more one sees it the more one loves it, the more one understands it, the more one is grateful for the true intoxication with Beauty it offers to wondering eyes.[3]

---

3. It was at the Champ-de-Mars Salon in 1895 that *The Gossips* was shown for the first time. I need not remind the reader that this was a major event. Although no title and no signature had labeled it for the curiosity of visitors, one understood that, whoever he was, the author was henceforth famous. We have not forgotten, moreover, the enthusiastic article devoted to it by our eminent colleague Octave Mirbeau, an article that was the first ray of sunlight, the first ray of glory to penetrate the retreat of the great artist. Several copies of *The Gossips* exist in marble, plaster, or onyx. The first of the marble copies was executed in 1896 (not without clumsy technicians first destroying several studies that could not be finished) at the behest of the Norwegian painter Fritz Thavlow. It was exhibited at the Champ-de-Mars Salon of 1897. Another marble copy, containing only the four gossipers without the partition that protects them, was sculpted for the Champ-de-Mars Salon for Monsieur Pontremoli. A copy in green onyx, which was exhibited at the Champ-de-Mars Salon in 1897, belongs to Monsieur P . . . Plaster copies, molded in gelatin on the first marble, have been acquired by the Museum of Geneva, which has relegated this masterpiece to the darkest corner, and by Messieurs Rodin, Octave Mirbeau, Gustave Geffroy, Robert Godet, Maurice Reymond, Adrien Demacle, Z . . . etc.

Appendix 2

Chronology

Year	Camille Claudel	Auguste Rodin
1862	3 February: marriage of Louis-Prosper Claudel and Louise-Athanaïse Cerveaux, at Villeneuve	Death of his sister Maria
1863	1 August: death of Charles-Henri, first child of the Claudels	
1864	8 December: birth of Camille Claudel	Meeting with Rose Beuret; *Man with the Broken Nose* rejected by the Salon
1866	26 February: birth of Louise Jeanne Claudel	Birth of Auguste-Eugène Beuret
1868		
1869		
1870	Louis-Prosper Claudel appointed to Bar-le-Duc	
1871		Military discharge for myopia; works for Count de Carrier-Belleuse in Belgium
1873		
1874		

6 August: birth of Paul Louis
Claudel

J.-B. Carpeaux: *La Danse*

19 July: declaration of war between
France and Prussia

March–May 1871: the Commune

Arthur Rimbaud: *A Season in Hell*

Appearance of word *impressionism*

Year	Camille Claudel	Auguste Rodin
1876	Louis-Prosper Claudel appointed to Nogent-sur-Seine; Camille meets Alfred Boucher	
1878		
1879	Louis-Prosper Claudel appointed to Wassy-sur-Blaise	*The Age of Bronze*
1880	Arrival in Paris	Commission for *Gates of Hell*
1881	Enters Colarossi academy atelier at 111, rue Notre-Dame-des-Champs	
1882	Camille received by Paul Dubois, director national École des Beaux-Arts [Society of Fine Arts]; exhibits *Head of Old Woman*, or *Old Hélène*	Series of busts of writers and artists
1883	First meeting with Auguste Rodin; portrait of Mme. B; *Bust of Paul Claudel at age 13*	26 October: death of his father

Paul Claudel	*Era*
	World's Fair in Paris
Enters secondary school Louis-le-Grand; death of grandfather Athanase Cerveaux	
Writes *L'Endormie*	
	Death of Wagner

Year	Camille Claudel	Auguste Rodin
1884	*Paul Claudel at age 16* *Bust of Louis-Prosper* Portrait in oil of Mme. Louis-Prosper Claudel; works with Rodin	Commission for *Burghers of* *Calais*
1885	Works with Rodin *Old Woman: Hélène* (terra cotta)	*L'Aurore* [Dawn]
1886	Clos Payen–Neubourg Folly *Paul Claudel at age 18* *Bust of Rodin* (terra cotta)	Rents Clos Payen *Thought* *The Kiss/Fugit Amor*
1887	Works as technician at Rodin's atelier, rue de l'Université *Bust of Young Girl* *Louise* (bronze) *Portrait of Rodin* (oil) *Torso of Woman* (plaster) *Young Roman*	Named chevalier of the Legion of Honor
1888	*Paul Claudel at age 20* (pastel) Sculptures of Ferdinand de Massary *Louise de Massary* (pastel) *Bust of Rodin* (plaster) *Çacountala* or *Abandonment* Champs-Élysées Salon	

Paul Claudel	*Era*

Reads Rimbaud   Death of Victor Hugo

25 December: Paul Claudel's
conversion at Notre-Dame

Writes *Une Mort prématurée*

Year	Camille Claudel	Auguste Rodin
1889	*The Prayer* *Charles Lhermitte* Monument for Villeneuve rejected	Major Exhibition of Rodin and Monet; commission for *Victor Hugo* *Saint Georges* *The Eternal Idol*
1890	Travels to Touraine Anjou, Château of Islette, Azay-le- Rideau	Travels to Touraine Anjou
1891	13 February: Claude Debussy – farewell letter to an unknown woman	Commission for *Balzac*
1892	New address: 113, boulevard d'Italie *Bust of Rodin* (bronze)	Named officer of the Legion of Honor; inauguration of *The Lorrain* at Nancy *Convalescence* *Farewell*
1893	*The Waltz* (plaster) *Clotho* (plaster) Champ-de-Mars Salon Articles by Geffroy and Mirbeau in the *Revue encyclopédique*; Camille alone at Islette	Rodin succeeds Dalou as president of the Société nationale des beaux-arts
1894	Camille breaks with Rodin *The Vanished God* (plaster)	

Paul Claudel	Era
Tête d'Or	World's Fair, Paris; The Eiffel Tower
La Ville	
	Claude Monet, *Les Nymphéas*
La Jeune Fille Violaine	
Departs for U.S. *L'Échange*	
Departs for China	

Year	Camille Claudel	Auguste Rodin
1894	Portrait of *The Little Châtelaine* Champ-de-Mars Salon Camille at Guernsey during the summer	
1895	*Study of a Japanese* (plaster) *Jeanne as a Child* (marble) *The Painter* (bronze) *The Gossips* (plaster) Study Admiring article by Mirbeau	3 June: inauguration of *The Burghers of Calais*
	May: relations resumed with Rodin Group *Çacountala*	
	10 October: gift to the Museum of Châteauroux; polemics over *Çacountala* (marble)	Rodin buys villa Brillants at Meudon 19 December
1896	Sends 19 sculptures to exhibition in Geneva	
1897	Commission for monument to Daudet (friend of Paul Claudel) rejected *Clotho* at the museum of Luxembourg *The Waltz* *Portrait of Mme D* *The Gossips* (jade) in May Article by H. de Braisne	

Paul Claudel *Era*

•

La Ville, second version

Year	Camille Claudel	Auguste Rodin
1897	becomes member of Société des beaux-arts November: commission for ten busts of Rodin in bronze Camille is ill	
1898	Leaves blvd d'Italie and moves to 63, rue de Turenne *Hamadryad* (marble and bronze) *Deep Hearth Thoughts* (for Peytel family) *Bust of Mme X* Definitive break with Rodin, end of 1898	*The Kiss* *Balzac* Exhibition at Galérie des Machines
1899	Change of address: 19, quai de Bourbon (January) *Portrait of M. le compte* *Clotho* (marble) *Maturity* (plaster) *Statue of Perseus*, maquette Exhibition Salon des beaux-arts *The Paths of Life* Salon de la nationale; meets with General Tissier	
1900	Desire to follow Paul to the consulate	Rodin Pavilion at Alma
1901	Article by Camille Mauclair	

Paul Claudel	Era
Travels in China, Japan, Syria, and Palestine	
	The Dreyfus affair; Pierre and Marie Curie discover radium; first houses of reinforced concrete
Stay in Legugé	World's Fair
Departs for China	

Year	Camille Claudel	Auguste Rodin
1902	Tissier orders cast of group *Paths of Life* *Perseus* (marble)	
1903	Article by Reval on Camille *Maturity*, 2nd project (bronze) Letters to E. Blot, her agent *Abandonment* (marble) *Figure on Knees* *Female Faun* (plaster) *Siren* *Hearth* *Chill* *Perseus* (bronze) Meets Henry Asselin	Named commander of the Legion of Honor; Isadora Duncan dances for him
1904		Beginning of his liaison with the Duchess de Choiseul
1905	Summer, stays with Paul in the Pyrenees *Fortune* (bronze) *Portrait of Louis-Prosper Claudel* (pencil) *Paul Claudel at age 37* (bronze) *Vertumnus and Pomona* (marble) *Abandonment* *Woman Warming Herself* (marble) *The Siren*	

Paul Claudel

Era

Claude Debussy: *Pelléas et Mélisande*
Death of Dalou

Returns from China
Partage de Midi
Marries Reine Sainte-
Marie-Perrin

Third departure for China

Year	Camille Claudel	Auguste Rodin
1905	November: Camille falls ill 4–16 December: last Major Exhibition by Camille Claudel, at Eugène Blot's gallery; 13 sculptures	
1906	Beginning of Camille's fugue states; destruction of her sculptures	21 April: inauguration of *The Thinker* in the Panthéon
1908		Rodin at Biron residence (Rodin Museum)
1912		Break with Duchess de Choiseul
1913	Death of her father Louis-Prosper, 3 March; 10 March, arrest and incarceration of Camille Claudel at Ville-Evrard; in July, incarceration at Montdevergues	Rodin suffers a stroke
1914		
1917		14 February: death of Rose Beuret; 19 November: death of Auguste Rodin
1918		

Returns to France;   Opening of Paris Métro,
departs for Prague   subway system

Article on Camille

Hamburg
Le Pain dur

3 August: declaration of war

6 March: death of Claude Debussy

Year	Camille Claudel	Auguste Rodin
1919		
1924		
1929		
1933		
1939		
1943	19 October: death of Camille Claudel at the asylum of Mondevergues	
1955		

Paul Claudel	Era
Le Soulier de satin	

Travels

Death of his mother, Louise

1927–1933: commentary on
the Bible

Declaration of war

First production of
Le Soulier de satin at the
Comédie-Française, directed
by Jean-Louis Barrault

23 February: death of Paul Claudel

Author's Acknowledgments

First, I must express my deep gratitude to my father, who, when I was very young, took me across the ocean, where I discovered the New World. An architect who designed beautiful houses, he would have been so happy to see this book translated into the American idiom.

Next, I would like to thank and express my affection for Geneviève Laverne, without whom Camille Claudel never would have been introduced to our friends at Mercury House. Thanks to her warm enthusiasm, Camille and I were accepted. I have truly fallen in love with the country and the faces, which even now that I am back in France, still fill my heart.

I would like to mention every one of them, but that is impossible.

My thoughts go to Anne Dickerson, who was one of the first to read this book and has never ceased to surround it with tenderness; to Thomas Christensen, perspicacious in his comprehension of the fragility of artists, the kind of editor many writers would love to have; and to all his colleagues at Mercury House.

I think also of Harry Parker, who opened the California Palace of the Legion of Honor and unwrapped Camille's bust of Rodin for me. I am still moved by the recollection of all those works being protected after the earthquake. I thank him for his bright and comforting welcome.

I think of Dr. August Coppola, who shared my love for Camille; of Mr. Goery Delacôte of the Exploratorium, who instinctively understood the terrible childhood of all "Camille Claudels"; of Mr. Yvan Roé d'Albert, consul general of France, and his wife.

I will not forget Henri Monjauze, Bernard Brasseur, and so many others – Michèle Heuzé, Caroline Eades – who, at one time or another, helped to forge this lasting bond among America, Camille, and me.

And then there were the sculptors – Christian Lazard, Bruce Beasley, and many others – whom I now remember with a sort of sad respect.

It all began ten years ago in a little theater. Now I also thank the Berkeley Repertory Theatre, Sharon Ott, and Susan Medak, whose support never flagged. We shared across the miles the same disappointments and the same dreams.

Finally, my thanks to Michel Laverne, who always opens the doors of his home in Oakland and who speaks so highly of his American friends and of the country where he would like to remain forever.

To all of them a kiss from the bottom of my heart.

Anne Delbée
Paris, 4 July 1992

Translator's Acknowledgments

I would like to give special thanks to Carol Christensen for her meticulous copyediting, to Hazel White for her careful supervision throughout production, and to Thomas Christensen for his editorial enterprise and encouragement. Indeed, the entire Mercury House staff deserve my gratitude for their enthusiasm and hard work.

Finally, I would like to thank Carol Drucker for her steady support, and not least my husband, Robert Alter, for his astute insights and unflagging faith in my work.

About the Author

Anne Delbée is an author, playwright, producer, and actor. In 1982, Delbée created both the play *Une Femme* (A Woman) and the book of the same title, catapulting the unknown sculptor Camille Claudel to worldwide recognition for the first time. Delbée is a founder of the Go Theater and creative director of the National Drama Center in Nancy. She lives in Paris with her daughter and is currently working on a biography of Jean Racine.

Carol Cosman has lived and studied in France. She is the translator of Jean-Paul Sartre's multivolume biography of Flaubert, *The Family Idiot*. She is also coeditor of an anthology of twentieth-century women poets in translation, *The Other Voice*, and of *The Penguin Book of Women Poets*. She lives in Berkeley, California, with her husband and two sons.

This book was designed by Vic Marks and typeset by The Typeworks. The typefaces are Linotype Centaur and Arrighi. The photograph section was designed by Sharon Smith. The copyeditor was Carol Christensen. Production was coordinated by Hazel White. Printing and binding were done by R. R. Donnelley and Sons, Harrisonburg, Virginia.